PENTECOST AND MISSIONS

PENTECOST AND MISSIONS

By

HARRY R. BOER

WM. B. EERDMANS PUBLISHING CO.
GRAND RAPIDS, MICHIGAN

Fifth printing, June 1979

Dedicated To

All my colleagues in the several Branches of the Sudan United Mission, the Church of the Brethren and the Dutch Reformed Church Missions, and to the seven Churches of the Fellowship of Churches of Christ in the Sudan that have, under God's blessing, grown out of their witness in Northern Nigeria

Contents

Chap.		Page
	Foreword by Dr. W. A. Visser 't Hooft	9
	Author's Preface	11
I	THE ROLE OF THE GREAT COMMISSION IN MODERN MISSIONS	15
2	THE GREAT COMMISSION AND MISSIONS IN THE NEW TESTAMENT	28
3	PENTECOST AND MISSIONS—AN HISTORICAL SURVEY	48
4	THE MOVEMENT OF THE SPIRIT IN THE HISTORY OF REDEMPTION	65
5	THE MEANING OF PENTECOST	76
6	PENTECOST AND THE WITNESSING CHURCH	98
7	THE ENDS OF THE EARTH AND THE END OF TIME	135
8	PENTECOST AND THE WITNESSING CHURCH IN ACTION	161
9	PENTECOST AND THE WITNESS OF THE CHURCH IN UNITY	186
10	QUENCH NOT THE SPIRIT! (PENTECOST AND THE PRACTICE OF MISSIONS)	205
	NOTES	255
	INDEX OF AUTHORS	261
	INDEX OF BIBLE PASSAGES	263

Foreword

WHEN doctors' theses arrive on my desk I lay them aside in the unfounded hope that I may find time to read them later on. But it happens sometimes that even the first casual glance gives the impression that here is a study which may be vital for one's work. This happened to me when I received Dr. Boer's *Pentecost and the Missionary Witness of the Church* and the impression was fully confirmed when I took time to read it.

Dr. Boer's study is so very relevant for our thinking about mission and unity, precisely because it is wholly concentrated on the study of the structure of biblical thought. He shows us that we have far too often tried to found our theology of missions on certain parts of the New Testament which speak explicitly about the missionary task of the Church. What we need and what he gives is a theology of mission which has its basis in the total kerugma. Only thus do we begin to see that the missionary witness is not one among several aspects of the task of the Church, but that it is rooted in the very being of the Church.

In this way the profound relation between witness and unity is also seen in a new light. We learn again that we are not to advocate unity with secondary and utilitarian arguments. We are called to witness in the unity of the Spirit because that belongs to the very nature of the Church of Pentecost. And we are told why according to the New Testament this unity must take visible form.

The future of missions and the future of the ecumenical movement will in the last analysis depend on the solidity of their biblical foundations. This book can render a very real service in helping the Churches to rediscover these foundations.

W. A. VISSER 'T HOOFT

Author's Preface

THE International Missionary Council declared in one of its findings at Tambaran, "At this stage in the history of the Church and the nations, the Council is convinced that the churches in all parts of the world should examine themselves anew and should turn again to the intensive practical study of the life and teaching of Jesus Christ and of the essential features of the New Testament Church, which from the day of Pentecost manifested a powerful corporate and individual witness entirely out of proportion to the insignificant human means employed." Tambaran Series, Vol. III, p. 420.

During the years that have passed since 1938 the need of re-examining the theological bases on which the missionary witness of the Church rests has been intensified in a degree that no one could then foresee. World War II and the convulsions that have followed and continue to follow in its wake have had the profoundest effects on the Church's missionary activity. The Communist revolution has forced the discontinuance of the witness of the Western Churches in China and in other sections in the Orient. In still other large missionary areas the continuance of their witness is surrounded by varying degrees of uncertainty. These developments have laid upon the younger Churches missionary responsibility in a measure unknown to them before.

As the missionary community leaves, or is confronted with the possibility of having to leave, work to which so much energy and self-dedication have been given, searching questions are being asked about the quality and permanence of the work that has been done. Have we everywhere brought into being a Christianity, and established the kind of Churches, that can develop without us? Have we in our mission work always laid the emphasis where it needed most to be placed? Do those who have come to know Christ through our witness have an adequate understanding of the witnessing task that has now wholly fallen, or may soon wholly fall, upon them?

These questions cannot fail to lead to renewed study of what the Bible, and particularly the New Testament portion of it, has to say about the bases that should underlie the missionary witness of the Church. Such study, in turn, may not fail to devote large attention to the missionary activity of the Church of New Testament times "which from the day of Pentecost manifested a powerful corporate and individual witness entirely out of proportion to the insignificant human means employed". Can we, can the younger Churches, recapture the secret of that success?

The following study is concerned with the significance of Pentecost for missions. The writer has been surprised to discover that exceedingly little theological attention has been devoted to this subject. Much curious interest has been shown in the "speaking with other tongues", recorded in Acts 2, but there has been very little concern to understand the meaning of the event that launched the Church on her missionary course. Much has been written about the work of the Holy Spirit in the salvation of men, but very little about His crucial significance for the missionary witness of the Church. The subject has not been wholly ignored but, while it deserved to be central in missionary reflection, it has been allowed to remain at the periphery.

Before the significance of Pentecost for the missionary proclamation of the Church could be fruitfully discussed three related subjects needed first to be investigated. The Great Commission has stood central in conscious missionary motivation during the past century and a half. Is this centrality, in the form in which it has existed, justified on the ground of the New

Testament data? The negative answer that is discovered to this question is the first step that prepared the way for the discussion of the missionary significance of Pentecost. The second step is a review of the relationships that have historically been seen between Pentecost and missions, and the third is a discussion of the place of Pentecost in the whole of the history of redemption. To a discussion of these matters the first five chapters are devoted.

Against the background so established, chapters six to ten have been written which deal with the subject proper of this book. Chapters six to nine are predominantly exegetical in nature, but they are related at many points to recent and contemporary missionary thought. In the last chapter some suggestions are made respecting the practical significance of the findings of the preceding study. Some of the questions taken up are questions of a controversial nature. The Church has seldom been and perhaps will never wholly be of one mind as to the concrete methods by which her witness must be expressed in the world. The writer is convinced, however, that broad and serious reflection on the rich data found in the New Testament concerning the indissoluble relationship between Pentecost and missions cannot fail to lead to a greater unity in striving.

The present study appeared originally in 1955 as a doctoral dissertation* written for the Department of Missions of the Free University, Amsterdam. It owes a great deal to the stimulation and helpful criticism of my faculty sponsor, Professor J. H. Bavinck. Some alterations have been made. Material in languages other than English has been translated or omitted; the five original rather long chapters have been re-divided; the notes have been greatly curtailed, and here and there modification by addition or deletion has been effected.

It is the hope of the writer that this volume on the missionary meaning of Pentecost may help to strengthen the witness of the

---

* Entitled: *Pentecost and the Missionary Witness of the Church.*

Church by calling her to a greater awareness of the extent and depth of the work of the Holy Spirit in her witness, without whose power and blessing her proclamation is in vain.

HARRY R. BOER

Theological College of Northern Nigeria
Gindiri, Barakin Ladi.
October 1, 1960

Chapter 1

THE ROLE OF THE GREAT COMMISSION IN MODERN MISSIONS

A COMPARISON of the bases that have consciously undergirded the missionary witness in the most recent and in the very earliest periods of the history of the Church reveals a striking double contrast. The first contrast is the exceedingly heavy emphasis that has been placed on the Great Commission in the missionary motivation of the Church during the past one hundred and fifty years, and the apparently complete absence of this motivation as a conscious factor in the missionary life of the early Church. The second is the slight attention that missionary thought has paid to the significance of Pentecost for the Church's witness in the world during the past century and a half, and the emphasis in the Acts of the Apostles on Pentecost as not only initiating but as wholly conditioning the missionary witness and expansion of the early Church. The emphasis, therefore, which the modern period has laid on the Great Commission and Pentecost is in each case in inverse ratio to the emphasis given them in the missionary thought of the first generation of Christians. This is a very remarkable and significant contrast.

In chapters one and two we shall set forth the first part of this contrast, namely the roles which the Great Commission has consciously played in the latest and in the earliest periods of missionary expansion. If the thesis is found to be true that the Great Commission, so far as can be determined from the New Testament record, was not a conscious ingredient in the missionary thinking of the early Church, then, obviously, an inquiry into the missionary significance of Pentecost will be invested with a new urgency. The Church has always recognized the New Testament as presenting the norm for her missionary labor. The New Testament also unfolds the story of the most intensive and fruitful expansion of the Church in the course of her history. At the beginning of this history, indeed, coinciding with the very day on which the missionary witness of the Church began, stands the Pentecost event. If the reason for the phenomenal missionary expansion of the early Church is not to be found in her conscious obedience to the command of Christ then, doubtless, Pentecost merits first consideration in an effort to determine wherein her success did lie.

The great things that have been done during the past century and a half of missionary witness on the part of the Church are known to all. Yet the Church of apostolic times manifested no such consciousness of the Great Commission as we have, as will become evident below, and her missionary successes, it will be agreed, simply dwarf ours when the size of the witnessing Church, the number of her missionaries, her material resources, theological understanding, and means of travel and communication are taken into account. Whether or not there is a connection between this contrast in missionary fruitfulness and the differing bases on which the earliest and the most recent Church carried on her missionary witness must be left to later consideration. We wish to begin our study by noting in this first chapter the prominence of the Great Commission in recent times and, in the second chapter, its total want of prominence or even reference so far as our record of the early Church's missionary motivation goes. When this has been done the way will be open for a relevant discussion of the New Testament conception of the place of Pentecost in the missionary proclamation of the Church.

In the last decade of the 18th century William Carey launched his powerful plea for missionary witness in the non-Christian world. This plea marked the beginning of the great century and a half of missionary proclamation at the tapering end of which we now find ourselves. If we were to select a single effort by Carey which would be considered pre-eminently influential in sending the modern missionary movement on its way it would doubtless be the publication in 1792 of his booklet, *An Enquiry into the Obligations of Christians to use Means for the Conversion of the Heathen*.[1] The first section of his book, which also constitutes its theological argument, is entitled, "An Enquiry whether the Commission given by our Lord to His Disciples be not still Binding on Us". Lamenting the want, in his own time, of the zeal and perseverance that characterized the early Christian obedience to Christ's command, Carey takes direct issue with "an opinion existing in the minds of some, that because the apostles were extraordinary officers and have no proper successors, and because many things which were right for them to do would be unwarranted for us, therefore it may not be immediately binding on us to execute the commission, though it was so upon them". Christ's command, said Carey, is binding on men today as it was binding on the apostles. If this be not true, he argued, then the command to baptize should also be restricted to the apostles, then all such ordinary ministers who have endeavored to carry the gospel to the heathen have acted without warrant, and whoever goes now to preach the gospel to them goes without authority if he have not a special commission from heaven. Then also the promise, "Lo, I am with you always, to the end of the world" must be limited to the apostles. The command has not been repealed, there continue to be subjects to obey it, there has been no counter revelation to nullify it, and nothing stands in the way of obeying it. Therefore, Carey concludes, Christ's mandate remains in effect and requires the obedience of Christian men and women.

That Carey should press these thoughts seems strange to us for whom the validity of Christ's command is not even remotely a matter of dispute. But they were as strange in Carey's time because of their unusual and even radical character as they seem to us because of their obviousness. Clearly, Carey was grappling with a view that was powerful and dominant in his day. This view we must briefly examine before we can further outline the place which the Great Commission has occupied in the Church since the days of Carey.

In the conception of the Reformers and of the majority of seventeenth-century theologians the Great Commission was binding *only* on the apostles. When they died Christ's command died with them. It does not extend to the Church which the apostles founded. From the death of the apostles onward the Church expands through witness in her immediate community or as a result of being scattered on account of persecution. Christian governments have the duty of seeing to it that the gospel is preached to subjects under their authority in non-Christian areas. The Church, however, has no mandate to preach the gospel and found churches in distant parts. The authority of each minister or bishop is limited to the congregation or area over which he has been placed. Material from the writings of the Reformers and of leaders in the post-Reformation Church setting forth this view is so abundant that even a cursory survey would lead us much too far afield. We shall therefore limit this discussion to a few representative citations.

Calvin distinguished between two kinds of offices in the Church—the temporary and the permanent. To the former class belong the apostles, evangelists and prophets, to the latter pastors and teachers. It was the task of the apostles to preach the gospel everywhere in obedience to the command of Christ. The evangelists engaged in this work also, but they were clothed with less dignity than the apostles. Such were Luke, Timothy and Titus. These offices existed only during the time in which churches had to be established in areas where they did not yet exist. In times of great need God may again raise up apostles and evangelists to lead churches back to the truth who have fallen prey to anti-Christ but, even so, these offices would be of a temporary nature. This the office of prophet is also. It is clothed by men who excel in gifts of revelation. If there are such today they are less conspicuous than in the early Church. Pastors and teachers serve the Church permanently. Of these the task of pastor is the more inclusive. It is the same as that of the apostles with this exception: the authority of pastors is limited to their own churches.[2] Even more clear is Calvin's commentary on 1 Cor. 12: 28:

> . . . for the Lord created the apostles, that they might spread the gospel throughout the whole world, and he did not assign to each of them certain limits or parishes, but would have them, wherever they went, to discharge the office of ambassadors among all nations and languages. In this respect there is a difference between them and pastors, who are, in a manner, tied to their particular churches. For the pastor has not a commission to preach the gospel over the whole world, but to take care of the Church that has been committed to his charge.

Luther's view is like that of Calvin:

> That the apostles entered strange houses and preached was because they had a command and were for this purpose appointed, called and sent, namely that they should preach everywhere, as Christ had said, "Go into all the world and preach the gospel to every creature". After that, however, no one again received such a general apostolic command, but every bishop or pastor has his own particular parish.[3]

How, then, are we to conceive of the progress of the gospel in the world? It was *in principle* declared to the whole world by the apostles. The work begun by them continues in ever widening circles to extend to men everywhere. This is not done by means of a self-conscious missionary program, however, but it is effected through the preaching and especially through the dispersion of Christians attendant upon persecution:

> This preached message is like a stone thrown into the water: it makes ripples and circles around itself which move farther and farther outward, the one pushing the other, until they reach the

water's edge. Although it may become quite still in the middle, yet the ripples do not rest but move outward. So it goes with the preaching of the gospel: it began with the apostles and continues on and on. Preachers carry it forward, it is hunted and persecuted from place to place, yet continues to be made known to those who have not heard it before although in the middle where it first began it may have completely disintegrated and become heresy.[4]

The views of Melanchthon, Bugenhagen, and Zwingli are similar to those of Calvin and Luther. None envisions an organized missionary program and the general view is that the Great Commission ceased to be in effect when the apostles died. Bucer stands out among the Reformers as a man with missionary concern. In his book *Von der waren Seelsorge* he expresses his dismay over the fact that Christian men are willing to go to distant parts and exert themselves in many ways to further their material enrichment, but that there is little concern for the spiritual welfare of those with whom they commerce. It is significant that he wishes the elders of the Church to take this concern in hand. But even Bucer did not free himself from the Reformation conception that the Great Commission was limited to the apostles:

> What Christians in general and the civil authorities neglect to do with respect to seeking the lost lambs, this the elders of the Church shall undertake to make good in every possible way. *And though they do not have an apostolic call and command to go to strange nations*, yet they shall not in their several churches . . . permit anyone who is not associated with the congregation of Christ to be lost in error.[5]

In 1592 Adrian Saravia, a Dutch political refugee residing in England, took issue with the reigning conception. Having become a convinced Anglican he published a booklet vindicating the episcopal system. In the course of his argument he adduced the binding character of the Great Commission.

> The command to preach the gospel to the gentiles pertained not only to the age of the apostles, but to all future times to the end of the world.[6]

The execution of the Great Commission requires apostolic authority and this only bishops standing in the line of apostolic succession possess. Perhaps the fact that Saravia's plea for missions stood in the context of and in subordination to his larger interest of defending episcopacy was the reason for its ineffectiveness. In any case, there is no evidence that any action followed upon his writing.

Saravia's argument gave occasion to Joh. Gerhard to give classic formulation of the post-Reformation view of the Great Commission entertained by most 16th- and 17th-century theologians. Defining the apostolate, he said that in it three things are to be considered: first, that it involves the teaching of the gospel and the administration of the sacraments, with the power of the keys; second, the supervision of the Church of Christ; third, the power of preaching the gospel in the whole world, along with which came the gift of miracles, authority and infallibility. The apostolate proper really consists in the third consideration, and there is no successor to it. It is a temporary and extraordinary office. There follow some texts such as Mark 16: 20 and Romans 10: 18 that the gospel was preached everywhere by the apostles, after which comes the conclusion: "Therefore with the apostles this mandate and authority ceased."[7]

There were protesting voices, but they did not avail to break down the existing dogmatism concerning the apostolate. Chief among these was a German nobleman, Justinianus von Welz, 1621-68. Distressed by the spiritual coldness of the Church and the neglect of her missionary calling he made passionate appeals for a deepening of the spiritual life and for student-volunteers to preach the gospel in non-Christian areas. It was with words such as these that he assailed the disregard of Christ's command to disciple the nations:

> Why do we regard the false pretences of some learned people more highly than the clear word of Christ in Matt. 28: 19: Go and teach all nations, baptize them in the name of the Father,

the Son and the Holy Spirit, and teach them to do all things that I have commanded you. From this every unprejudiced reader who loves the truth can easily judge that this command of Christ affects the contemporary Church, and must therefore conclude: If Christ has commanded the apostles to teach Christians to do all things that he commanded them to do, he must also have commanded them to teach Christians that they should at all times send out qualified men and say to them: Go to this or that land, teach and instruct its people in the Christian faith, baptize, etc. For how is it possible that Christ should have commanded the apostles to teach Christians all that he had commanded them, and the apostles were to keep all the commandments but not this one: Go and teach all nations, etc.? But since the apostles have caused this command to be written also, they have done their part. Therefore I ask why we Christians want to be so disobedient and do not desire to follow the command of Christ.[8]

Wolfgang Gröszel, in his fine study, *Die Mission und die evangelische Kirche im 17 Jahrhundert*, has fully set forth and documented the well-nigh unbelievable view of missions to which the Lutheran Church subscribed during the 17th century. Not only Lutheran theologians who had fallen prey to scholastic theology and dead orthodoxy, but also men in whom spiritual vitality was more vigorous, were unable to free themselves of a false conception of Christ's command. It was reserved for the Pietists to break through the prevailing missionary indifference and open the way for missionary effort. The organized Church, living by the accepted theology of her leaders, followed slowly.

It is against this background of Reformation and post-Reformation thought that Carey's reference to "an opinion existing in the minds of some, that because the apostles were extraordinary officers and have no proper successors, and because many things which were right for them to do would be unwarranted for us, therefore it may not be immediately binding on us to execute the commission, though it was so upon them" must be understood. England's religious background since the Reformation was predominantly Calvinistic. The Genevan Reformers had been her theological if not her ecclesiastical teachers. Calvin's *Institutes* had appeared in six editions in the English language and his commentaries on 1 Corinthians and Ephesians in at least one edition each. We have already noted that in each of these three works Calvin unambiguously limits the task of universal gospel proclamation to the apostles. Since Carey was, after leaving the Anglican communion, a "particular", i.e. Calvinistic, Baptist, and a widely read man who was also conversant with the Latin language, he doubtless had the Reformation understanding of the Great Commission in mind when he wrote the above words.

To the idea that the Church had no duty to preach the gospel to men in distant places there was added, in Carey's time, the notion in certain Calvinistic circles in England, reminiscent of the Scottish Marrow controversy some decades earlier, that the unregenerate had no duty to believe the gospel. Nothing, it was held, must be addressed to the unregenerate in the way of exhortation except what relates to external obedience. Andrew Fuller, Carey's life-long friend and co-laborer at home, took sharp and prominent issue with this view. He did so particularly in his book, *The Gospel Worthy of All Acceptation*, which appeared in 1784. A representative opponent whom Fuller quotes had set forth the pseudo-Calvinistic conception by a comment on John 6: 29, "This is the work of God that ye believe in him whom he hath sent". He wrote:

> The words contain a declaration that believing in Christ for salvation is necessary to the enjoyment of eternal life, and that faith in him is an act acceptable and pleasing to God, but afford no proof that it is required of men in a state of unregeneracy. To declare to unregenerate persons the necessity of faith in order to salvation, which is what our blessed Lord here does, falls very far short of asserting it to be their present duty.[9]

Fuller himself phrased the issue thus:

> The question is not whether unconverted sinners be the object of exhortation; but whether they ought to be exhorted to perform

spiritual duties? It is beyond all dispute that the scriptures do exhort them to many things. If, therefore, there be any professors of Christianity who question the propriety of this, and who would have nothing said to them except that "if they be elected they will be called", they are not to be reasoned with, but rebuked, as setting themselves in direct opposition to the word of God. The greater part of those who may differ from the author on these subjects, it is presumed, will admit the propriety of sinners being exhorted to duty; only this duty must, as they suppose, be confined to merely natural exercises, or such as may be complied with by a carnal heart destitute of the love of God.[10]

Fuller's insistence on the duty of all men everywhere to believe the gospel, and especially the appearance of his book, had a profound influence on Carey.

When Fuller had published his treatise, Carey had drawn the practical deduction—"If it be the duty of all men, when the Gospel comes, to believe unto salvation, then it is the duty of those who are entrusted with the gospel to endeavor to make it known among all nations for the obedience of faith".[11]

It appears, then, that a concrete theological discussion involving so basic an issue as the free offer of the gospel played a determinative role in the crystallization of Carey's missionary vision. His argument for missions was simple but clear: If all men are in duty bound to believe the gospel when they hear it, then it must be preached to them by those who have the gospel. When he sought action on this conclusion, however, he found the Reformation interpretation of the Great Commission standing in his way. It was therefore to the discrediting of this interpretation and to the defense of the continually binding character of Christ's last command that he addressed himself in his *Enquiry*. Carey's plea and the particular form in which he cast it had, it is clear, a definite theological and historical background, as did that of von Welz a century and a quarter before him.

Once the eyes of the Church were opened to her missionary duty the command of Christ around which Carey had so effectively centered his appeal became the basis on which the missionary witness of the Church was consciously built. There is little doubt that the historical and theological background out of which Carey's emphasis on the Great Commission arose was soon lost to sight. The emphasis alone remained, working powerfully in its own right. This is evident in many of the leading figures and movements that have carried the gospel witness to the far ends of the earth. Lashing his fellow ministers with unrestrained charges of "the habitual, open violation of Christ's command . . . without shame, and almost without an effort to the contrary", the Rev. Melville Horne, a clergyman of the Anglican Church who had been chaplain of the British Colony in Sierra Leone, gave the initial impetus for the formation of the London Missionary Society.[12] The first public meeting of the LMS after the adoption of the resolutions bringing the organization into being was addressed by the Rev. Thomas Haweis, co-founder and leading spirit, in a sermon on Mark 16: 15–16 in which he endeavored "with great fervor and eloquence to impress on his auditory their solemn obligation to enter upon the work".[13]

Eugene Stock, in preparing his three-volume work on the history of the Church Missionary Society, entitled the first chapter "The Great Commission", and judges his work to be a recording of the obedience that has been given this command by the men and women of the CMS.[14] Henry Venn, the distinguished and powerful leader of the CMS during one of its most effective periods of service, commenting on the missionary motivation of the founders of the Society, said, "What could have been the moving cause which led such men to attempt so great a work? It may be replied that they were men of strong faith, that they were constrained by the love of Christ, that they were men of prayer. . . . The true answer we conceive is this: They were men who felt their individual responsibility to obey the command of Christ, 'Go ye into all the world and preach the Gospel to every creature'."[15]

25

When Adoniram Judson was asked whether he was moved to his missionary labors by faith or by love he replied that it was neither, rather that it was the missionary command of Christ that had come directly into his heart and with it the decision to obey this command, whatever might happen.[16] Robert Morrison (China), William Ellis (Madagascar and the South Seas), and W. G. Lawes (N. Guinea) were similarly motivated to their great missionary service. During July 1886, a meeting of two hundred and fifty-one students representing eighty-seven colleges was held at Mt. Hermon, Massachusetts, which proved to be the beginning of the Student Volunteer Movement. Before this memorable conference was concluded one hundred of those present had volunteered for missionary service. The most significant meeting of the conference was concluded by Dr. Wm. Ashmore of China with this challenge, "Show, if you can, why you should not obey the last command of Jesus Christ". John R. Mott, who played so prominent a role in the Student Volunteer Movement, regarded Christ's command as the "first and most important part of our missionary obligation".[17] In Europe it was not different. Gustav Warneck, in introducing his own understanding of the theological foundation of missions, reflected the reigning conception when he wrote, "Why do we do mission work? The shortest and most popular answer is: Because Jesus Christ has commanded it."[18] His son, Johann Warneck, observes,

> When we investigate the motives underlying the growing missionary activity of the past century, we discover that its root was and is in first instance obedience to the command of Jesus. This command was seen on the background of the personal experience of salvation which found Jesus as Saviour and Lord but which acknowledged him at the same time as the Saviour of all lost men. Pity for a godless world then necessarily entered the motivation to multiply the unfolding of missionary energy. But only as the idea of missions laid itself upon the consciences of men as a *command* of our Lord did the urge to missions grow in circles in which faith breathed obedience. The obligating reminder of the

26

command of Jesus, "Go ye into all the world" caused missionary life for a hundred years to grow and has maintained the vitality of that life up to this very day.[19]

From this summary review it is clear that the Great Commission has been the dominant motivation to missionary witness during the most flourishing and productive period in the century and a half that have elapsed since Carey published his *Enquiry* in 1792. It will also be clear that the emphasis on the Great Commission during this time was initiated in no small measure by historical circumstances.[20] The question naturally arises whether an emphasis whose origins lie embedded so strongly in reaction to a long held theological misconception is also a *scriptural* emphasis. Does our knowledge of the missionary mind and activity of the early Church bear out the thesis that the Great Commission was for her the foundation of gospel witness in the sense in which this has been the case during the past one hundred and fifty years? About the fact that Jesus actually gave the command to disciple the nations there can be no doubt. It comes too well authenticated in too many places to admit of question. This does not answer the question, however, what *role* it played in the missionary activity of the early Church. In the following chapter we shall endeavor negatively to define this role.

Chapter 2

THE GREAT COMMISSION AND MISSIONS IN THE NEW TESTAMENT

ADOLF HARNACK considers it one of the most striking characteristics of Acts that Luke raises and answers the question of how
the original Jewish-Christian evangelistic movement came to
engage in mission work among the gentiles. This is indeed the
question to which we must address ourselves. On the surface it
would seem that Luke considers missions to the gentiles to be a
natural outgrowth of the Great Commission as he records it. In
Acts 1: 8 he writes, "But ye shall receive power, when the
Holy Spirit is come upon you, and ye shall be my witnesses
both in Jerusalem, and in all Judea and Samaria, and unto
the uttermost part of the earth." Then after relating the
coming of the Spirit, 2: 1–13, he proceeds to give an account
of the expansion of the faith. This account follows the pattern
laid down in 1: 8. But is the development which Luke records
the result of conscious obedience to the Great Commission?
It is generally assumed that the same relationship which has
been conceived to exist between Christ's command and
missionary activity in modern times existed also in the minds
of the apostles and of the early Church. The early Church, it is
held, was a missionary Church because she was utterly obedient
to Christ's command. It is admitted by students of the question
that there are problems here. The direct statement of Nikolaus
Adler is rather exceptional, "Hardly had the Promised One
descended upon them but they began to execute the missionary
command" (Matt. 28: 19ff., Mark 16: 15).[1] Max Meinertz is
much more careful:

How is the actual transition from Jewish to gentile missions to be explained in terms of a real missionary command of Christ? I fully acknowledge the difficulties that appear here. At the same time, I do not regard them as insuperable; indeed, I believe that the command permits of being integrated in an adequately probable manner with the facts of history.[2]

It is clear that Meinertz acutely feels the need of harmonistic exegesis to relate command and witness in the early Church.

Gustav Warneck presents perhaps the best effort at harmonizing conscious obedience to the Great Commission on the part of the early Church with the New Testament data. Both because he presents his position so clearly and because we shall have occasion to refer to it several times in the course of the argument we shall quote the heart of his view in full:

It does indeed seem strange at first glance that neither the original apostles nor the "apostle to the gentiles" appeal to this command. Peter defended the baptism of Cornelius by reference to a special revelation and guidance from God (Acts 15: 7ff.), and Paul defends his activity as a missionary to the gentiles by adducing a specially given command (Acts 22: 21, 26: 17ff.; Gal. 1: 16; Eph. 3: 8, etc.). Quite apart from the fact that in both cases an abrupt calling would have lacked evidential quality, and that both were understandable only on the assumption that the right of receiving gentiles into the Christian Church, relative to the proclamation to the gentiles, had already been decided in principle, there was no reason why in this controversy the general missionary command should have been adduced as defense motif. This command as an article of high divine majesty about which there was no dispute was not questioned by any of the apostles. The controversy was not concerned with the question whether or not gentiles might be numbered among Christ's disciples, but *whether or not they had to be circumcised* (Acts 15: 1–5, 9–11, 16–20; Gal. 2: 3–5). Had not the first question been considered as resolved, the Jewish Christians would have appealed to the prohibition given in the first missionary instruction, namely to go nowhere among the gentiles. Therewith the whole question of accepting non-Israelites into the community of Jesus' disciples would have been invalidated. Since this did not happen, it must in the light of the basic significance of this question be presumed that a decision had already been reached, and that through an authority to whom all yielded. This authoritative decision, which must be assumed to have been a generally known and acknowledged one, cannot have been any other one than the Great Commission.[3]

Is Warneck's thesis correct? Is it true that the question of the relationship of the Church to the gentiles was solely one of conditions governing their entry into the Church and not one of entering her as such? How did the Church at Jerusalem conceive of this relationship? Is it true that the Great Commission was a silent presupposition in the mind of the apostles and of the early Church? Into these questions we must inquire.

The missionary witness of the Church that is related in Acts up to 9: 31 is limited to those who were members of, or more or less related to, the Jewish community. In 9: 31 we read, "So the Church throughout all Judea and Galilee and Samaria had peace, being edified; and, walking in the fear of the Lord and in the comfort of the Holy Spirit, was multiplied." This closes off Luke's description of missionary activity in the Jewish and Samaritan areas and is immediately followed by the events leading up to Peter's experience in Caesarea where the conversion of Cornelius and his household initiates his account of the Church's mission to the gentiles.

In the section that is concluded by 9: 31 there are two instances of missionary activity outside the strictly Jewish community. The first is the witness of Philip in Samaria with its rich results and endorsement by the apostolic group, 8: 4–25. The second is the conversion of the Ethiopian eunuch, 8: 26–39. Neither of these could, in the nature of the case, raise the question of the relationship of the Church to the gentiles. The Samaritans were not regarded as gentiles. Although the population of Samaria was heterogeneous, the Israelitish element was prominent and had set its religious stamp on the whole. There is doubt about the belief of the Samaritans in the resurrection, but they believed in the unity of God, in the existence of angels and devils, they regarded the Pentateuch as sole divine authority, they looked for a Messiah. The great stumbling-block between the two nations was the Samaritan insistence on Mt. Gerizim as the place from which God ought to be worshipped. Nevertheless, the Jews declared the food of the Samaritans to be lawful. Christian Jews, therefore, could have no objection to receiving Samaritan believers into their fellowship. A similar situation presents itself with respect to the Ethiopian eunuch. While he was "of another nation" in the sense of 10: 28 he was religiously closely related to the Jews as a "God-fearer". He could not be a proselyte in the full sense of the word because of his physical defect, but his relationship seems to have been as close as his condition permitted. It went so far as to constrain him to come to Jerusalem to worship. His association with the Jews probably stemmed from contact with a Jewish military colony in southern Egypt whose existence in apostolic times is likely. He must therefore be regarded as one of those gentiles who associated themselves in a general way with the religious conceptions and worship of the Jews.

It is clear, therefore, that from the day of Pentecost to Peter's contact with Cornelius the question of the Church's relationship to the gentiles and of the proclamation of the gospel to them had not in any concrete manner confronted the Church. Up to that point there is no evidence of consciousness of, much less of obedience to, Christ's command to disciple the gentiles on the part of the apostles or of the Church as a whole.

We meet the gentile problem for the first time, and that clearly and unambiguously, in the account of the conversion of Cornelius. It is interesting to note a curious absence in the scripture passages with which Warneck supports his thesis that in the Church-gentile question only the *manner* of the gentiles' entry into the Church was at stake. The texts which he cites are

Acts 15: 1, 5, 9–11, 16–20 and Gal. 2: 3–5. The omission that strikes attention is Luke's extensive description of Peter's experience in Caesarea, Acts 10: 1–11: 18. On the basis of the texts which Warneck adduces a good case can doubtless be made out for his thesis. But we do not meet the gentile problem for the first time at the Jerusalem conference recorded in Acts 15. We meet it for the first time, and, in Luke's estimation, very importantly, in Caesarea and in Peter's defense of his action immediately following his return to Jerusalem. To this complex of events Warneck pays virtually no attention. The light which Luke's account sheds on the attitude of the Jerusalem Church to the gentiles and to the proclamation of the Gospel to them is revealing.

Acts 9: 32–43 describes Peter's visits to Lydda and Joppa. These verses introduce his trance experience and the subsequent visit to Caesarea, the conversion of Cornelius and his household, and the reaction of the Church in Jerusalem to it, 10: 1–11: 18. It is no small space that Luke gives to this matter —sixty-six verses exclusive of the twelve that relate how Peter came to be in Joppa at the time of the angel's visit to Cornelius. In view of Luke's economy of statement and strict purposefulness in writing this must not escape notice. Particularly must Luke's extensive treatment strike our attention when we contrast it with the thirty-five verses devoted to the account of the crucial Jerusalem conference, Acts 15. Clearly Luke attached the greatest significance to the conversion of Cornelius. Why did he set forth this event so carefully and so fully?

It is significant that few have concerned themselves with this section of Acts more than have critical scholars. They have realized fully what is at issue here. Eduard Zeller rejects the historicity of the account. It is for him unthinkable that Peter should have baptized a gentile before the apostolic council at Jerusalem had taken place and before the missionary journeys of Paul had begun. Luke wrote his account with the idea of making Pauline universalism acceptable to Jewish readers.

Therefore he presents the first move of the Church in the direction of gentile missions as having been undertaken by Peter, the apostle to the Jews *par excellence*. O. Pfleiderer rejects the account for the same reason: Peter could not have anticipated Paul. Martin Dibelius sees Luke's purpose in presenting the conversion of Cornelius so carefully as an attempt to put an unanswerable argument in the mouth of Peter at the apostolic council related in Acts 15. The decision to permit the gentiles to enter the Church had been decided, "from early days" 15: 7, not by man, not even by so great a one as Peter, but by God himself through the obvious descent of the Spirit on non-Jews. The Cornelius account is therefore a calculated literary device to convince the reader of the God-willed character of the gentile mission.

The desire to eliminate the historical character of this account stems from the recognition of what Luke actually meant to say here. Luke's grand conclusion is 11: 18—"And when they heard these things they held their peace, and glorified God, saying, Then to the gentiles also hath God granted repentance unto life." This is the great decision of the Church after Peter had related all that occurred in Caesarea. Pfleiderer has put the matter plainly: "This conclusion of the account is obviously its real point: it is intended to show that the beginning of gentile baptism by Peter rested on divine instruction and that after initial doubts it was approved by the primitive Church."[4] There can be no doubt that this is indeed the great point of Luke's account. Even before Peter returned to Jerusalem word has arrived there concerning his preaching to gentiles. "Now the apostles and the brethren that were in Judea heard that the gentiles also had received the word of God" 11: 1. This was the rock of offense. The offense, to be sure, was expressed in a characteristically Jewish form: "And when Peter was come up to Jerusalem, they that were of the circumcision contended with him, saying, Thou wentest in to men uncircumcised and didst eat with them" 11: 2, 3. Peter understood that the ceremonial

c

objection covered a much more basic objection, namely that "the gentiles also had received the word of God". It is to *this* objection that he addresses himself in his defense. He testifies to his own ceremonial orthodoxy by relating his trance experience in Joppa. But God had contradicted his scruples. When the messengers from Cornelius arrived the Spirit had bidden him to go with them "making no distinction", 11:12. When he came to Caesarea, Cornelius related how the angel had told him to call Peter who would speak to him "words whereby thou shalt be saved, thou and all thy house", 11:14. Then, while he was addressing the group, the Holy Spirit had descended and conferred on them "the like gift as he did also unto us when we believed in the Lord Jesus Christ", v. 17. This is for Luke the central and conclusive fact in the Cornelius account. He mentions it no less than four times—three times in the immediate context and once again in chapter 15. He relates the descent of the Spirit and its effect on the group concerned, 10:44-46; it is the immediate occasion for Peter's question, "Can anyone forbid water that these should not be baptized, who have received the Spirit as well as we?" 10:47, 48; he relates it again in 11:15-17 where the account is immediately followed by the joyful acquiescence of the whole assembly and, finally, it is mentioned in Peter's testimony at the Jerusalem conference, 15:8, 9, ". . . giving them the Holy Spirit, even as he did unto us; and made no distinction between us and them, cleansing their hearts by faith".

Fully realizing the import of this happening and of the baptism which he had ordered to be administered, Peter had taken with him all the six brethren who had accompanied him from Joppa to Caesarea. That he asked them to go with him the thirty odd miles from Joppa to Jerusalem underscores his desire to authenticate with witnesses his minute report of the eventful happening in the house of Cornelius. The decision of the assembly that followed upon Peter's account contains not the slightest reference to the gentiles' relation to the Mosaic law.

It affected *one* and *only* one point: *salvation had come to the gentiles.* Through the descent of the Spirit, Jew and gentile had become like recipients of the grace of God. "And when they heard these things they held their peace, and glorified God, saying, Then to the gentiles also hath God granted repentance unto life" 11: 18. This was basic to the further expansion of the Christian Church. It was the *first* and *most decisive* happening in the clarification of the gentiles' relation to the gospel. Here it was made clear, not in terms of a general principle, but in the form of an acknowledgment of an evident gift of the Spirit to concrete gentile individuals, that *the gospel was intended for gentiles no less than for Jews.* It is not stated that God had given repentance to gentiles who had become proselytes, or to gentiles who really ceased to be gentiles, or to gentiles who would not have to become Jews first, but it is stated that God had granted repentance to gentiles without qualification.

The Church never again questioned this decision. It was questioned by a group within the Church, but they met with no support either from the Church as a whole or from any of the apostles. The decision later taken at Jerusalem, Acts 15, was a ratification, a further definition by way of negation, and as such an unambiguous reaffirmation, of this prior and more basic decision. At the Jerusalem conference it was established that *believing gentiles need not observe the law of Moses.* Before the Church effected this clarification it had already, in connection with the conversion of Cornelius, made the fundamental affirmation that gentiles *as gentiles* could be the recipients of salvation. When later developments threatened the integrity of this affirmation ("Except ye be circumcised after the custom of Moses, *ye cannot be saved*" Acts 15: 1) the Church acted and acted resolutely to safeguard it. The Jerusalem conference did not bring a new state of things into being. *It simply rejected a heresy.* The new state of things had been brought into being earlier at Jerusalem when the Church accepted as valid the conversion and baptism of Cornelius.

It is clear that in the judgment of Luke the receiving of the Holy Spirit by the household of Cornelius was the incontrovertible evidence that the barrier between Jew and gentile had fallen away. The Pentecost event that had so radical a significance for the Jewish disciples of Christ had no less significance for the gentiles. This the Church at Jerusalem recognized and joyfully acknowledged. Before this happened, the Church had undertaken no missionary effort outside the Jewish community. Jewish Christians had not been able to regard gentiles as heirs of salvation. After the conversion of Cornelius the missionary witness to the gentiles began. It is to the description of the development of this witness that Luke devotes the remainder of his book.

Having determined what the attitude of the Church to the gentiles was before the coming of the Spirit on the household of Cornelius, and what it became in consequence of this event, we must now more specifically face the question: What role did the Great Commission play as a motivating factor in the missionary witness of the early Church? Is it true, as Warneck claims, that the Great Commission was a silent presupposition underlying the witness of the earliest Christian community?

We can perhaps best seek a satisfactory answer to this question by following three main lines of inquiry. The leader of the apostolic group was Peter. It is reasonable to assume that in him the mind of the Church on this question found fair reflection. Was the Great Commission a factor in Peter's thinking? The Church as a whole faced the gentile problem. Did the Great Commission play a role in leading her to missionary witness among the gentiles? This is the second question we must answer. Finally, what role did Jesus' last command play in the mind of Paul, the great missionary of the early Church?

A. *Peter and the Great Commission*

Before Peter was called to Caesarea he gave expression,

according to Luke's report, to six utterances of a universalistic nature. They are:

1. Acts 2: 16, 17—but this is that which hath been spoken through the prophet Joel: And it shall be in the last days, saith God, I will pour forth of my Spirit on all flesh;
2. 2: 21—And it shall be, that whosoever shall call on the name of the Lord shall be saved;
3. 2: 39—For to you is the promise, and to your children, and to all that are afar off, even as many as the Lord shall call unto him;
4. 3: 25—In thy seed shall all the families of the earth be blessed;
5. 3: 26—Unto you first God, having raised up his Servant, sent him to bless you, in turning away every one of you from your iniquities;
6. 4: 12—And in none other is there salvation: for neither is there any other name under heaven, that is given among men, whereby we must be saved.

Of these verses 2: 16, 17, 21 and 3: 25 are quotations from the Old Testament, and 2: 39 is built around Isa. 57: 19 and Joel 2: 32. Only 3: 26 and 4: 12 are wholly Peter's own words. It would be hazardous to read into these expressions of Peter, whether quoted or original, the missionary vision which the Church later came to entertain. What distinguishes Peter's use of the Old Testament quotations from their Old Testament reference is that they are no longer regarded as prophecy that is to be fulfilled, but as prophecy that has gone into fulfilment. It is by no means clear, however, that in Peter's mind this fulfilment is to be accompanied by missionary witness. The words "and to all that are afar off, even as many as the Lord our God shall call unto him" in 2: 39 refer in Isaiah and in Joel to the Jewish people. Some see here implications for the universalism of the gospel, but in view of Peter's attitude to the gentiles at the time of his being called to Caesarea it is not likely that he had the gentiles in mind when he spoke these words. In 3: 25 and 26 there is manifest an awareness that the blessings of salvation are to be mediated to the world at large through the Jews to whom the gospel comes first, but there is no indication of the manner in which this is to be done. In 4: 12 the only name given under heaven among men brings salvation to "us", that is, to Jews.

How exceedingly careful we have to be in ascribing a consciousness of universalism in the missionary sense of the word to expressions of a universalistic nature such as Peter spoke is evident from the Jewish reaction to Paul's defense recorded in Acts 22. In verse 15 Paul quotes Ananias as bringing him a commission from God that he would be "a witness for him to all men of what thou hast seen and heard". This moved his intensely nationalistic and religiously exclusive audience not at all. It was when Paul became specific and mentioned the execrable word "gentiles" that his auditory showed of what cloth it was cut: "And he said unto me, Depart, for I will send thee forth far hence unto the gentiles. And they gave him audience unto this word; and they lifted up their voice, and said, Away with such a fellow from the earth: for it is not fit that he should live. And . . . they cried out, and threw off their garments, and cast dust into the air" vv. 21-23. From Peter's expressions alluded to above we conclude, therefore, that, although they manifest a certain awareness of the universal significance of the gospel, it is not warranted to understand them as reflecting a comprehension on Peter's part of the meaning of the Great Commission.

We must now refer again to Peter's visit to Caesarea. He was prepared for the events that were impending by experiencing a trance in which he was instructed no longer to distinguish between the ceremonially clean and unclean, 10: 9-16. This was followed by a revelation from the Holy Spirit to accompany the men who had been sent to him by Cornelius, 11: 12. These happenings, coupled with Cornelius' account of the angel's visit, 10: 30-33, crystallized for a moment Peter's unclear universalism, "Of a truth, I perceive that God is no respecter of persons: but in every nation he that feareth him and worketh

righteousness, is acceptable to him" 10: 34, 35. The paren-
thetical exclamation, "(he is Lord of all)", in verse 36, strength-
ens the words with which he began his address. It would seem
that Peter had broken through the religious prejudices of his
people. This, however, is far from being the case. All is neutral-
ized by the remarkable words in v. 42, "And he commanded us
to preach to the people, and to testify that he is the one ordained
by God to be the judge of the living and the dead." Is this a
reference to the Great Commission? If it is, Jesus' words are
here invested with a strange limitation. The apostles who are
witnesses to the resurrection have, according to Peter, been
instructed to preach *to lao*. The incongruity of this expression
in the present context requires closer examination.

The word *laos* (of which *to lao* is the dative with the article)
is a favorite word with Luke. He uses it 36 times in the Gospel
and 47 times in Acts, a total of 83 times, thus far more than
half of the 140 times the word is used in the New Testament.
It is Luke's favorite designation for the people of Israel as
God's people. In designating groups of non-Jewish people he
constantly avails himself of *ochlos*, which means crowd or
multitude. Luke uses *laos* (i.e., people) as a parallel expression
to *ethne* (gentiles), but only in the plural. In 10: 42 its singular
use clearly indicates the Jewish people. Whatever intimations
Peter may have had concerning a universal significance of the
gospel, in a concrete confrontation with gentiles he cannot hide
the fact of his particularistic conception of the *preaching* of the
gospel. Even in the flesh and blood presence of gentiles to whom
he had been supernaturally called with the explicit purpose of
speaking words whereby Cornelius would be saved, he and all
his house, 11: 14, it does not occur to Peter that the command
to preach the gospel which the Lord had given had reference
to the gentiles. The apt observation of Nösgen concerning
Peter's awareness of the universalistic implications of his
words in 2: 39 is highly applicable to Peter's entire attitude
up to this point. "The somewhat ambiguous expression wholly

reflects his own limited insight into the as yet hidden range of the fulfilment that has begun, as Peter himself ascribes such limited vision to the Prophets in 1 Peter 1: 11."[5]

The coming of the Spirit was for Peter the decisive event that resolved all uncertainty. Until this happened he was a man who is led bewildered into a new world which he enters obediently but hesitantly. But when God gave "the same gift" (Acts 11: 17) to gentiles as to Jews he suddenly understood that God had made Jew and gentile equal recipients of the grace that is in Christ. At this point all doubt vanished and hesitation was replaced by understanding and conviction. The gift of the Spirit to Cornelius and his family removed in Peter all the tension resulting from the contradiction between his ingrained Jewish exclusivism and the divine leading that required him to preach the gospel to gentiles. Any suggestion that the amazement of the men of the circumcision who had come to Caesarea with Peter, 10: 45, was not shared by him is removed by 11: 17, "who was I that I could withstand God?" So strong had Peter's practical and conscious particularism been that he surrendered it only in the face of an unmistakable divine revelation. When this took place Peter had to choose between submission and rebellion. His submission led him to become an ardent supporter of the universal mission of the Church even though he himself remained an apostle to the circumcision, Gal. 2: 7.

It will be plain that, so far as Peter is concerned, little can be said for Warneck's thesis that it was consciousness of the Great Commission that gave evidential value to God's special providences. On the contrary, it was these divine interventions that removed Peter's particularism and gave him a correct and practically useful conception of the universalism of the gospel.

B. *The Church and the Great Commission*

We have already seen that until the Church at Jerusalem heard of the visit of Peter to Cornelius she had not in any concrete manner been confronted with the problem of her relationship to the gentiles. The test of her attitude to the gentiles was the conversion of Cornelius. We have examined her reaction to this happening. We must now further examine this reaction from the viewpoint of the question we are considering in this section.

Chapter 11: 1, 2, relates that the apostles and brethren who were in Judea heard that the gentiles also had received the word of God, and that when Peter arrived in Jerusalem "they that were of the circumcision" took sharp issue with him because he had gone to uncircumcised men and had eaten with them. Are these identical with the "apostles and the brethren that were in Judea", or do they form a group of indeterminable size among them? Some choose the latter position, holding that the apostles and the remainder of the believers looked with approval or, at all events, not with disapproval, on Peter's action. For the larger part, exegetes understand the expression "they that were of the circumcision" to refer to the entire group of believers, that is, "the apostles and the brethren that were in Judea" Acts 11: 1. A number of considerations support this judgment: (a) Peter himself had come to the recognition of the gentiles' full participation in the gospel with the greatest difficulty and had yielded only to the clearly revealed will of God. There is no reason to believe that others entertained a less conservative view than he had. (b) The same expression, "they that were of the circumcision", is used in 10: 45 to describe all the six brethren who had accompanied Peter from Joppa to Caesarea. These men were witnesses for and supporters of Peter. Zahn, holding to a separate group in 11: 2, can hardly be said to meet the difficulty in which the reference to "they that were of the circumcision" in 10: 45 involves him by saying that here these words "must have another sense".[6] Moreover, (c) the Judaistic party cannot yet be said to have arisen within the Church. The issue on which the Judaizers took their stand required some time to crystallize and when it did it was a different issue from that which was decided in connection with the conversion of Cornelius. Here the question was, may gentiles as gentiles be the recipients of salvation? The question of the gentiles' relation to the law was not raised. For the Judaizers on the other hand, the issue was, must not gentiles, before they can be saved, submit to the Mosaic law? (d) Finally, and most importantly, the hearty response that met Peter's explanation of his action can hardly be confined to a group among his hearers: "And when they heard these things they held their peace, and glorified God, saying, Then to the gentiles also hath God granted repentance unto life" 11: 18. Such a spontaneous, whole-hearted rejoicing in the salvation of gentiles is nowhere in the New Testament attributed to Judaizers.

In summary, there seems to be no warrant to believe that awareness of the Great Commission played a role in the mind of the Church at Jerusalem when she took the great decision to acknowledge the equal share of the gentiles in the gospel and to validate Peter's baptism of the household of Cornelius. As Wikenhauser says, "The position which the primitive Church took with respect to missions to the gentiles is evident from this, that it required from Peter an accounting of his baptism of the gentile Cornelius."[7]

The conversion of Cornelius and its attendant legitimizing of the gentiles' participation in the gospel having been fully set forth, Luke now proceeds to a further description of the expansion of the faith in the gentile world. With the exception of chapter 12 the remainder of the book is devoted to this theme. Immediately following the account of the conversion of Cornelius, Luke relates that those who were scattered as a result of the persecution that arose after Stephen's death travelled as far as Phoenicia, Cyprus and Antioch. These, he explicitly states, spoke the word to the Jews only, 11: 10. This is wholly consonant with the pattern obtaining up to 9: 31. But there is also an important break in the pattern. There were some, we read, men of the Diaspora from Cyprus and Cyrene, who, on coming to Antioch, spoke to the Greeks also and preached Christ to them, vv. 20, 21. Whether this took place before or after the conversion of Cornelius is difficult to determine. In favor of placing it after is the place which Luke gives it in the ordering of his account. In favor of placing it before is the fact that Luke relates this preaching to the scattering of Christians that followed the stoning of Stephen. This would seem to have taken place some time before the visit of Peter to Caesarea. The argument that the preaching to the Greeks would hardly have been undertaken without the prior validation recorded in 10: 1–11: 18 is not conclusive. Nothing is said about the decision of the Church at Jerusalem, and it is significant that only men from the Diaspora spoke to the Greeks. It is very much a question whether these less ceremonially bound Jews, aflame with Pentecostal fire, would feel the need for permission from the leaders of the Church in Jerusalem to testify to the hope that was in them. There can be no doubt, however, that when news of this witness finally reached Jerusalem the decision concerning Peter's action in Caesarea had been rendered. This is evident from the fact that the Church sent Barnabas to supervise this work among the gentiles, and that he, a Levite, Acts 4: 36, wholly endorsed it. What is more important to note is that this first recorded voluntary witness of Jewish Christians to gentiles was not undertaken by the apostles to whom Jesus had given the Great Commission, but by men to whom Jesus had given no command to witness to the gentiles and concerning whom we have no reason to believe that they had received it through the apostles. There is mention here only of an uncommanded, undirected, spontaneous witness to the faith on the part of lay-Christians.

It will not be necessary to pursue this inquiry further by investigating the motivation that led gentile Churches to their missionary witness. It may suffice to state that there is no evidence that consciousness of the Great Commission constituted an element in their motivation. We may close this part

43

of the discussion by stating that there is no ground to believe that awareness of the Great Commission played a role in launching the Church on her missionary labors.

C. *Paul and the Great Commission*

We must, finally, inquire whether awareness of the Great Commission played any role in the missionary thinking of the apostle Paul. Is it true, as Warneck holds, that Paul's special calling to missionary service derived its binding character from the Great Commission as an underlying assumption in all the missionary labor of the early Church and that therefore Paul also shared that assumption? There is no evidence that the apostles or anyone else ever communicated the command of Jesus to Paul. This is particularly remarkable in view of the fact that Luke, in speaking about Paul and in quoting him, clearly and repeatedly indicates the nature of the imperatives that moved Paul to his missionary labors. Three days after Paul's encounter with the exalted Christ on the Damascus road the Lord commissioned Ananias to restore to Paul his lost vision. To Ananias' protestations that this man was an enemy of the faith the Lord answered, "Go thy way, for he is a chosen vessel unto me, to bear my name before the gentiles and kings, and the children of Israel" 9: 15. This is the first indication of Paul's missionary destiny. Immediately after his conversion he preached in the synagogue at Damascus, 9: 20–22, and disputed with the Grecian Jews in Jerusalem where he had to flee from Damascus, 9: 23–29. In Jerusalem also Paul found himself in danger of his life, and brethren took him first to Caesarea, then to Tarsus, 9: 30. It was from there that Barnabas called him to assist in the work at Antioch where together they labored a whole year, 11: 25–26. These events were preparatory to his being designated by the Holy Spirit to be sent out with Barnabas on a missionary tour to Asia Minor, 13: 1–3. The first recorded statement of Paul's own declaration concerning his missionary motivation we find in Acts 13: 46–47. In the

44

concrete context of rejection by Jews and acceptance by gentiles he says jointly with Barnabas, "It was necessary that the word of God should first be spoken to you. Seeing ye thrust it from you, and judge yourselves unworthy of eternal life, lo, we turn to the gentiles." Then, validating his turning to the gentiles by appeal to a special revelation from God, he does not adduce as his warrant the Great Commission, but a quotation from Isaiah, "For so hath the Lord commanded us, saying, I have set thee for a light to the gentiles, that thou shouldest be for salvation to the uttermost part of the earth." Luke's next reference to Paul's commission to preach to the gentiles is made in connection with Paul's defense before the Jews in his famous "Speech on the Stairs". There Paul states that God had revealed to him through Ananias that he would be "a witness for him unto all men" of what he had seen and heard, 22: 15, and that God had said to him directly in a trance which he had experienced in the temple, "Depart, for I will send thee forth far hence unto the gentiles" 22: 21. In his defense before King Agrippa he relates the words that Christ spoke to him on the Damascus road, ". . . delivering thee from the people, and from the gentiles, unto whom I send thee, that they may turn from darkness to light . . ." 26: 17, 18. Finally, we note Paul's testimony in his letter to the Galatians: immediately after his conversion he did not confer with flesh and blood, nor did he go to Jerusalem to those who were apostles before him, but he went away into Arabia and returned again to Damascus, 1: 15–17. In all these statements of motivation and the manner in which he came to his missionary calling we search in vain for any indication that the Great Commission was the moving factor or even a moving factor in Paul's witnessing ministry.

It is clearly not possible, in view of the foregoing, to accept the view that an awareness of the Great Commission was the element that gave a binding quality to the direct revelation that Paul had received as warrant for his mission to the gentiles. Just as Peter, and the Church at Jerusalem, and the Christian

Jews of the Diaspora were brought to a missionary vision without manifesting any knowledge of the Great Commission, so Paul was led into his prodigious missionary labors without evidencing any such knowledge.

In concluding this chapter a final question must be asked. Can it be that the early Church did indeed entertain the Great Commission as a silent presupposition but viewed its execution in terms of traditional Jewish proselytizing? Is it possible that the apostles and Jewish believers regarded it as their task to move gentile converts or prospective converts to the faith to become Jews as a condition of entry into the Church? We have already seen that the Church at Jerusalem, after the coming of the Holy Spirit on the household of Cornelius, did not entertain the possibility of receiving gentile believers in this manner. But can we not say, in fairness to Warneck, that *before* this event occurred the Great Commission may have been understood as a command to proselyte gentiles into the Jewish nation as a means to membership in the Church? This would mean that the Jewish Christians were indeed aware of the Great Commission but simply misunderstood it. It would remove the remarkable difference of non-awareness and emphatic awareness that we have discovered between the early Church and the Church in the modern period with respect to Christ's command.

A simple but conclusive fact militates against this supposition. This fact is that the Jerusalem Church did not lift a finger to carry the Great Commission, so understood, into effect. The judaizing element in the Church later attempted this form of evangelism, but their effort was never regarded as legitimate. Neither before nor after the conversion of Cornelius did *the Church* attempt or validate such a means of reaching the gentiles with the gospel.

In view of the conclusions of this chapter it must seem strange indeed that Luke should so prominently mention the Great Commission in Acts 1:8, build up his whole account in terms of

THE GREAT COMMISSION: NEW TESTAMENT

the geographic expansion indicated in Christ's command, and yet say nothing further about it in the remainder of his work. Here we may anticipate our later concern with this problem by saying that the Great Commission played a powerful role in the missionary witness of the early Church from the day of Pentecost to the present. It can be said that it always has been, is now, and always will be the heart and soul of all true missionary witness. But its meaning for and place in the life of the missionary community must, we believe, be differently construed than is customarily done. The Great Commission, as we shall have occasion to see, derives its meaning and power wholly and exclusively from the Pentecost event.

Chapter 3

An inquiry into the significance of Pentecost for the missionary witness of the Church requires that we acquaint ourselves with the relationships that have been seen between Pentecost and missions in the past. It is the purpose of this chapter to present a brief historical survey of these relationships. The magnitude of the Pentecost event and its intimate association with the beginning of the missionary endeavors of the Church give reason for entertaining high expectations of an historical inquiry such as is here undertaken. These expectations are disappointed. Few, if any, areas of theological investigation have been left so unexplored as the field on which we here enter. It is true, correlation between Pentecost and missions there has always been. Never has the great power of the Pentecost event and its gift of the Spirit by which the missionary enterprise is borne forward and made effective been wholly out of the mind of its agents. "So bright a light", said Roland Allen, "could not be wholly hid."[1] The power of the Spirit in the missionary witness of the Church has been great, but the light of understanding as to the nature and practical missionary significance of this power has been dim. Allen asks, "How, then, has this revelation been treated by the great teachers of our day?" He answers, "I venture to say it has been practically ignored. . . . In almost every recent work on the Holy Spirit a sentence here and there suggests it, i.e., the relationship of the Spirit to missions. But where to find any full statement of its profound significance I do not know."[2]

Even so, the history of the relationship must be set forth. An exhaustive inquiry is not intended. We shall consider the purpose of our investigation to be achieved when the characteristic viewpoints that have engaged the mind of the Church shall have been outlined. These may be subsumed under four main heads. Pentecost has been seen as providing the Church with

A. *Temporary linguistic endowment for evangelistic purposes*
B. *A symbol of the universalism of the gospel*
C. *Spiritual empowerment for missionary witness*
D. *An eschatologically qualified missionary task*

Both because of its relatively new emphasis and the close connection which it sustains to the argument of this dissertation a survey of the views that have been expressed about Pentecost in its relation to missions as an eschatologically qualified task will be omitted in this chapter. The subject and the men who have given attention to it will be taken up in the course of the argument. The others are not mutually exclusive. The first held the field prominently until the forepart of the 19th century. The second and third have always been present in greater or less degree. Until about one hundred years ago, however, they were quite overshadowed by the linguistic consideration. When this view moved into the background the others came much more into their own. There is discernible, therefore, a marked difference between the accents that missionary thinkers and exegetes of the past century and those who reflected on the missionary significance of Pentecost before them have laid on Pentecost as a symbol of the universalism of the gospel and as providing the Church with power for her missionary task. It is to these more recent expressions that we shall call attention. We shall first consider the view that Pentecost provided:

A. *Temporary linguistic endowment for evangelistic purposes*

Although the Church Fathers who commented on Pentecost universally understood the speaking in other tongues of

Acts 2 : 4 as the ability of the apostles (or of the apostles and the disciples as a group) to speak languages previously unknown to them, not all related this phenomenon explicitly to missionary activity. Among those who do, Eucherius, bishop of Lyons (died about 450), is one of the earliest known to us. In reply to the question, how the coming of the Spirit before the ascension (John 20: 22) is to be distinguished from his coming at Pentecost, he answers: at the first coming of the Spirit the apostles were qualified to forgive sins, to baptize and to administer the Spirit to believers. After the ascension, that is, at Pentecost, the apostles obtained the grace of the Holy Spirit in the work of virtue, strength of body, and in the receiving of various languages by which they would be able to preach the gospel to all the nations.[3] A similar thought is attributed to Chrysostom: the apostles received the gift of tongues since they were about to go everywhere to preach. The Syrian, Isho'dad of Merv, Nestorian bishop of Hadatha about 850, writes that the gift of tongues was given to the apostles, among other reasons,

> because with *diverse tongues* they were to preach to the strange *tongues* in the world. . . . And *some* hand down, that to the Twelve alone the gift was given, that they might speak with all *Tongues;* but to others was given each a *tongue*, the one which he was destined to preach in the region to which he was sent by the Spirit; and not only this, but what was more wonderful, while one of the apostles was speaking with any *tongue*, whatever it might be if it happened that there were sitting before him possessors of other *tongues*, every one of them understood the word which was being spoken by the apostles according to his *tongue*; for the Spirit formed his voice by means of the air in the ears of the hearers according to the speaking of the *tongue* of each.[4]

Theophylact, archbishop in Bulgaria about 1078, further enlarges on the missionary significance of Pentecost. Why did flames of fire descend on the heads of the apostles? Because the apostles were ordained and appointed teachers of the whole world, and as the placing of the hand on the head is a fit symbol of ordination, so here the tongues descended on the heads of the apostles to indicate their universal task. For the discharge of this task they were equipped with the ability to speak the required languages.[5]

The view current before the Reformation was continued in the Reformation and in the post-Reformation period well into the 19th century. It finds expression in Calvin. The tongues of fire signify the purifying power of the gospel and the apostles are endowed with the gift of speaking foreign languages in order to the carrying out of the Great Commission outside the borders of Israel. Pentecost has permanent meaning for the Church, but this consists in the soteriological operations of the Spirit which also constrain the believer to make with his tongue a true confession. Peter's quotation from Joel, "And your sons and your daughters shall prophesy" Acts 2: 17, refers to the enlightenment of the mind and the impartation of the grace of salvation. The promise, "and ye shall receive the gift of the Holy Spirit" 2: 38, applies to a certain extent to the entire Church, but its primary significance was limited to Peter's hearers on whom also the gift of languages hitherto unknown to them was conferred.[6] Luther's understanding is much like Calvin's. The Holy Spirit had worked long before in the hearts of men to bring them to faith, to enlighten, to strengthen and to comfort. But now he does so "completely and openly". At Pentecost the Kingdom of Christ was revealed to the whole world. As an instrument in the universal dissemination of the gospel, the ability to speak languages not spoken by them before was given to the apostles. To the Greeks they preached in Greek, to the Romans in Roman, to the Egyptians in Egyptian, to the Persians in Persian. "Wherever the apostles and their disciples came to a people they began to preach in the language of that people."[7] Benedicto Aretio, 1607, wrote that God, being pleased to use the ministry of men to move the hearts of hearers, conferred at Pentecost the gift of languages "since in the whole world there ought to be Doctors in order that the ignorance of languages should not impede the course of the gospel".[8] Joannis Lorinie, S.J., 1609, commenting on the pride of men that brought about the multiplicity of languages, observed that it was therefore fitting "for the bringing together of men in the one as it were spiritual ark of the Church, that the knowledge of distinct languages be communicated, as can be observed in most of the Fathers".[9] Liberto Fromondo, 1654, carefully avoiding identifying himself with it, reports an interesting exegesis of the "tongues of fire", Acts 2: 3, current in his day: "Some think single tongues, two-forked, three-forked or four-forked, etc., tongues to have appeared according to the number of languages of which each one received gifts and in proportion to what was needed for themselves for the promulgation of the gospel to the nations to which they were sent, or for other purposes." He himself understands that the disciples were endowed with "other languages, that is, diverse from their mother tongue, which they had never spoken before", and these, along with Sapientia, Scientia, and Miraculi, were given in so far as "they were necessary for the propagation of the gospel".[10] Similar exegeses are given by Philippus van Limborch, Johannes Gerhardus, Johannes Plevier, Hugo Grotius, Andrea Andriessen, and others.

Eduard Zeller, reviewing the earlier interpretations of the central Pentecostal phenomenon of speaking with tongues, wrote with complete justification, "This phenomenon has been regarded by the whole of the older exegesis, so far as our knowledge goes, as a miraculous speaking in foreign languages. The Christians who had gathered had, according to the old interpretation, suddenly spoken in languages until then unknown to them, and this was the result of a miraculous working of the Spirit, an ability which remained with them in the interest of the apostolic proclamation of the gospel."[11] As late as 1840 the distinguished missionary, Alexander Duff, could write, "Take the gift of tongues:—wherein did it consist? Was it not this:—that into whatever city or region an apostle entered, he found himself instantly, without any previous study, and solely by supernatural communication, enabled to address the native inhabitants in their own vernacular dialect."[12]

The correlation between Pentecost and missions set forth and illustrated above was destined in the course of the next one hundred years well-nigh wholly to disappear from academic circles, whatever their theological viewpoint might be. The next view to be considered is the conception that Pentecost provided

B. *A symbol of the universalism of the gospel*

The past century of discussion about Pentecost has been largely controlled by the interest to remove or retain the supernatural character of the event and of the phenomena associated with it. One learned treatise after another has flowed from the pens of scholars, probing in every conceivable way into the meaning of the Pentecostal phenomena and especially into the "speaking with other tongues". In this discussion detailed studies involving exegetical, historical, psychological and *religionsgeschichtliche* considerations so completely dominated the inquiry that the place and significance of Pentecost in the history of redemption were but little advanced beyond the insights obtaining in 1850. In 1905 K. F. Nösgen, complaining that Pentecost as a revelatory event was virtually being ignored in contemporary theology, observed, "Also in the third edition of the *Theol. Realencycl.* no article is devoted to the subject."[13] One of the finest studies that appeared in the course of the debate was Nikolaus Adler's *Das erste christliche Pfingstfest, Sinn und Bedeutung des Pfingstberichtes Apg 2, 1-13*. While Adler broke a noble lance for the wholly supernatural character of the Pentecost event and of the Pentecostal phenomena, his specifically theological reflection on the meaning of Pentecost

53

occupies only 23 of the 166 pages of his book, and the insights which he offers in them can hardly be said to constitute the chief contribution of his book. This lies rather in the thorough-going manner in which he refutes the thesis that Pentecost is explainable in terms of purely intra-cosmic factors. So to explain Pentecost was especially attempted by the Tübingen School. Interpreting the early history of the Church as a process whereby a synthesis was effected between the Judaistic and the universally minded Pauline parties in the Church, it regarded the Pentecost narrative as a mythical account origin-ating in the early Christian community to explain the unknown origin of the Church. This conception in turn paved the way for viewing the Pentecost account as a composite narrative arising out of sources whose origins are obscure or no longer determinable. The appearance of A. Harnack's *Die Apostel-geschichte* in 1908 had a sobering influence on the critical dis-cussion about Acts and therefore indirectly on the discussion centering around Pentecost. Although Harnack was fully as liberal and critical as the Tübingen scholars, he was led by purely literary considerations to uphold the Lukan authorship of Acts. He also drew attention to the missionary character of the book and to the far-reaching significance which its author ascribed to the Spirit in setting forth the missionary expansion of the early Church.[14]

In the course of this discussion a significant development took place with respect to the understanding of the relationship between Pentecost and missions. Many scholars who con-cerned themselves with the Pentecost account continued to see a close connection between it and the missionary witness of the Church, but completely abandoned the older conception of this relationship. The view that the disciples were endowed with the gift of languages to preach the gospel in foreign countries was surrendered. Even those scholars who accept the speaking with tongues as a speaking in foreign languages, notably N. Adler and Th. Zahn, do not conceive of this as having had missionary labor among the gentiles as its purpose. The emphasis in the interpretation of Pentecost in its significance for missions was transferred from the idea of a linguistic preparation of the Church for its missionary task to that of a symbol of the universal significance of the gospel and of the Church that it brings into being.

Two streams of interpretative thought are here discernible which may be characterized as critical and conservative. By critical in this connection is meant that scholarship which denies the historicity and supernatural character of the event as related in Acts. By conservative is meant that scholarship which understands the account in Acts 2: 1–13 as reflecting faithfully an historical and supernatural occurrence that introduced the Holy Spirit into the Church.

Representative of the more extreme type of critical thinking is Eduard Zeller, disciple of F. C. Baur, founder of the Tübingen School. That some historical event should lie at the basis of the Pentecost story is theoretically possible, but the likelihood of this is so remote that it is hardly worth entertaining. Nevertheless, it was clearly the purpose of the writer of Acts to set forth Christianity as a universal religion, "the new religion intended for all nations". This is particularly indicated by the obvious intent of the author to present the speaking with "other tongues" as a speaking in foreign languages. The linguistic confusion of Babel occasioned by the sin of man was at Pentecost undone through the unity of understanding in the diversity of languages, an emphasis that is further stressed by the list of nations whose representatives shared the phenomenal oneness of the Spirit.[15] Otto Pfleiderer, continuing the Tübingen tradition in the interpretation of Pentecost, understands that "the universality of the Christian faith . . . has in the Pentecost miracle been illustrated by means of an allegorical picture".[16] Johannes Weiss conceives the theme of Acts to be a defense of the Christian religion written for gentile Christians and directed against the Jews with the aim of showing how Judaism

55

was replaced by Christianity as the religion destined for universal acceptance. Pentecost is, accordingly, "the symbolico-typical representation of missions to the gentiles which are to proceed from 'the apostles'".[17] K. L. Schmidt finds an historical basis for the imaginatively elaborated Pentecost account in "a grand mass ecstasy" and considers that the writer presented this in the form which he chose in order to indicate the destiny of Christianity as a religion of universal scope.[18]

Adolf Harnack regards the Acts of the Apostles as a book written with the central purpose of showing "the power of the spirit of Jesus in the apostles historically set forth", and manifesting itself principally in the missionary expansion of Christianity. When Luke wrote his account Christianity had already spread far beyond the borders of Palestine and the Pentecost story served to present an "anticipatory portrayal" of the conquests that were to mark the course of the expansion of the faith. While acknowledging the historicity of Pentecost as little as any of his liberal contemporaries, Harnack nevertheless makes a distinct advance on them. He has caught the indissoluble relationship which Luke conceived to exist between missions and the Spirit. The power of the Spirit manifest in the apostles finds in the missionary expansion the historical movement through which it comes to expression. Within this context Pentecost is the impressive "portrayal" depicted at the beginning of the book to dramatize the theme of the Expansion.[19] In relating his understanding of the Spirit to missions Harnack does little more than get beyond his thematic statement. The erroneous conception which he has of the "Spirit of Jesus" makes further correlation between the Spirit and missions quite impossible. A position similar to Harnack's but even less developed is presented by F. J. Foakes Jackson and Kirsopp Lake. The Pentecost narrative betrays clearer marks of legendary influence than any other chapter in Acts. Nevertheless, the "gift of the Holy Spirit" is the most important constant factor throughout the first generation of the Church and it was the Spirit that led the Church onward to the evangelization of the gentiles.[20]

In common with representatives of the critical view, theologians belonging to the conservative direction see the Pentecost event as pointing to the claim of Christianity to be a worldwide religion. For them, however, the Pentecost account is not a construction reflecting a wholly fictitious drama or one that has some no longer determinable religious experience of the early Church as its basis. The events related in Acts 2: 1–13 are history. The speaking with tongues may be referred to as a symbol of the universal diffusion of the gospel (Nösgen) or as a "pointer" (Adler) to this fact, but symbol and pointer rest in a supernatural historically manifest reality that promises to effect what symbol and pointer indicate. There is, therefore, only formal similarity between the two groups.

Alongside the agreement among conservative theologians concerning the missionary significance of Pentecost there is considerable divergence as to the manner in which the "speaking with other tongues" is to be understood. Among those who understand this phenomenon as a speaking in foreign languages may be mentioned Gotthard Victor Lechler, Th. Zahn, Karl F. Nösgen, and the Roman Catholics N. Adler and A. Steinmann. Others see in it a form of inspired speech akin to the glossolaly of which Paul speaks in 1 Cor. 12. Representative of this view are F. W. Grosheide, J. M. S. Baljon, F. F. Bruce, and the Roman Catholic A. Wikenhauser. Richard B. Rackham puts forward a view which, considering the uncertainty surrounding the specific nature of the speaking with "other tongues", is attractive because of its very indefiniteness: "The apostles speak with *other tongues*: for this voice of the Spirit speaking in humanity is something new: it is the new 'law or word of the Lord going forth from Jerusalem'. The apostles 'sing a new song'. But this new speech is to continue, for the apostles only *begin to speak*. It will also heal the divisions caused by the confusion of tongues at Babel."[21] Abraham Kuyper, on the other hand, finds in the "speaking with other tongues" a speaking of the language that was spoken in Paradise. Notwithstanding these differences, there is general agreement on the missionary significance of Pentecost. F. F. Bruce's understanding of the speaking in tongues at Pentecost may be regarded as typical:

> The content is more important than the manner. On the present occasion, the content of the ecstatic utterances was "the mighty works of God", and the range of the languages in which these were proclaimed suggests that Luke thought of the coming of the Spirit more particularly as a preparation for the world-wide proclamation of the gospel. The church of Christ still speaks in many tongues, and if her speech is not now of the supernatural order that marked the day of Pentecost, the message is the same —the mighty works of God.[22]

In closing this section allusion must be made to the relationship that has been found between the Pentecostal speaking with tongues and the rabbinic tradition respecting the giving of the law at Sinai. When God gave the law, Rabbi Jochanan taught, every word that issued from His mouth divided itself into seventy languages so that every nation might hear the divine commandments in its own speech.[23] A segment of New Testament scholarship has found in this Jewish tradition an explanation of the Pentecost account and particularly of its universalistic reference. The descent of the Spirit from above, the speaking with other tongues, the list of nations represented, and the universalistic reference of the whole, are said to be an obvious borrowing from the tradition to explain the beginning of the Church. Adler has subjected this claim to searching examination and convincingly demonstrated its untenability.

The conservative understanding of the Pentecost account holds common ground with the earlier Reformation and post-Reformation interpretation in viewing Pentecost as both an historical event and as having significance for the missionary witness of the Church. It deepens the conception of this significance, however, by pointing to a relationship that is both prophetic in character and abiding in meaning.

We must next briefly examine the view that Pentecost provided

C. *Spiritual empowerment for missionary witness*

In the views so far discussed the significance of Pentecost was seen to rest chiefly, in one way or another, in the phenomenon of speaking with tongues. We must now discuss a conception which largely passes over considerations of phenomena but brings to the fore the idea of the endowment of the Church with power for the discharge of her missionary mandate. This conception is derived less from the Pentecost account itself than from Jesus' promise of the Spirit, "But ye shall receive power when the Holy Spirit is come upon you: and ye shall be my witness . . ." Acts 1: 8, and from the effect of the gift of the Spirit on the life of the Church. It is doubtless this aspect of Pentecost that the International Missionary Council had in mind when it called attention to the "powerful corporate and individual witness" manifested by the early Church from the day of Pentecost onward.[24] We meet here an understanding of Pentecost in its missionary significance which is more than an objective theological formulation concerning the universalism of the gospel. The idea of Pentecostal endowment of the Church with power for her missionary labors makes Pentecost contemporaneous, as it were, with all the ages of the Church's history. The Spirit is the continuing dynamic in the life of the witnessing Church and of her witnessing servants. It is therefore significant that the finest expressions of this view come not from exegetes and dogmatic theologians, but from men who either through direct missionary labors or through the study of missions are intimately identified with the struggles, problems, and successes of the missionary witness of the Church.

Albert von Ostertag, historian of missions, compressed into one sentence the living and indissoluble relationship between

Christ's command and the execution of it by the Church in the power of the Pentecostal Spirit:

> The early Church, the Church founded at Pentecost, is the blessed fellowship of saints and beloved of God, filled with the Spirit of Christ. She received from her Head not merely the command, but also the inner, mighty, irresistible drive of life and love to transmit to her environment the life she has received in the same way in which she herself obtained it.[25]

Robert E. Speer, commenting on the relationship between Pentecost and missions, observes that the missionary enterprise is a spiritual enterprise whose ends, methods, and motives are spiritual. Therefore there is a most close tie between the discharge of the missionary task and the Spirit of the loving God. The Holy Spirit alone can reveal to the Church her missionary character; He alone can prepare the world for the Church's mission. It is the Spirit who must lift the Church out of her self-centredness into a vision of life and service in imitation of Christ; only He can teach the hearts of men that every Christian has a call to missionary service. In the same manner John R. Mott, supporting with many illustrations his central thought, "The Superhuman Factor" in missions, writes:

> Missionaries, native Christian workers, and leaders of missionary activities on the home field, while they differ on nearly all questions pertaining to plans, means, and methods, are absolutely united in the conviction that the world's evangelization is a divine enterprise, that the Spirit of God is the great missioner, and that only as He dominates the work and workers can we hope for success in the undertaking to carry the knowledge of Christ to all people. They believe that He gave the missionary impulse to the early Church, and that today all true mission work must be inaugurated, directed and sustained by Him.[26]

J. H. Bavinck, the Dutch missionary thinker, sees rich Pentecostal and missionary significance in Paul's words, "For in one Spirit were we all baptized into one body, whether Jews or Greeks, whether bond or free; and were all made to drink of one Spirit"

1 Cor. 12: 13. Pentecost is no less than the divine proclamation that the "middle wall of partition between us" has been openly broken down. That which separated the world into two camps fell away at Pentecost and there came into being one world that was destined to be the domain in which Christ would gather His Church. Pentecost is the announcement that God's ultimate intention with respect to the world has begun to go into effect. God will gather His congregation from every tongue and generation and people. That is to say, the missionary program was announced, the power of Christ was declared over all the nations of mankind. The Church that has Pentecost standing at the beginning of her history is the Church that has received the Comforter, the Comforter in whom Christ Himself accompanies His people. It is the Church that has a powerful program requiring activity and exertion in every area of her life. But it is most particularly the Church that has a mandate to draw all the world within the circle of the light that is Christ.

At the international missionary conference held at Willingen in 1952 F. W. Dillistone related Pentecost intimately to the missionary task confronting the Church today. The manifestation of the Spirit at Pentecost began with communication and brought into being a community. The situation of brokenness and estrangement in our contemporary world is a renewed challenge to present the gospel of reconciliation in the power of the Spirit who from the beginning has been the Spirit of Witness for the Church and the Spirit of Worship in the Church.[27]

No review of the place which the Spirit as power occupies in missionary literature may fail to mention the name of Roland Allen. He is pre-eminently the missionary thinker of the Spirit. Allen's conception of the missionary task finds in the doctrine of the Spirit its determinative factor, and from it he drew important conclusions for the practical execution of the work. It is best at this place only to mention him and to leave more extended references to his thought for later consideration.

Hendrik Kraemer calls attention to the fact that at the very moment in which the Church was born her missionary task also began. A clearer and more striking demonstration of the fact that Church and missions constitute a natural, an essential unity is hardly conceivable. Kraemer rightly emphasizes that the whole manner of the Pentecost event underscores this. Church means missions and missions mean Church. The first activity of the Church was a prophetic missionary witness. The descent of the Spirit made the disciples apostles, i.e., missionaries. One might almost say, it *branded* them as apostles. The world-embracing missionary vision is expressed in prophetic reality in the speaking with tongues. At Pentecost the whole of God's redemptive purpose with the world was for a moment set off in bold relief. The Beginning and the End was revealed: the Beginning of the Church's missionary course throughout the world, and the End when the whole world shall have been gained for the gospel. Pentecost is the fulfilment of the promise: You shall receive the power of the Holy Spirit and you shall be my witnesses, Acts 1: 8. But, more than this, in the Pentecost account an illustration is given of the thought that has in recent years so frequently been expressed, namely that the Church and her missionary task must be seen eschatologically. The Church lives between the first and the second coming of Christ. She is conscious of being the uniting element between these two events, and she must express herself in terms of this consciousness. The Church is an interim phenomenon and her characteristic activity in the interim period is missionary activity. Judging by the Pentecost account we may say that both Church and missions are creations of the Holy Spirit and are both taken up as essential elements in the divine plan for the world.[28]

D. *Missions as an eschatologically qualified task*

Since we shall have occasion to introduce the eschatological significance of Pentecost for the missionary witness of the

Church again and again in the course of the argument, we shall not enter further upon the question at this point.

It is evident from the foregoing brief review that Pentecost has not played a determinative role in missionary theological thinking. Suggestive, even penetrating, thoughts have been presented but, except by Roland Allen, a missionary theology centering around Pentecost and its continuing meaning for the Church has not been developed. Nowhere is this more plainly evident than in Gustav Warneck's *Evangelische Missionslehre* which is undoubtedly the fullest and ripest statement of the theology of missions that has been written. Here and there a sentence indirectly indicates an awareness of the role which Pentecost plays in the missionary witness of the Church: the missionary power revealed in the early Church did not arise simply out of obedience to the external command, but it was expressive of an urge to witness which had its roots in the new spiritual life; the Holy Spirit serves to remind the Church of her mandate to witness when her missionary zeal becomes cold; the driving power of the promised Holy Spirit is, along with Christ's universal power, the scriptures that had to be fulfilled, and the authority lying in Christ's being sent by the Father, the ground for the giving of Christ's command to disciple the nations. Such occasional observations clearly do not give to Pentecost a central and determinative role in the construction of Warneck's missionary conception. The elements for the development of the missionary significance of Pentecost are there, but they receive no elaboration. For Warneck the missionary task, so far as its theological formulation is concerned, rests on other bases. Even less is said about the significance of Pentecost for missions by Julius Richter in his *Evangelische Missionskunde* and by F. E. Daubanton and the Roman Catholic J. Schmidlin in their systematic treatments of the theory of missions. Representative missionary magazines like the *International Review of Missions*, the *Evangelische*

Missionsmagazin, and the *Allgemeine Missionszeitschrift* reflect, in attention they have devoted to the subject in the course of the years, the general lack of interest indicated above.

So far as we can determine, Roland Allen's judgment concerning the interest of his British theological contemporaries in the significance of Pentecost for missions is a judgment that applies with equal force to the missionary thought of the Church as a whole. "How then has this revelation been treated by the great teachers . . . ? I venture to say it has been practically ignored. So bright a light could not be wholly hid. . . . But where to find any full statement of its profound significance I do not know."

Chapter 4

THE MOVEMENT OF THE SPIRIT IN THE HISTORY OF REDEMPTION

THE significance of Pentecost for the missionary witness of the Church can be measured only against the background of the role which Pentecost plays in the entire history of redemption. While endeavoring not to lose ourselves in this much broader subject, some indication of what the outpouring of the Holy Spirit means for the onward movement of the redemptive process should be given. The perspectives thus gained will have to be alluded to again and again in the treatment of the subject proper.

The first of many commentaries that have been made on the Pentecost event was made by the apostle Peter. It is significant that the very first word which he spoke about it declared it to be an event of profound eschatological import: "But this is that which hath been spoken through the prophet Joel: and it shall be in the last days, saith God, I will pour forth of my Spirit on all flesh" Acts 2: 17. It would indeed be difficult to find a biblical passage that indicates a greater cleavage between what had been and what became than is found in the first thirteen verses of the second chapter of Acts. The extent of this cleavage is indicated by the difference between John's "For the Holy Spirit was not yet" ch. 7: 39, and Peter's "Being therefore by the right hand of God exalted, and having received of the Father the promise of the Holy Spirit, he hath poured forth this which ye see and hear" Acts 2: 33. This cleavage is at the same time, however, the deepest point of continuity between the old and the new dispensations. Pentecost is the fulfilment of Old Testament prophecies concerning the coming of the Spirit, and it marks the incipient realization of the promise given to Abraham, "In thee shall all the families of the earth be blessed" Gen. 12: 3. At Pentecost a distinct period in the divine economy of redemption was introduced, the characteristic feature of which is the presence of the Holy Spirit. We may therefore say that after Creation and Incarnation the outpouring of the Spirit is the third great work of God.

Before we can discuss the place which Pentecost occupies in the history of redemption we must first speak a word about the relationship of the Holy Spirit to creation. In the understanding of the Old Testament the Spirit is the principle of creation and of life in the natural world. He brooded upon the face of the waters in the beginning, Gen. 1: 2; the Spirit of God has made man, the breath of the Almighty has given him life, Job 33: 4, and all the host of heaven were made by the breath of his mouth, Ps. 33: 6. Luther taught that only Christians have the sanctifying Holy Spirit, but the life-giving Spirit informs all men of wisdom, insight and prudence.[1] Calvin describes the Spirit as diffused over all space, sustaining, invigorating, and quickening all things, both in heaven and on earth, while his transfusion of vigor into all things, breathing into them being, life and motion, is plainly divine.[2] The substratum of the life of man and of nature, the vital power informing and sustaining all cosmic processes, is the Spirit of the living God. This life-giving and life-sustaining function of the Spirit forms the basis for and finds its parallel expression in the redemptive renewal of the life of man and of nature. The operations of the Spirit in creation and redemption are therefore not disparate activities. Redemption has no meaning apart from creation. The Redeemer-God and the Creator-God are one. Redemption means the redemption of *creation*. The Spirit who brooded over the face of the waters in the beginning is the same Spirit who is the life of the *new* creation. The work of the Spirit in creation and in redemption is *one* work that brings the whole of created reality to its ultimate destiny.

66

The central event that marks the participation of the Spirit in the effecting of the new creation is Pentecost. Since Pentecost does not stand in isolation from but is intimately related to the work of the Spirit in the whole of redemptive history, an inquiry into the significance of Pentecost must be preceded by a delineation of the role of the Spirit in this history. We shall limit this delineation to a description of the movement of the Spirit in the redemptive process.

In the realm of the natural the work of the Spirit is, as far as our knowledge goes, undifferentiated. In the sphere of redemption, on the other hand, the operations of the Spirit present themselves in several distinct though not unrelated stages. The movement of the Spirit in the discharge of His redemptive function pursues a course consisting of a process of contraction followed by a process of expansion, culminating in His indwelling of the universal Church as the manifestation of the new humanity. This movement may be described as follows:

A. *Universal concern with mankind*
B. *Limitation to Israel*
C. *Concentration in the Messiah*
D. *Diffusion through the apostles*
E. *Indwelling in the Church universal*

The central point of the movement is Christ. *To* Him all the work of the Spirit tends, *from* Him the Spirit and His work flow to effect the regeneration of men and of the cosmos. The movement is from the many to the One and from the One to the many. The redemptive line as moving from universalism to universalism through a process of contraction and expansion has been effectively set forth by O. Cullmann in his well-known work, *Christ and Time*. Here we are concerned only with the movement of the Spirit in this process.

A. *Universal concern with mankind*

In the pre-Abrahamic period God's redemptive work was not bound to a particular nation or group of men. It was therefore universal in extent. Although there is no specific reference to a soteric operation of the Spirit during this period, that operation comes indirectly to expression in the delineation of the redemptive line passing from Adam and Seth through Noah to Abraham. When this line had progressed to Noah its integrity was threatened by gross apostasy manifesting itself especially in inter-marriage between those whose life was directed Godward and those whose life was not. At this point God sought to safeguard the integrity of the line that was to issue in the Messiah by the judgment of the deluge. The post-diluvian humanity, however, proved no more responsive to the divine will than the pre-diluvian. Its pride and disobedience found climactic expression in the building of the tower of Babel. With this second manifestation of universal intransigence God effected a severe limitation in the scope of His soteric dealings with men. This limitation was effected through the calling of Abraham. To him and to his descendants was given the special function of preserving in its integrity the messianic line culminating in the coming of Christ and in the second universal diffusion of the grace of redemption. Even so, God never wholly relinquished His hold on the nations whom He continued both to bless and judge. God's mercy and God's judgment prevented their complete moral and spiritual disintegration and preserved them for an eventual confrontation with the redeeming Spirit. The withdrawal from them of the Spirit in His soteric activity was effected with a view to their ultimate salvation. In the very act of calling Abraham, God made plain the universalistic reference of his call to separation, "in thee shall all the families of the earth be blessed" Gen. 12: 3.

B. *Limitation to Israel*

During the period of Old Testament particularism the activities of the Spirit come to expression in a consistently characteristic manner. He descends intermittently and abides for a time on particular men or classes of men to achieve a particular purpose. In this manner He confers gifts of wisdom and skill,[3] of rulership and military prowess[4] and, especially, of prophecy.[5] Sufficiently akin to this activity to be classed with it is that manifestation of the Spirit whereby He removes a man from one place to another either physically or in a vision. His descent is always occasional in character. This so characteristic activity of the Spirit in the Old Testament bears a distinctly soteric character. The descents of the Spirit and the endowments which He confers qualify Israel's leaders to govern the chosen people and guide them to the fulfilment of their redemptive role. He equips workmen to build the tabernacle in which God will dwell and in which sacrifice will be made to Him. It is in the prophetic sphere, however, that the Spirit most prominently expresses Himself. Through the prophets on whom the Spirit descends the divine word is made known by which Israel is called from its waywardness to obedience. In the ruin of its sin and international involvements, it is presented with the hope of the Messiah who will effect its deliverance. The Old Testament passages that speak of this hope are of a distinctly eschatological nature. The prophets of Israel foretell the coming of the Suffering Servant and of the new age that the outpouring of the Spirit will inaugurate. The Spirit will be pre-eminently concentrated in the Messiah and He will wholly indwell the people of God who shall live in the eschatological period. The abiding presence of the Spirit will be, as Eichrodt has said, "the central wonder of the new aeon", in which He will no longer appear "start-wise" but He will exercise "an enduring influence on men".[6] Here Incarnation and Pentecost and the new period in the economy of redemption that shall be inaugurated by them are adumbrated.

We find only faint traces in the Old Testament of an indwelling of the Spirit in God's people as a body and in its members individually, both of which are so characteristic of the Spirit's presence in the Church of the New Testament. Taken by itself, David's prayer "Take not thy Holy Spirit from me", Ps. 51: 11, seems to indicate such an indwelling. Apparently David here prays that the Spirit enabling him to live righteously as a member of the covenant community be not taken from him in punishment for his sin. It is questionable whether this psalm in its entire Old Testament context allows this interpretation. It is difficult to square with the unvarying emphasis on the occasional character of the Spirit's operations in the old dispensation. O. Procksch suggests that "the poet experiences already in the present, by virtue of the Spirit, participation in the messianic time".[7] It is more likely that David, remembering how Saul was deprived of the Spirit of rulership with which he had been anointed, besought the Lord that his sin of adultery and murder might not be followed by a similar punishment. Such an interpretation would be supported by the view of K. Bornhäuser that, in the light of verse 12, David must have had reference to the Spirit of rulership.[8] This verse reads, "With the *ruach nedibah* strengthen me". The Septuagint renders *ruach nedibah* as "spirit of rulership"; so that the passage could mean, "With the Spirit of rulership strengthen me". The word *nedibah* can mean nobility, highness and, therefore, by extension, rulership. It is generally translated in the sense of willingness or freedom, however. Even if certainty could be achieved here the problem of how to understand "thy Holy Spirit" in verse 11 would remain. In Hag. 2: 5, "So my Spirit remaineth among you, fear you not", the presence of the Spirit is mentioned in connection with the rebuilding of the temple. There is indicated, therefore, a characteristic occasional operation of the Spirit. But since the rebuilding of the temple was not the task of a few but of the whole people, 1: 14, we may see here a striving of the Spirit to communicate Himself to the entire covenant community. In this passage and, to some extent, in Isa. 63: 11, indications of the occasional character of the Spirit's presence are accompanied by suggestions of a larger presence.

While the activity of the Spirit centers pre-eminently in His occasional descent on specific men for specific purposes, evidence of a more diffused presence of the Spirit in the congregation as a whole seems, therefore, not to be entirely absent. This intimation of a more pervasive presence of the Spirit in Israel should make us careful not to minimize the place which the Spirit took in the moral and religious life of the Old Testament covenant community. The several passages suggesting a wider presence of the Spirit may not improperly be regarded as evidence of a larger activity than is revealed. It is indeed impossible to read the intensely spiritual utterances of the Psalmists and the Prophets, and the accounts of the lives and actions of men and women on whom no descent of the Spirit is related, without being deeply impressed with the Spirit-derived life and worship that often obtained before the coming of the Holy Spirit at Pentecost. In the following chapter we shall suggest the reason for the occasional and in many respects obscure activity of the Spirit in the Old Testament dispensation.

C. *Concentration in the Messiah*

Intense messianic concentration is characteristic of the Spirit's work in the Gospels and in the first chapter of Acts. The manifestations of the Spirit are there almost wholly centered in or around Jesus as though in preparation for a mighty dispersion. The Spirit is mentioned in connection with the birth of John the Baptist, Luke 1: 15, 67, the forerunner of Him who will establish the Kingdom. The birth of Jesus stands wholly under the sign of the Spirit.[9] John prophesies of Him that He will baptize with the Spirit,[10] and when he baptizes Jesus the Spirit descends on Him in the form of a dove.[11] It is the Spirit that drives Jesus into the wilderness to be tempted.[12] For the discharge of His messianic labors He is endowed with the Spirit without measure, John 3: 34. Jesus appropriates to Himself the prophecy of the coming of the

71

Spirit of the Messiah, Luke 4: 18, and Matthew also sees in Him the fulfilment of prophecy concerning the messianic Spirit, 12: 18. Jesus casts out demons by the Spirit of God, Matt. 12: 28, He commands baptism to be done in the name of Father, Son and Holy Spirit, 28: 19, and through the Holy Spirit conveys His last instructions to the apostles whom He has chosen, Acts 1: 2.

There are two passages in the Gospels that speak of a personal indwelling of the Spirit: "If ye, then, being evil, know how to give good gifts unto your children, how much more shall your heavenly Father give the Holy Spirit to them that ask him" Luke 11: 13, and the Spirit passages in Jesus' interview with Nicodemus, John 3, especially "Except a man be born of water and the Spirit, he cannot enter into the Kingdom of God" v. 5. Neither of these references is easy to understand. They are so characteristic of the post-Pentecostal relationship between the Spirit and the believer that it is difficult to understand their meaning for the time when "the Spirit was not yet". Some regard Jesus' words to Nicodemus as an anachronistic reference on the part of John to the Spirit-conferring baptism that was later to be practiced by the disciples. There is no need, however, to refer the expression "water and Spirit" to the later rite of Christian baptism or to suggest that Jesus did not actually speak these words. John's baptism in the waters of the Jordan was well known, as was also his prophecy of baptism by the Spirit which the Messiah would confer. It was reasonable to expect that a religious leader in Israel would be acquainted with this teaching that was working a spiritual revolution among the people. Moreover, John, more than the synoptists, thought and wrote in terms of the Pentecostal Spirit. This led him on at least one occasion to quote Jesus as presenting the work of the Spirit as present reality while with the use of an editorial insertion he added that this was said of the Spirit that was yet to come, John 7: 38, 39. It is entirely conceivable that in 3: 5 John quotes Jesus after a similar fashion without adding editorial comment upon the futuristic reference of the Lord's teaching. The coming of the Spirit was no longer distant; it was imminent. The Lord in whom the kingdom was present reality was already before the Pentecostal manifestation of it speaking in terms of the new condition of things that would obtain with the coming of the Spirit. On other occasions Jesus did not permit the inability of His hearers to understand Him to withhold Him from speaking about things that they would understand later.[13] The urging of Jesus to ask for the Holy Spirit, Luke 11: 13, and His speaking of the Spirit as present before He had been poured out, John 3: 5–8, may be regarded as a divine pedagogy that prepared Jesus' hearers for the coming of the Spirit. When Jesus spoke these words the Spirit "was not yet" John 7: 39. The not-yetness of the Spirit in the Church, His concentration in Jesus, and Jesus' speaking of Him as present reality, all emphasize the imminence of His being poured forth. When Jesus departs the Spirit will come.[14]

D. *Diffusion through the apostles*

Although the apostles do not receive the Spirit in a different manner than the Church receives Him there belongs to them, as distinguished from other men, a special function in the diffusion abroad of the Pentecostal Spirit. They are the official and unique leaders of the Church. They have no successors. In so far as we can speak of an apostolate today that apostolate belongs to the entire Church, not to any particular man or group of men. In preparing the Church for her awaiting task Jesus dealt with her through the apostles. It is they who during three years accompanied Him and lived in His school, they were eyewitnesses of the resurrection, to them he gave the Great Commission wherein he set forth the central task of the Church in the time between the parousias. It is they who are told to wait in Jerusalem for the descent of the Spirit, and it is upon them that He bestows the symbol of the coming Spirit by breathing on them, John 20: 22, preceding and following His spiration with the mandate by which they were to live. They are sent ones. After Pentecost the kerugma is especially carried out by them, and the missionary expansion of the Church stands wholly under their leadership and guidance. It is pre-eminently through the apostles that the Spirit sent forth by Christ is transmitted to ever-widening circles. They are, under Christ, the founders of the New Testament Church.

E. *Indwelling in the Church universal*

At Pentecost the Holy Spirit made the Church as body of Christ His dwelling place. In distinction from the limiting of His operations to Israel in the old covenant and from concentration in the Messiah in the Gospels He became, after Pentecost, universal in His activities. The Church, moreover, became consciously aware of the presence of the Spirit in her midst and lives and acts in His power. The change that Pentecost effected in the relations of the Spirit to men was, therefore, radical. From Pentecost on, the abundance of the Spirit's activity in the Church is testified to in so many ways that even the roughest kind of classification of His activities seems to be quite impossible. In view of the larger attention that will be given to the nature of the Spirit's indwelling of the Church, it will suffice here merely to indicate the manifold character of His operations. He renews us, Titus 3: 5, dwells in us, Rom. 8: 11, confers gifts, 1 Cor. 12, and rich fruits of the Spirit, Gal. 5: 22. He is our access to the Father, Eph. 2: 18, and makes intercession for us, Rom. 8: 26. The Spirit is the means of fellowship, Phil. 2: 1, of prayer, Eph. 6: 18, of joy, 1 Thess. 1: 6, of worship, Phil. 3: 3. He wars against the flesh, Gal. 5: 17, will at last quicken our mortal bodies, Rom. 8: 11, and changes us into the image of the Lord from glory to glory, 2 Cor. 3: 18. The gospel is preached with the Holy Spirit sent down from heaven, 1 Pet. 1: 12, only through the Spirit can men confess that Christ is Lord, 1 Cor. 12: 3; He makes men able ministers of the new testament, 2 Cor. 3: 6. At Pentecost the fullness of the Spirit was poured out, and the universalism with which God began His dealings with men at their creation was re-initiated with a view to their redemption.

Chapter 5

WHAT is the significance of Pentecost in the whole of redemptive history? This we must ascertain before we can discover its significance for that particular redemptive activity known as missions. In endeavoring to do this we must necessarily limit ourselves to a few major aspects from which the significance of Pentecost can be viewed. We shall try to resolve the problem of selection posed by the abundance of scriptural material available by examining four aspects of the question which seem to be most promising in making possible a penetration to the meaning of the Pentecost event. We shall seek to answer the following questions: (*a*) What is really meant by the "outpouring of the Spirit"? Was not the Spirit present before? How must we understand that the Spirit *came* at Pentecost? (*b*) What function most centrally describes the totality of the many activities in which the Spirit poured out at Pentecost engages? (*c*) Since the life of the New Testament Church is circumscribed by so much of sin and imperfection, how are we to conceive of the manner in which the Spirit is present? The results which the inquiry into these questions produces may then be brought together by viewing, (*d*) the Pentecost event as an eschatological phenomenon. We treat, therefore:

A. *The coming of the Spirit*
B. *The Spirit as the Giver of life*
C. *The Pauline conception of the Spirit as Earnest and as First-fruits*
D. *The eschatological significance of Pentecost*

A. *The Coming of the Spirit*

In the Old Testament and in the gospels the Spirit is treated both as one who *already is* and as one who *is yet to come*. These two themes are not, as such, irreconcilable. The New Testament speaks of the Kingdom that is and of the Kingdom that is yet to come. Here the difference is one of presence in principle and of coming in full realization. Can we relate the presence of the Spirit before Pentecost and His coming at Pentecost in this manner? This is indeed open to question. The coming of the Spirit at Pentecost is nowhere presented as the consummation of an already existing reality. The advent of the Spirit is presented in both the Old Testament and in the Gospels as the coming of a *new* factor. The Spirit will be "poured out", Joel 2: 28; God will give a new heart and a new spirit, and will take away the stony heart, Ezek. 11: 19; God's Spirit will cause men to walk in His statutes and keep His judgments, 36: 27; when the Spirit shall have been poured out all who shall call on the name of the Lord shall be delivered, for in mount Zion and in Jerusalem shall be deliverance, Joel 2: 28ff. In the Gospels this emphasis is even stronger. When the Holy Spirit comes He will reprove the world, guide the disciples into all truth, show them things to come, glorify Christ and, having received from Him, shall show it to them, John 16: 8, 13, 14. The disciples can do nothing until the Spirit comes, they must wait for Him in Jerusalem, Luke 24: 45ff., but when they are empowered from on high they shall witness to Christ to the ends of the earth, Acts 1: 8. Nowhere, however, is the matter put so strongly, we may say, so absolutely, as in John 7: 39b. There we read that the Holy Spirit *was not yet*. We are confronted, therefore, by two apparently contradictory theses. On the one hand, our review of the operations of the Holy Spirit in the Old Testament and in the Gospels plainly indicates that He was active before Pentecost. On the other hand, we also discovered that before Pentecost the Spirit *was not*. We shall approach the problem posed by this apparent contradiction by inquiring into the meaning of Jesus' words, "for the Spirit was not yet", John 7: 39b.

The exegesis of this clause usually accepts as starting point the fact of the Spirit's manifest operations in the Old Testament and then attempts to understand John's words in the light of these earlier activities. This method of approach to the text unavoidably leads to severe strictures on the absoluteness with which John expresses himself. F. Büchsel is representative of many exegetes when he writes that obviously John cannot mean that there was no Spirit before Jesus was glorified since Jesus had the Spirit, and it cannot be denied that the prophets before Him had the Spirit also. He must mean, therefore, that "in comparison with the possession of the Spirit which the Church had since Jesus' glorification it can be said that the Spirit had not been".[1] John, then, availed himself of a sort of literary license whereby a very large difference of degree in the Spirit's presence is described as a difference between non-presence and presence of the Spirit. Others understand John to mean that after Jesus' exaltation the Spirit entered upon a new function, a new activity, in which He had not engaged before and, considered from that aspect, He may be considered not to have been before. So Herman Bavinck considers the significance of the coming of the Spirit to lie in the fact that He gives to the New Testament Church an independent existence, cuts her loose from priest and law, from temple and altar, dwells in her, and spreads the Church over the whole world and to all peoples. This distinguishes the New Testament functioning of the Spirit from the Old Testament when there was also "all kinds of activity through gifts of the Holy Spirit".[2]

H. B. Swete writes, "But the experience of the primitive Church was but a continuation and enlargement of the experience of the Church of Israel which is expressed in the Old Testament. The New Testament doctrine of the Spirit begins where the Old Testament doctrine breaks off. . . . His presence under the New Covenant is manifested in new ways. . . ."[3] The variations in which the peculiar function of the Spirit in the New Testament is presented are many, but common to them all is the conception that in the New Testament period the Holy Spirit enters upon enlarged activity or upon particular operations in which He had not engaged before.

This understanding would seem to be open to several strictures. It leaves unclear the relationship between the Spirit's activity in the Old Testament and the work of Christ. The basis for the outpouring and work of the Spirit in the New Testament is the work of Christ in cross, resurrection and ascension. But what is the basis for the soteric operations of the Spirit in the Old Testament? Is it not the work of Christ also? But how do the foregoing interpretations establish a connection between the two? Further, if the Spirit merely entered upon a new *function* at Pentecost how can scripture legitimately speak of an outpouring of *the Spirit*? Moreover, the advent of the Spirit did not bring into being an improved form of an old situation, but a wholly new situation. We must, therefore, take the expression "the Spirit was not yet" seriously. It constitutes an unambiguous statement which, according to accepted rules of exegesis, should be understood literally unless good ground can be adduced for not so understanding it. The New Testament presents significant material suggesting that a literal understanding of "the Spirit was not yet" is not incompatible with the fact of the soteric operations of the Spirit in the Old Testament. The exegeses of John 7: 39b that were briefly reviewed above all take as their point of departure the prior operation of the Spirit and endeavor to understand the statement that the Spirit was not yet from that point of view. The exegesis in this section will reverse the usual procedure and take its point of departure from the text that is being exegeted, and we shall then inquire how the prior operations of the Spirit are to be reconciled with a literal acceptance of the sense of John's words.

79

The passages in the New Testament to which we wish to call attention in this discussion are:

1. Acts 7: 51, 52a

> Ye stiffnecked and uncircumcised in heart and ears, ye do always resist the Holy Spirit: as your fathers did, so do ye. Which of the prophets did not your fathers persecute? and they killed them that showed before of the coming of the Righteous One; of whom ye have now become betrayers and murderers.

In this and in the following passages we are dealing with the problem of apparent anachronism. The Holy Spirit who was operative in the old dispensation is presented in these verses not simply as the Holy Spirit without further qualification, but *He is identified with the Holy Spirit poured out at Pentecost.* A striking instance of this is given in Stephen's scorching denunciation of the Sanhedrin. The Holy Spirit whom the Jewish leaders resisted is evidently the Pentecostal Spirit. Their resistance manifested itself in a resisting of the preaching, Acts 6: 8–15, and the preaching is a direct outgrowth and expression of the Spirit's presence in the Church. That same Spirit, said Stephen, their fathers resisted in persecuting the prophets. Before discussing the implications of this identity concept we must take note of several other striking manifestations of it in the New Testament.

2. 1 Cor. 10: 1–4, 9a

> For I would not brethren, have you ignorant that our fathers . . . did all eat the same spiritual food; and did all drink the same spiritual drink: for they drank of a spiritual rock that followed them: and the rock was Christ. . . . Neither let us make trial of the Lord as some of them made trial.

Arresting here is the use of the word *spiritual*, and its identification with Christ. The Israelites ate spiritual food, drank spiritual drink, drank from a spiritual rock, and this rock was Christ. The spiritual is in its Pauline use Spirit-derived, 1 Cor.

2: 13, 12: 1ff. Only the Spirit can bring the spiritual into being. The spiritual drink of the Israelites Paul identifies with Christ. He evidently refers here to the Christ of history who is now glorified. In verse 9 Paul admonishes his readers not to tempt the Lord as the Israelites tempted Him. The use of Lord instead of God, the strong support for Christ instead of Lord in alternative readings, and the natural identification of Lord with Christ in v. 4, strengthen the view that Paul had in mind here the Christ whom the Church knew and worshipped. *Him* Paul sees active in the Old Testament period in the form of a Spirit-derived spiritual reality. For Paul, then, the Christ whom he knew and the Spirit that informed the Church of which he was a member were active in the Old Testament covenant community. We have here, therefore, an instance of the typical Pauline conception of the intimate and inseparable relationship between Christ and the Spirit (2 Cor. 3: 17), which is a distinctly post-Pentecostal relationship. And this Christ-become-spirit was active in the old dispensation.

3. Gal. 4: 28, 29

> Now we, brethren, as Isaac was, are children of promise. But as he that was born after the flesh persecuted him that was born after the Spirit, so also it is now.

We are doubtless to understand Isaac's being born after the Spirit as in the first instance the physical power with which God worked in Abraham and Sarah to effect the birth of Isaac. This physical manifestation of the power of the Spirit had intense spiritual background, however. Through it the line of God's redemptive purpose in Christ was borne onward. It also occasioned one of the greatest displays of faith in the Old Testament. In Rom. 4: 18–24 Abraham's faith in the integrity of God's promise to give him a son is not only presented as being reckoned to him for justification, but it is equated with our belief in God who raised Christ from the dead. Isaac's being

F

"after the Spirit" is for Paul *the same* as our being "after the Spirit". Therefore he regards the reason for the persecution of his brethren to be the same as that for the persecution of Isaac—both are born after the Spirit. Moreover, Isaac, as we are, was a child of promise. To be a child of promise means to be a recipient of the Holy Spirit that has been given to the gentiles, Gal. 3: 14. Paul understood, then, that the Spirit poured out at Pentecost is the Spirit by whose power Isaac was born. Paul knows no other Spirit than the Spirit who indwells the Church.

4. 1 Peter 1: 10, 11

Concerning which salvation the prophets sought and searched diligently, who prophesied of the grace that should come unto you: searching what or what manner of time the Spirit of Christ which was in them did point unto, when it testified beforehand the sufferings of Christ, and the glories that should follow them.

When Peter speaks here of the Spirit of Christ we understand him to mean the Spirit of the historical and exalted Christ. The Spirit in these verses is consequently the Spirit given to the Church at Pentecost. It is the Spirit of Pentecost who inspired the prophets of the old covenant. Some take the first mention of Christ in v. 11 to refer to the pre-existent second Person of the Trinity. This understanding labors under the difficulty that "Christ" is used in the same verse in an unambiguously historical sense. Moreover, "Spirit of God" would be a much more natural reference to the Spirit in the setting of the Old Testament and to His relationship purely to the second Person of the Trinity than "Spirit of Christ". Others regard the Spirit of Christ as the Spirit of Christ in the New Testament sense, but reject the idea that the prophets in whom the Spirit worked were the prophets of the old dispensation. They were the prophets of the early Church, Eph. 3: 5ff. The sufferings and glories alluded to by Peter are not the sufferings and glories of Christ, but the sufferings undergone by the missionarily expanding Church for Christ's sake and the glories that will follow upon these sufferings.

The forced character of this exegesis could be examined at length. Here we wish to point out that the reference of all witness in the Old and in the New Testaments is Christ, not the sufferings and glories of Christians. For the prophets the time of the fulfilment of prophecy was uncertain, unknown. That fulfilment is now history and it makes possible the preaching of the gospel by the Holy Spirit sent down from heaven, v. 12. The sufferings and the glories of Christ foretold or witnessed before by the prophets are therefore the work and the reward of Christ seen by them from afar through the illumination of the Spirit. These now form the burden of New Testament proclamation, they are the gospel. The words, "not unto themselves but unto us they did minister", v. 12, are strikingly akin to the thought expressed in Heb. 11: 40 that they of the old dispensation "without us should not be made perfect". Both indicate the futuristic reference of the entire Old Testament.

The thought of a soteric operation of the Spirit of Christ poured out at Pentecost during the time of the earlier dispensation is therefore by no means strange to the writers of the New Testament. They knew only one Spirit, the Spirit given to the Church at Pentecost. This was the Spirit who not only dwelt in the Church of their time, but who nourished the children of Israel on their wilderness journey, who was resisted by the unbelieving in the days of the prophets, whose bearers were persecuted by those not having Him in the days of the patriarchs, and who spoke about Christ's sufferings and glories through the prophets.

The New Testament seems to leave little alternative to regarding the work of the Spirit in the Old Testament as the retroactive work of the Spirit of Pentecost in the time when He was not yet poured out, in the time when there was not yet a basis for his operation in the life, death and resurrection of Christ.

Christ had not yet been glorified in the time of the old dispensation. Nevertheless, the Spirit that was poured out at Pentecost
worked under the old covenant, albeit differently, less clearly,
less powerfully than under the new covenant. On basis of the
scriptural data we can only affirm *that* this happened, we
cannot explain *how* this happened. We are here dealing with a
work of God, not with a work of men. God transcends the time
categories with which we are familiar and the time limitations
under which we live. He does indeed adapt His redemptive
actions in incarnation, cross, resurrection, ascension, Pentecost
and consummation to the time conditions which He has
created for man. These actions all follow an understandable
chronological sequence. The *effects* of these actions as they
come to expression in the work of the Spirit do not follow a
chronological sequence. Even the historic, chronologically
successive redemptive actions with which we are familiar have
this background of timelessness. We were chosen *in Christ*
before the foundation of the world, Eph. 1 : 4; the names of the
saints have been written in the book of life of *the Lamb that was
slain from the foundation of the world*, Rev. 13: 8; the death of
Christ, who offered Himself through the eternal Spirit, redeemed the transgressions that were done under the first
testament, Heb. 10: 14, 15. And how shall we understand that
one day is with the Lord as a thousand years, and a thousand
years as one day, 2 Pet. 3: 8? John was not treading on wholly
strange ground, therefore, when he taught that until Pentecost
the Spirit *was not*, while being at the same time, as we must
assume, fully aware of the work of the Spirit before Pentecost.

We must conceive of the operations of the Spirit before
Pentecost, then, as an arching backward, of the historical
reality that did not exist until Pentecost. In thus effecting
earlier operations of the Spirit of Pentecost God preserved
both the unity of the redemptive process, and the unity
of the congregation of the Old Testament with the Church
of the New Testament. But in this unity the first period

is characterized by that distinctive mode of operation of the Spirit that is appropriate to His retro-active activity. It is shadowy, unclear, coming to consciously felt expression only at particular times, on particular men, for particular purposes. When we ask why the Old Testament presents the work of the Spirit in the sphere of redemption as bearing a chiefly "start-like" or occasional character, rather than as a constantly operative factor (as in the New) it is difficult to find an answer. We can only suggest that the constant operations of the Spirit which were undoubtedly present, though not described, required an intensification to make possible the tasks of establishing forms of worship, of judging, military leadership, and, especially, of prophecy. This divinely effected intensification could then be described as a "descent" or as a "being seized" by the Spirit. We are left in uncertainty here, however. The central affirmation about the presence of the Spirit in the Old Testament that can be made with scriptural warrant is that it was a retro-active effect of the presence of the Spirit given to the Church at Pentecost. The redemptive process of the old dispensation was as a moon that had no light of itself but received and reflected light from the sun that had not yet appeared in the horizon. The effulgence of the Sun of righteousness that had not yet risen with healing in his wings benefited Israel with the light and warmth of true grace through a reflection upon her of the Pentecostal glory that had not yet come.

If the Spirit who spoke through the prophets of Israel was not the Spirit of Christ given at Pentecost, there is little alternative to the vague and hardly acceptable view set forth by Swete, "The Holy Spirit with which he [Joh. Bapt.] was filled was not the new spirit of Christ and the Christian Church, but the spirit which gave to the saints of the Old Testament the strength and wisdom which was theirs . . . the spirit and power of Elijah, the prophet-preacher of northern Israel."[4] Such a conception is wholly wanting in the integration that exists in scripture between the work of the Spirit in the old dispensation

85

and his work in the new. Karl Barth, on the other hand, sees the giving of the Spirit as an event whose effect is limited neither forward nor backward to the happening on the day of Pentecost. The similarity of the view set forth in this chapter to his, as also the illuminating accompanying reference to the retro-active effect of the resurrection of Christ on His miracle-working activity during His ministry, merit a rather full quotation.

> It is hardly the view of the New Testament that only after Good Friday and Easter there were people who had received the Holy Spirit. How were we otherwise to understand the fact that also before this time faith is in all seriousness attributed to Jesus' disciples and to non-disciples? . . . One might also ask whether all of Jesus' miraculous deeds are not to be regarded as, so to speak, backward extending rays of the glory of the Risen One, whether indeed the whole of the life of Jesus is not to be viewed in this light. . . . Also John 20: 22 and the Pentecost account in Acts 2 are certainly to be understood as the express and solemn witness to an event which is chronologically to be limited neither forward nor backward.[5]

A too scrupulous reading of the last sentence might lead to the conclusion that the Pentecost *event* is limited neither forward nor backward. That is hardly Barth's intention. It is the *effect* of Pentecost that is not limited to the day of outpouring. Barth does not indicate the limit backward of the Pentecostal "rays". The limit, if we would set one, lies in Paradise where the first announcement of salvation to fallen man was an anticipation of the grace that was to be revealed in Christ and given to the Church at Pentecost.

The understanding of the Spirit's activity in the old dispensation as outlined in this section casts a clarifying light on phenomena and passages in both the Old and the New Testaments which on a different basis remain wanting in satisfactory explanation. It accounts, on the one hand, for the shadowy and passing character of Old Testament religion and, on the other, for the evident spiritual life, holiness and true religion that were present under the old covenant. It accounts,

86

on the one hand, for the contrast which John draws when he writes, "The law was given through Moses, grace and truth became through Jesus Christ" 1: 17, and, on the other, for the fact that Paul can describe the law as being "spiritual", Rom. 7: 14. We understand why John the Baptist, greater than any born of women under the old dispensation, was less than the least in the new aeon ushered in at Pentecost, Luke 7: 28, for he lived in but the pre-dawn of reflected glory, while the least in the New Testament "now" lives in the light of the fully present Spirit. We understand, too, why the saints of the Old Testament could not be made perfect without us, Heb. 11: 40. The Spirit who worked in them could do so only because He was to come as the life-giving Spirit indwelling the New Testament Church. In all this it becomes plain how fully true it is that before Pentecost "the Spirit was not yet". It was not until Pentecost that the new aeon, of which the Spirit is the informing and vital principle, was given to the Church to usher her into the endless life of heaven.

B. *The Spirit as the Giver of life*

The Spirit having come at Pentecost, what is His central function in the new aeon which He revealed? What do we mean when we say that the Spirit is the vital and informing principle of the new age? It was earlier suggested that the activities of the Spirit as described in the New Testament are so varied that they seem to defy all classification. While this is true, it is not difficult to subsume all His activities under one inclusive head—the Spirit poured out at Pentecost *conveys life*. Life is the term whereby especially Paul characterizes all those virtues, graces, and dispositions, whether ethical or religious, that the Holy Spirit works in the hearts of men.[6] That the bestowal of life should be the central function of the Spirit in the new aeon is not surprising. The bestowal of life in the realm of the natural was the central function of the Spirit in the work of creation. Since redemption is the renewal and

87

reconstitution of the created world there is also needed a renewal and reconstitution of its life. This renewal, also called a new creation in the New Testament, 2 Cor. 5: 17; Gal. 6: 15, is the work of the Spirit. The function of the Spirit in the re-creation of the world, therefore, parallels His function in creation. In the redemptive operations of the Spirit life is lifted to a higher, to an indestructible, to an incorruptible level, and abides forever. The Church is an epistle of Christ, written with the Spirit of the living God through the ministry of the Spirit which gives life, 2 Cor. 3: 3–6. Christians live in the Spirit and are therefore appealed to to walk in the Spirit, Gal. 5: 25. This walk manifests itself in love, joy, peace, long-suffering, gentleness, goodness, faith, meekness, temperance, vv. 22, 23, all of which are not so much nine disparate fruits of the Spirit as collectively and representatively the *one fruit* of the Spirit as the Giver of life. Christ was raised from the dead by the Spirit of Holiness, Rom. 1: 4, that we, being raised with Him, may walk in newness of life, Rom. 6: 4ff. In Rom. 8: 13 the sharpest of contrasts, life and death, is presented in the form of the contrast: Spirit and flesh.

The life that the Spirit brings into being receives a strongly eschatological coloring from the fact that it is so intimately related to the resurrected and exalted Lord. Here two closely associated factors must be taken into account: the relationship between the risen Christ and the Spirit, and the relationship between the believer and the risen Christ expressed in the well-known Pauline formula "in Christ". So close and intimate is the union between Christ and the Spirit that Paul can say "now the Lord is the Spirit", 2 Cor. 3: 17. The connecting link between the believer and the Spirit is the mystical incorporation of the believer "in Christ". So intimate is the union of the believer with the Spirit-conditioned Christ that he who is joined to the Lord "is one spirit" (with Him), 1 Cor. 6: 17. There is, then, a relationship between Christ and the Spirit that is expressed in terms of identity, and a spiritual relationship between the believer and Christ that Paul likens to the chaste union of husband and wife, 1 Cor. 6: 15ff. But we can go further than this. The believer is described as being not only "in Christ" but also "in the Spirit". In several places Paul applies the expressions "in the Spirit" and "in Christ" to the same matter:

To be	(a)	But of him are ye *in Christ Jesus*, 1 Cor. 1: 30.
	(b)	But ye are not in the flesh but *in the Spirit*, Rom. 8: 9.
To speak	(a)	in the sight of God, speak we *in Christ*, 2 Cor. 2: 17.
	(b)	no one can say, Jesus is Lord, but *in the Holy Spirit*, 1 Cor. 12: 3.
To be sanctified	(a)	them that are sanctified *in Christ Jesus*, 1 Cor. 1: 2.
	(b)	being sanctified *by the Holy Spirit* (alternative reading: *in the Holy Spirit*), Rom. 15: 16.
To be justified	(a)	but ye were justified *in the name of the Lord Jesus Christ* and *in the Spirit* of our God, 1 Cor. 6: 11.

The union believer-Christ-Spirit is therefore expressed by Paul in varied forms indicating the intimacy of the relationship: Christ is the Spirit, the believer is united to Christ as wife is to husband, the believer is in Christ, and he is also in the Spirit. This relationship centers, as we have seen, in the resurrection of Christ. If the Spirit of Him that raised up Jesus from the dead dwell in us, He that raised up Christ Jesus from the dead shall give life also to our mortal bodies through His Spirit that dwells in us, Rom. 8: 11. The central redemptive action from which the Spirit draws the life which He confers is the resurrection of Christ. Doubtless this explains the heavy emphasis on the resurrection of Christ that is found in the preaching of the early Church. It was the supreme evidence of the reality of the new life that was being offered by the missionary Church to the dying world. The substratum of the life that is to come, the determinative and constitutive element of the new existence, is the Holy Spirit mediated to men through union with Christ. Therefore Vos can say that in Christ this Spirit "is none other than the Spirit of the consummate life and consummate glory, the circumambient element of the eschatological state in general".[7] This life is already now reality for the Church. She and her members are partakers of the new aeon into which the Holy Spirit at Pentecost introduced the Church.

In John's writings the concept of life is prominent, and for pregnancy and depth parallels that of truth. It is the essence of what Jesus came to bring. It may be called the heart of His revelation. He calls Himself the life, 11: 25, 14: 6, the bread of life, 6: 35, 48, the light of life, 8: 12, He dispenses living water, 4: 10, He is the living bread and those who eat Him shall live forever, 6: 51, His words are spirit and life, 6: 63, they are words of life eternal, 6: 68, He came to give the world life, 6: 33, 10: 10. Now this life is by John intimately related to the Spirit. The rivers of living water that will flow from the belly of him who believes in Christ find their source in the Spirit that is to be poured out at Pentecost, 7: 38, 39. In words almost identical to Paul's "the life-giving Spirit" he speaks of "the Spirit that gives life" 6: 63. The Spirit generates the new birth, 3: 5ff., and thus provides the substratum for the new state of the believer. On this substratum this new state not only rests, but out of it its several manifestations take their rise. What is born of God overcomes the world, 1 John 5: 4, and whoever does righteousness is born of God, 2: 29. Therefore, when out of all available possibilities he chooses a word that shall describe what Christ and the Spirit shall bring into being he chooses the comprehensive expression "eternal life".

C. *The Pauline conception of the Spirit as Earnest and as First-fruits*

In the two preceding sections we found that the Spirit took up His dwelling-place in the Church at Pentecost, and that His central function is to confer life. But how, in the midst of so much of imperfection, sin and death, must we understand the life-giving Spirit to be present? What is the relation of the presence of the Spirit to the whole of the redeemed life that is yet to be revealed? Paul's conception of the Spirit as earnest and first-fruits can best shed light on this question. In Acts 2 the descent of the Spirit is accompanied by dramatic manifestations and, in a reduced degree, a visibly manifest power of the Spirit continues to characterize the whole of Acts. It was Paul who was given to see the passing character of the extraordinary gifts of the Spirit and the abiding character of His hidden operations in the Church. This comes most notably to expression in 1 Cor. 13. Upon concluding his discussion of the gifts of the Spirit, 1 Cor. 12, among which healing, miracle working, speaking with tongues and interpreting are mentioned, he admonishes his readers to covet earnestly the greater gifts, and these are faith, hope and love, of which the greatest is love, ch. 13. But how must the presence of the Spirit who works faith, hope and love in the Church be understood?

The Holy Spirit is constantly present and constantly operative in the Church as earnest or first-fruits of the complete redemption that is to be revealed. Paul refers to the Spirit as earnest in three places, 2 Cor. 1: 22, 5: 5; Eph. 1: 14, and as first-fruits but once, Rom. 8: 23. These expressions are so concisely descriptive of the manner in which Paul conceived the Spirit to be present in the Church, however, that they merit close attention. Paul meant to say that the entire, undivided Spirit indwells the Church, and that this indwelling is the guarantee of the complete redemption which includes prominently the redemption of the body. The words "first-fruits of the Spirit" or "earnest of the Spirit" are sometimes understood to mean a part of the Spirit, an initial instalment of the Spirit. This they do not mean and cannot mean. In Eph. 1: 13, 14 Paul writes that the Spirit of promise by which his readers were sealed *is* the earnest of our inheritance. Earnest and Spirit are here entirely convertible terms. The word *arrabon* is probably derived from Semitic commercial usage and means a pledge, money given as guarantee that the full price of a purchase will be paid. The pledge that God will wholly effect the redemption that He has promised is, then, the Spirit who indwells the Church. The same thought is expressed by "first-fruits" in Rom. 8: 23. Here the thought is not that the Spirit is the harvest of which some first-fruits have been given, but the first-fruits *are* the Spirit. The whole, the undivided Spirit is the guarantee that all the fruits of Christ's work will one day be harvested. The believer is "in the Spirit", the Spirit of God dwells in him, vv. 9, 11, he puts to death the deeds of the body by the Spirit, v. 13, and he has received the Spirit of adoption enabling him to cry Abba, Father, 8: 15. In 2 Cor. 1: 22 the "earnest of the Spirit" is not further defined, but there is no reason to believe that it bears a different meaning than *arrabon* does in Eph. 1: 14, or than "first-fruits" in Rom. 8: 23. The New Testament nowhere speaks of a second or larger outpouring of the Spirit. There is only one Pentecost, and at that Pentecost the Spirit was once for all given to the Church. The earnest "consists in the Spirit, the genitive being epexegetical, just as in Gal. 3: 14 the 'promise of the Spirit' means the promised thing consisting in the Spirit".[8] John Owen observes, "It is not any act of the Holy Spirit on or in us that is called His being an 'earnest'. It is He Himself who is the earnest."[9]

Paul's view of the Spirit as earnest and first-fruits is, further, a distinctly eschatological conception. The Spirit is an anticipation in this life of the full and perfect redemption that is still outstanding, and, conversely, he makes the Christian long for and, in a sense, project himself into the time of full redemption. This Paul would certainly seem to mean when he writes in Rom. 8: 23, ". . . ourselves also, who have the first-fruits of the Spirit, even we ourselves groan within ourselves, waiting for our adoption, to wit, the redemption of our body". The presence of the Spirit in the Church is therefore a harbinger of the End. In this expectation and longing for the End the believer does not stand alone. The whole creation waits and longs for the revealing of the sons of God, vv. 18ff. The Spirit as the already present power and life of the new aeon creates in those who have Him a yearning to share that power and life without the encumbrance of the unredeemed body and its evil affections, and this yearning finds a mute but eloquent reflection in the creation of which man is head. In Eph. 1: 13, 14 the Spirit is "the earnest of our inheritance until the redemption of the purchased possession", which is reinforced by 4: 30 where believers are admonished not to grieve the Holy Spirit whereby they are "sealed unto the day of redemption". More fully than in any of the foregoing does 2 Cor. 5: 1ff. describe the eschatological redemption of the body of which the Spirit is earnest. When the earthly house of our tabernacle is dissolved we have a building from God, a house not made with hands, eternal in the heavens which, when we enter it, will swallow up mortality by life. Now the God who has prepared us for this very thing is the God who has given us the earnest of the Spirit as guarantee that we shall one day enter upon this new mode of existence. The presence of the Spirit in the Church is therefore a clearly eschatological phenomenon. The first-fruits are a part of the harvest as well as a promise of the full harvest, and the earnest is a part of the purchase price as well as a promise that the full price will one day be paid. The End is here in the Spirit, and the central function of the Spirit in the time of the End is to confer the life that shall come to full manifestation at the consummation of the present dispensation.

D. *The eschatological significance of Pentecost*

When we endeavor to compress into one comprehensive statement the meaning of the coming of the Spirit as dispenser of life in the form of earnest and first-fruits we can perhaps best say: at Pentecost the Church was introduced into the new and unending aeon which is life eternal. This constitutes Pentecost a pre-eminently eschatological event. In his illuminating work, *The Pauline Eschatology*, Geerhardus Vos makes the observation that the Spirit's operations in the application of Christ's work to the individual have so much occupied the attention of theologians that His eschatological significance has been obscured.[10] Doubtless a major reason for neglecting this important aspect of the revelation concerning the Spirit is the traditional limiting of eschatology to the return of Christ and the events immediately attending it. This approach to eschatology was never able to do justice to the many references in the New Testament that the last days are *now*,[11] and to the work of the Spirit in and his significance for the eschatologically qualified New Testament present. It had the effect of retaining in the thinking of the New Testament Church the Old Testament conception of the day of the Lord as a point or a very brief period at the end of history, unmodified and undifferentiated by the decisive historical event of Christ's coming and work. The new emphasis that representatives of recent eschatological thought have brought to the fore, is that the End is not simply that point of time coinciding with the return of Christ, but that the End began to be realized at Christ's first coming and will culminate in His second. O. Cullmann has described the relationship of the first to the second coming of Christ as that of a decisive and successful D-Day that guarantees the certainty of Victory Day. In terms of such an understanding the New Testament expressions "last days", "last time", "the ends of the ages" can be invested with a meaning that the older view of eschatology was never able to attribute to them. The period lying between the first and second parousias, therefore, occupies a distinct position in the divine economy of redemption. It is the period of the end, the period that Old Testament eschatology, because of its lack of historical perspective, telescoped into one undifferentiated event.

Into this period the Church was introduced at Pentecost. Its characteristic feature is the presence of the Spirit which radically qualifies the entire dispensation that Pentecost inaugurated. The Spirit carries into history the fruits of Christ's work, thereby in principle concluding one period of time and in principle initiating another. The fullness of time in which God sent forth His Son, Gal. 4: 4, is, consequently, not merely an appropriate time in the history of men, not merely a time characterized by a proper confluence of circumstances in the then obtaining world, but that moment when God sovereignly judged that the End of time should be introduced. At that moment Christ's coming cast the old aeon into its death throes and initiated the life of the new and unending aeon. At Pentecost this turning-point of the ages was publicly declared and made manifest through the outpouring of the Life of the new aeon into the hearts of men.

The last days which find their beginning at Pentecost, therefore, consist of the incompatible conjunction or coexistence of the old aeon hastening to its final end and the new aeon moving to its consummation. The Pauline contrasts of sin and grace, flesh and Spirit, old man and new man, first Adam and last Adam, natural body and spiritual body, serve to indicate the extent and comprehensiveness of the duality characterizing the present dispensation. Here "old" and "new", "first" and "last" must not be regarded as contrasting only ethical states, but also and not least New Testament time concepts. Even "natural" and "spiritual" carry this connotation with Paul: "that is not first which is spiritual, but that which is natural and *afterward* that which is spiritual" 1 Cor. 15: 46. Sin, the flesh, the old man, are not merely evil, ethically unacceptable to God; they are in a very real sense *old*, that is, about to disappear, vanishing, robbed of vital strength, ready to die. And grace, the spiritual, brought into being by the last Adam, the man from heaven, creates the *new* man who is young, going from strength to strength, whose years shall not end. On countless mission fields the heart of this thought has been grasped by converts, often almost instinctively and with unreflective simplicity, and comes to expression in the adoption of a new name signifying a break with the old life, in the revolution in their religious thinking, speech, family and social relations, in the awakening of gratitude, in a new attitude toward death and the world of spirits, in the desire for instruction, development of prayer life, and in the recognition of evil as sin against God.

Old Testament prophecy, looking at the coming salvation from the viewpoint of its fruits, associated it particularly with the gift of the Spirit; the New Testament, having a deep regard for the historical events that brought this salvation into being, sees the crucified and risen Christ as its effecting Agent, and the Holy Spirit poured out at Pentecost as the substratum and pervasive element of the life which that salvation has brought into being. But Christ's work up to His session at the right hand of God and the outpouring of the Holy Spirit are in reality no more than distinguishable aspects of the one redemptive work of God.

It is against this background of two overlapping aeons that the missionary task of the Church must be viewed. It is also this background that gives to that task its meaning and relevance. These two aeons, wholly incompatible while yet inseparably conjoined, are constantly in conflict with each other. The struggle of flesh lusting against Spirit, and Spirit against flesh, is all-embracing, ranging from internal personal conflict ("who shall deliver me from the body of this death!" Rom. 7: 24) to external universal conflict ("marvel not if the world hate you", i John 3: 13), and involves even nature groaning in its waiting for the revelation of the sons of God, Rom. 8: 19ff. From the side of the old aeon this conflict takes the form of indifference, hostility and hatred, but from the side of the new it expresses itself in the form of reconciliation and overcoming love. The center from which this reconciling activity radiates into the world is the Church. It is the body of those who, with all their shortcomings, have the gift of the Spirit. The existence

96

of the Church as body of Christ indwelt by the Spirit, and her proclamation of the gospel as the means of communicating the life that the Spirit gives her, is an ineradicable feature of the inter-parousia period. She preaches the "already now" of the new age in the "still here" of the old. Missions could not exist in the time before Pentecost because the Spirit "was not yet" to make a diffusion of His life possible, nor shall missions exist after the return of Christ because the old aeon which alone constitutes the area of missionary penetration will then have been finally and irrevocably separated from the new.

Chapter 6

AT the beginning of the history of the New Testament Church stands the Pentecost event. It does not stand *approximately* at the beginning, or as a first among several significant factors, but it stands *absolutely* at the beginning. It stands at the beginning because it is the fountain-head of the life of the Church. It does not, however, stand in *isolation* from preceding and succeeding redemptive history. The outpouring of the Spirit is the fulfilment of Old Testament promise, and it is the source from which the Church derives the Spirit who indwells her. Pentecost marked the introduction of the Church into the new aeon in which she finds herself, and it cast retro-active glory throughout the Old Testament dispensation of promise. When it is understood that Pentecost stands at the *beginning* of the history of the New Testament Church, that the *life* of the Church is derived from the poured-out Spirit, and that the life of the Church finds, as we shall see, her central expression in *witness* to the crucified and risen Lord, the indissoluble relationship between Pentecost and the missionary witness of the Church will be clear.

The inclusive head under which the varied activities of the Spirit in the new aeon can be subsumed is, we found, the conferring of *life*. It is characteristic of life to seek to impart itself. Life cannot be self-contained. It must be productive of new life. This is true also, and pre-eminently, of the life of the Spirit, John 6: 63. The condition of receiving the life of the Spirit is the hearing of the gospel, on the one hand, and faith embracing the proclaimed word on the other. The gospel is the word of life, Phil. 2: 16, it is the power of God to salvation, Rom. 1: 16, it brings life and immortality to light, 2 Tim. 1: 10, and surpasses the ministration of the letter in glory, for the ministration of the Spirit gives life, 2 Cor. 3: 6–12. It was a recognition of the central function of preaching, and of faith as the proper response to it, that constrained Paul to write, "For whoever shall call on the name of the Lord shall be saved. How then shall they call on him in whom they have not believed? and how shall they believe in him whom they have not heard? and how shall they hear without a preacher? and how shall they preach except they be sent? even as it is written, How beautiful are the feet of them that bring glad tidings of good things!" Rom. 10: 13–15. S. J. W. Clark, who impressed Roland Allen as a man who had a true vision of the missionary task, listed as first among the fundamental principles on which an indigenous Church should be established "that the Missionary must realize that his work is to hand on to others Life . . . that he is the channel through which Life comes to others".[1] Christ whom we preach is the resurrection and the life, John 11: 25, and His words are spirit and life, 6: 63.

The preaching of the gospel is the central task entrusted to the Church in the period called "the last days". This is the period lying between the incarnation of Christ and His return in glory. It is the time between the times. This time stands wholly under the sign of *eschatological proclamation*. The proclamation of the Church is a sign of the end. It may be said that it is *the* sign of the end. The last days were for the Church heralded by the Pentecostal speaking with tongues which initiated the witness of the Church, and they shall end when the gospel shall have run its course through the world. "And this gospel of the kingdom shall be preached in the whole world for a testimony unto all nations; and *then* shall the end come" Matt. 24: 14. Before the consummation of all things can take place "the gospel must first be preached to all nations" Mark 13: 10. When the disciples ask Jesus whether He will "at this time" establish the kingdom, He tells them that the Father has set times and seasons within His own authority, but that they must preach the gospel to the uttermost part of the earth, Acts 1: 6–8, and promises them His presence in the discharge of this task "even unto the consummation of the age", Matt. 28: 20. The inseparable conjunction of old aeon and new aeon during the inter-parousia period, and the dominant centrality of the gospel during this period, is nowhere so dramatically pictured as in the sixth chapter of Revelation. The Rider on the white horse, who is the Word of God, 19: 13, has been given a crown of victory and he goes forth conquering and to conquer, but alongside him ride the red, black, and pale horses of War, Famine, and Death, Rev. 6: 1–8. In the time between the times the concurrent judgment of God and the gospel of God point to the consummation of history.

The life of the Spirit is therefore communicated by the preaching of the gospel in the eschatologically qualified "now" of the interparousia period. *This* time, this *now*-time, is the time of apostolic paraklesis, "Behold, *now* is the acceptable time, *now* is the day of salvation" 2 Cor. 6: 2. The witness of the New Testament Church with which the Acts and the epistles acquaint us is pre-eminently a missionary witness. The New Testament witness knows no boundaries, acknowledges neither limits nor exceptions. Christ's mandate is that His witness be carried to the "uttermost part of the earth".

When we discuss the relationship of Pentecost to the witnessing Church we must qualify the Church in the sharpest possible manner as being *in her nature* a witnessing community and that she is this precisely because she derives her life from the Pentecost event. Witnessing is not one among many functions or activities of the Church; it is of her essence to witness, and it is out of this witness that all her other activities take their rise. When we speak of witnessing in this section we do not refer to missionary witness alone, but to the entire complex of her proclaiming activity of which the missionary proclamation is an essential part. We wish here to affirm that witnessing as such, of which the missionary proclamation is a specific expression, lies imbedded in the nature of the Church. Whatever more may or must be said of the Church—that she is the Body of Christ, the congregation of believers, the mother of the faithful—she, being all these, and because she is all these, is a witnessing, a proclaiming community. Witnessing does not exhaust the description of the nature of the Church, but without it her nature cannot be adequately described. The Church is both a living and a life-communicating body, and the manner in which her life is manifested, sustained, and transmitted is the proclamation of the gospel. We shall develop this thought in terms of four considerations:

A. *The Witnessing Spirit*
B. *The Pentecostal Reconstitution of the Church*
C. *The Great Commission as Law of the Church's Life*
D. *The Reticent Spirit*

A. *The Witnessing Spirit*

It is remarkable and worthy of careful note, that in describing the work of the Spirit as it comes to manifestation at Pentecost, Luke centers attention on one central effect of the descent of the Spirit. It is the phenomenon of speaking with "other tongues". The "sound as of the rushing of a mighty wind" and the "tongues parting asunder like as of fire" Acts 2: 3, 4, are mentioned but are not elaborated. What Luke places prominently central is "they were all filled with the Holy Spirit, and began to speak with other tongues, as the Spirit gave them utterance" 2: 4. This thought he emphasizes by relating the reaction of the Jewish populace, and by recounting Peter's sermon. Although the phenomenon of "speaking with other tongues" is the unique characteristic of Pentecost, it is nowhere explained. It is neither for Luke nor for any other writer of the New Testament a matter of interest to shed light on its nature. Liberal scholarship has endeavored to discredit the supernatural character of the Pentecostal speaking with tongues, and conservative scholarship, often thinking to defend scripture by speaking where scripture is silent, has, to the extent that it has done so, done little more than propose interesting theories. After more than a century of debate on whether the speaking with other tongues was a manifestation of mass ecstasy, a speaking in foreign languages, in the language of heaven, or in the language of Paradise, something akin to Corinthian glossolaly, a hearing wonder, a speaking wonder, or a hearing *and* a speaking wonder, we are little advanced beyond the point where the debate began. No one can say how the speaking with other tongues took place. We can only say *that* at Pentecost there was a dramatic praising of God's great works in "other tongues". The undeniable actuality of the *that*, and the complete absence of the *how*, on the score of the Pentecostal speaking with tongues, should not surprise us. It is characteristic of *all* the work of the Spirit that only its actuality, never its manner, is evident. We do not know how the Spirit descended, how He indwells the Church or the believer, how He affects heart and mind, how He achieves the wonderful things that are done in His power. The Spirit blows where He lists, we do not know whence He comes or where He goes. That is the kind of Spirit with whom we have to do. We are confronted only with the *fact* of His presence, with the *power* of His presence, with the *effects* of His presence. The being filled with the Spirit at Pentecost manifested itself in *irrepressible speaking* about the great works of God that came forth from the human spirit wholly seized by the divine Spirit. Pentecost momentarily placed in sharp and dramatic relief that the Church that had come into being in her New Testament form is a speaking, proclaiming Church and that she addresses all men and all nations with her message. More Luke did not say in giving prominence to the "speaking with other tongues" and there would seem to be no reason to believe that he meant to say more than that. "The Holy Spirit is the qualification for speaking about Christ; he is the panoply of the prophets and the apostles, he is the calling of the Church to the ministry of the Word. . . . If we ask, what is the 'meaning' of the Spirit, we must answer: it consists in this that he is the Gift of speaking about the mighty acts of God."[2]

The first effect of Pentecost that we are able to comprehend in the light of our own experience is Peter's great sermon. It also provides the only interpretation that the Bible gives us of the speaking with "other tongues": "this is that which hath been spoken through the prophet Joel: 'And it shall be in the last days, saith God, I will pour forth of my Spirit on all flesh, and your sons and your daughters shall prophesy . . . yea and on my servants and on my handmaidens in those days will I pour forth of my Spirit and they shall prophesy' " Acts 2: 16–18. With this quotation from Joel, Peter begins his inspired witness to the saving work of Christ. It is clear that in Peter's sermon we meet a form of witness that is altogether different from that presented by the speaking with tongues. It is the form of witness we meet everywhere in the primitive Church and later. The difference between the two types of speaking can perhaps best be so described: *the speaking with other tongues dramatically demonstrated the witnessing character of the Church; Peter's sermon set the pattern through which that witnessing character finds normal and continuing expression.* The one was passing, the other is abiding. The one is descriptive of impulse bringing momentum into being, the other of momentum continuing irresistibly on its course. Both establish that the central task of the Church is to witness to the great works of God in the power of the Spirit. And this task is eschatologically qualified. It takes place "in the last days". The proclamation of the gospel as a sign of the end was initiated by the outpouring of the Spirit.

The second consideration to which we must turn in order to understand the significance of Pentecost for the witnessing Church is the meaning of "Paraclete" in the discourses of Jesus presented in John 14, 15, 16. Nowhere in the scriptures before the book of Acts do we find so full and specific an account of the work that the coming Spirit will perform in the Church as in Jesus' description of the functions of the Paraclete: (*a*) He shall be with the disciples forever, and shall be in them, John 14: 16, 17, (*b*) He is the Spirit of truth, 14: 17, 15: 26, 16: 13, (*c*) He will teach the disciples all things, bring to remembrance all that Jesus said to the disciples, He will guide them into the truth and show them things to come, 14: 26, 16: 13, (*d*) He shall speak what He shall hear from Christ and shall declare it and shall glorify Christ, 16: 13–15, (*e*) He shall bear witness to Christ and (in immediate conjunction with this) the disciples also shall bear witness, 15: 26, 27, (*f*) He will convict the world of sin, of righteousness, and of judgment, 16: 8–11. It is clear that the words, *teach, remind, guide, show, convict, witness* massively indicate the teaching and witnessing function of the Spirit. The Spirit is a Teacher and Witness, and as such He is in the disciples and will be with them forever. This becomes even more significant when it is considered that the Paraclete as the subject of this teaching and witnessing activity is the "Spirit of truth". In John's writings "truth" has a particularly pregnant meaning. It is revelation, and it is mediated to men in the person and words of Christ. Grace and truth came through Jesus Christ, 1: 17, Jesus is the way, the truth, and the life, 14: 6. Jesus speaks the truth, 8: 40, 45, and bears witness to the truth, 18: 37. When John says that the devil is a murderer from the beginning, and does not stand in the truth because he is a liar, 8: 44, he indirectly teaches that the truth that is in Christ confers life, as indeed he calls Christ the truth and the life. The truth that confers this life is therefore not an abstract, static, timeless reality but it is concrete in the person of Christ and in the *communicated, understandable human word*. Jesus rebukes the Jews because He *says* the truth and yet they do not believe Him. He that is of God *heareth* the *words* of God, 8: 45–47. Similarly, John the Baptist *witnessed* to the truth, 5: 33, and the *hearing* of the apostolic word identifies one as knowing the Spirit of truth, 1 John 4: 6. Revelation, oral communication, life—these are essential elements in the Johannine truth concept. The Holy Spirit as the Spirit of truth is the "other Paraclete" who will take the place of Jesus as the Bearer of the revelation, the Power of its communication, and the Transmitter of its life. This is the Spirit of truth who informs and conditions the life of the New Testament Church, teaching, reminding, guiding, showing, convicting, and witnessing. How can the Church, having its life so determined, be other than a witnessing community?

Quite another question is why the Spirit, having these functions, should be called "Paraclete". Much attention has been given to this question, but a satisfactory answer has not been found. The problem of the name "Paraclete" arises from the fact that a want of correspondence or analogy seems to exist between the *name* and the *functions* ascribed to the Spirit. In Greek usage a parakletos is a helper, an advocate. In rabbinic literature the Greek word is taken over in the form of *p^eraklet* and applied to angels, men, sacrifice, feasts, fulfilment of the law, repentance, good works, alms, and in one place to the Holy Spirit, all of whom serve as pleaders for sinners before the bar of God's judgment.[3] This thought lends itself entirely to explain the use of Paraclete in 1 John 2: 1, "And if any man sin, we have a Paraclete with the Father, even Jesus Christ the righteous". Here function and name cover each other completely since the juridical activity of Christ in this verse stands prominently on the foreground. But this is by no means the case with *parakletos* in John 14, 15, 16. Only by a forced construction of the functions of the Paraclete can *parakletos* be made to describe them. Of the several solutions that have been attempted, that one seems most attractive which relates *parakletos* to the verb *parakaleo* and its substantive *paraklesis*.[4] In general Greek usage *parakaleo* means to call to one's side, beseech, exhort and, infrequently, to comfort. Often, however, exhortation has the value of comfort so that the two meanings may be said to coalesce. In the canonical section of the LXX the Hebrew word for comfort is generally rendered by *paraklesis* or, verbally, by *parakaleo*. In the apocryphal section, these words more generally mean exhortation, to exhort. Barrett notes that *parakaleo* is used in the LXX especially in connection with the comfort of the messianic age and calls especial attention to Isaiah's "Comfort ye, comfort ye my people", 40: 1. It was in waiting for the coming of this comfort that Simeon looked for the *paraklesis* of Israel, Luke 2: 25. The background against which this comfort must be seen is the oppressiveness of this present age. Paul gives classic expression to this comfort in 2 Cor. 1: 3ff., "Blessed be the God and Father of our Lord Jesus Christ, the Father of mercies and the God of all comfort, who comforteth us in all our affliction, that we may be able to comfort them that are in any affliction, through the comfort wherewith we ourselves are comforted of God". This is the comfort of the messianic age that has already dawned, and it forms the burden of the apostolic preaching. Barrett suggests that in the early Church the application of *paraklesis*, as exhortation, to the preaching arose out of the use of *paraklesis* as comfort. Whether this relationship actually obtained between the two senses in which *paraklesis* and *parakaleo* were used is uncertain, but there can be no doubt that these words are used to indicate "the convert-gaining proclamation of the apostolic preaching".[5] If Barrett's suggestion is correct, the name given to the content of the preaching, namely comfort, was applied by the early Church to the act of its presentation, namely the kerugma. When we now consider the functions ascribed to the Paraclete, "it will be difficult to resist the view that the Paraclete is the Spirit of Christian paraclesis".[6] The Paraclete is then the Spirit of witness who exhorts men to accept the comfort of the messianic age.

This construction, like all constructions that cannot penetrate to the mind of the writer, is not devoid of difficulties. It does not satisfactorily bridge the gap between the juridically colored *parakletos* and the hortatory, emotionally-laden *paraclesis* and *parakaleo*. Moreover, *parakletos* appears nowhere in the New Testament outside of the Johannine writings, and *paraclesis* and *parakaleo* appear nowhere in the Johannine writings. Barrett's suggestion has, however, this very great advantage: it unites in one fully consistent and internally coherent pattern the functions of the Paraclete, the content of the preaching, and a prominent New Testament description of the apostolic kerugma. For the rest, the view remains a hypothesis. Barrett's evaluation of the solutions proposed by others applies to his own also: "It seems, then, that in spite of the labors of scholars the background of John's thought about the Paraclete-Spirit has not yet been satisfactorily illuminated, nor has the source of his language been made clear."[7] The difficulties attending the attempt to ascertain the meaning of *parakletos* as used in the Gospel of John have no bearing, however, on the functions which Jesus ascribed to the coming Paraclete. These are plain. Whether we call Him Helper, Advocate, Comforter, Teacher, or simply retain the name Paraclete, His activity is clearly defined. He is Christ's witness in and through men to the Church and to the world. This is the Spirit who is the life and who determines the task of the New Testament Church.

When next we examine the several versions in which the Great Commission has come to us we find the same inescapable correlation between witnessing and the Spirit that was discovered in the Paraclete passages and in the Pentecost account. This correlation is made very explicit by Luke. The apostles are to be witnesses of Jesus, preaching repentance and remission of sins to all nations, beginning from Jerusalem. To this end He will send them the promise of the Father, but they must wait in Jerusalem until they are clothed with power from on high, Luke 24: 47–49. In Acts 1: 8 Jesus tells the disciples that they shall receive power when the Holy Spirit shall have come upon them. When that empowerment has come they shall be His witnesses in Jerusalem, in all Judea and Samaria, and to the uttermost part of the earth. In this connection we must not fail to note the encouragement and the promise that Jesus gave the twelve when He sent them out on their preaching tour in Israel. They would be delivered up to councils and synagogues, and be brought before governors and kings for His sake for a testimony to them and to the gentiles. But when they are delivered up they must not be anxious how or what they shall speak. It will be given them in that hour what they shall speak, for it is not they who speak, but the Spirit of their Father that speaks in them, Matt. 10: 17–20. In Matt. 28: 20 the correlation between Pentecost and the witnessing activity of the apostles is stated indirectly but unmistakably. Jesus, having commissioned them to make disciples of all nations, promises them "lo, I am with you always, even unto the end of the world". Clearly, Jesus is present in the witnessing Church that is built on the foundation of the apostles only in the Spirit. He is present in the Church in the "other Paraclete". Therefore the writer of the conclusion to the Gospel of Mark can say with complete propriety, "And they went forth, and preached everywhere, the Lord working with them" 16: 20. Since we shall have more to say about the relationship between Pentecost and the Great Commission later in this section we shall not further elaborate the matter at this point.

In discussing the relationship between Pentecost and the *witnessing* Church so far, we inquired into the meaning of the Pentecostal speaking with "other tongues", into the functions ascribed to the Paraclete and the meaning of His name, and we touched on the relationship between the Great Commission and Pentecost as that relationship comes to expression in the several versions of the Great Commission. What we discovered in this discussion substantiates the thesis of this sub-section that the Spirit who indwells the Church and constitutes her life is a Spirit of witness. Pentecost means witness and power for witness. We must now turn to the book of Acts to see whether this theme is sustained.

The Acts of the Apostles is the only book in the New Testament that deals exclusively with the history of the Church. It is a book of action, of dramatic action. The theme that is presented in 1: 8 controls the entire book: "But ye shall receive power, when the Holy Spirit is come upon you: and ye shall be my witnesses both in Jerusalem, and in all Judea and Samaria, and unto the uttermost part of the earth." Chapter 2, vv. 1–13, relates the fulfilment of the first part of this verse, and from 2: 14 on to the end of the book the progress of the gospel from Jerusalem to Rome is depicted. Two things stand out with great clarity in Acts: the irresistible missionary expansion of the Church, and the power of the Spirit in that expansion. The missionary witness of the Church begins *at the precise moment* of the descent of the Spirit, and the place and power of the Spirit to that witness are repeatedly attested in the book to its very end. Therefore Wikenhauser thus formulates the theme of Acts: "*The universal expansion of Christianity begun in the power of, and effected by, the Holy Spirit.*"[8] In so characterizing Acts Wikenhauser does not stand alone, but rather expresses a consensus of authoritative opinion. In a later section we shall indicate the intimate and vital role which Acts presents the Holy Spirit as playing in the witness and expansion of the early Church. He launches the witness at Pentecost and guides it at every turn until the grand climax is reached in Paul's arrival in Rome. The prominence of the Spirit in Acts wholly warrants the conclusion of Wikenhauser, "What the apostles do is not their work, but the work of God's Spirit which works in them".[9]

In summary: *It may without exaggeration be said that the preponderance of emphasis in all that Jesus says about the coming Spirit, and the preponderance of emphasis in Luke's account of the coming of the Spirit at Pentecost and in his description of the missionary expansion of the Church in the remainder of Acts, lies on the witnessing activity of the Spirit and of the recipients of the Spirit.* It is *at Pentecost* that the witness of the Church began, and it is *in the power of the Pentecostal Spirit* that this witness continues to be carried forward.

When we next examine the activity of the Spirit in the epistles this well-nigh exclusive association of the Spirit with witness wholly disappears. While emphasis on the witnessing activity of the Spirit is far from being absent, as we shall see below, it no longer dominates the description of the work of the Spirit. He is now presented as the distributor of diverse gifts in the Church, 1 Cor. 12; Heb. 2: 4, the earnest of our inheritance, Eph. 1: 14, the means of access to the Father, 2: 18, the sphere in which Christian love obtains, Col. 1: 8, the means of sanctification, 1 Pet. 1: 2, the ground of unity, Eph. 4: 3, and the fruits of the Spirit are love, joy, peace, longsuffering, kindness, goodness, faithfulness, meekness, self-control, Gal. 5: 22, 23. These and many more passages like them indicate the new aspects from which the work of the Spirit in the Church is regarded. How must this almost abrupt change in the New Testament description of the work of the Holy Spirit be understood?

We have repeatedly called attention to the scriptural emphasis that it is the work of the Holy Spirit *to confer life*. We have also seen that the means he has selected to transmit life is *the preaching of the gospel*. There can be no Christian life, i.e. there can be no manifestation of the fruits of the Spirit, apart from a prior acceptance of the gospel. This means that the witness of the Spirit in the proclamation of the Church is the basis out of which all the other activities of the Spirit in the Church take their rise. Once the Spirit has begotten men to a new life through the kerugmatic activity of the Church the varied manifestations of the new life will follow. Therefore the Church is first and last a witnessing, a proclaiming community. She is, in the new creation, precisely because of her nature as witnessing body, the "mother of all living". Now Jesus, in describing the work of the coming Spirit in the Paraclete passages and in the giving of the Great Commission, and Luke in the writing of Acts, were concerned with the basic, the determinative, activity of the Spirit in the Church. They were concerned to depict that activity through which the Spirit originatively, generatively, brings into the lives of men the life of the new aeon. This activity is the witness of the Spirit in the witness of the Church. It was left to the writers of the epistles to describe the several manifestations of the life which the witnessing activity of the Spirit would bring into being. Therefore there is found in the epistles primarily a testimony to the varied manifestations of the life of the Spirit in those who have in faith accepted this witness.

Even so, a careful reading of the data reveals how large is the place which the epistles give to the witnessing function of the Spirit. We shall cite only some representative passages: Paul's speech and preaching were not in enticing words of man's wisdom, but in demonstration of the Spirit and of power, 1 Cor. 2: 4; he speaks words which not man's wisdom teaches, but which the Holy Spirit teaches, comparing spiritual things with spiritual, 2: 13. No man speaking by the Spirit of God calls Jesus accursed, and no man can say that Jesus is the Lord save by the Holy Spirit, 12: 3. The Church at Corinth is an epistle of Christ ministered by him, written not with ink, but with the Spirit of the living God, 2 Cor. 3: 3. Paul is an able minister of the new testament, not of the letter, but of the Spirit, for the letter kills, but the Spirit gives life, 3: 6. The mystery of Christ was in other ages not made known to the sons of men as it is now revealed to the holy prophets and apostles by the Spirit, Eph. 3: 5–7. The gospel does not come to us in word only, but in power and in the Holy Spirit, 1 Thess. 1: 5, it is received with joy in the Holy Spirit, v. 6, and it is preached to us with the Holy Ghost sent down from heaven, 1 Pet. 1: 12.

Recalling the intimate association between glorified Christ and the life-giving Spirit, the Spirit-conditioned character of the preaching is seen in a new perspective when we note how frequently Paul stresses that it is done *in Christ*. Though the Corinthians have ten thousand instructors in Christ, yet have they not many fathers, *for in Christ Jesus* he had begotten them through the gospel, 1 Cor. 4: 15. The Ephesians have heard Christ and were taught *in him*, 4: 20, 21. Paul does not, as many, corrupt the word of God, but in the sight of God he speaks *in Christ*, 2 Cor. 2: 17, he speaks before God *in Christ*, 12: 19, he speaks the truth *in Christ*, his conscience bearing him witness *in the Holy Spirit*, Rom. 9: 1. He greets Priscilla and Aquila, his helpers *in Christ*, Rom. 16: 3, and warns Archippus to take heed to his ministry which he had received *in the Lord*, Col. 4: 17. That which is done in Christ, and that which is done in or through the Spirit, may be distinguished as that which is done in the power of the objective Giver of the Spirit and that which is done in the power of the Spirit as the subjectively received Gift. This distinction, while helpful and perhaps necessary, may not forget, however, that the Giver is Himself in a very real sense the Gift. Christ is with the witnessing Church to the end of the age in the Spirit, He indwells the Church in the Paraclete.

It is evident, therefore, that there is a surprising and unanimous testimony in the New Testament to the relationship between the Spirit poured out at Pentecost and the witness of the Church. The Paraclete passages, the several versions of the Great Commission, the Pentecost account, the emphasis in the remainder of Acts, the direct testimony of the epistles, and the indirect testimony through the Pauline formula *in Christ*— all underscore that the root activity of the Spirit in the Church is to effect witness to Christ. The acceptance of this witness by men is the condition for the further manifestation of the life of the Spirit in the Church which is so prominently put forward in the epistles. We must now further inquire how this intimate association between Spirit and witness affects the nature and task of the Church.

B. *The Pentecostal Reconstitution of the Church*

The profound effect which Pentecost had on the life and work of the Church is underscored and grows in clarity when we contrast the New Testament *ekklesia* with the Old Testament *kahal* (congregation). A farther-reaching change in the constitution of a religious community is hardly conceivable than that which Pentecost effected in the internal and external structure in and through which the life of the people of God expressed itself. Up to Pentecost the central place of worship had been the temple; the central office-bearer, the priest; the central cultic object, the altar; the central cultic act, sacrifice. With the coming of the Spirit this entire cultic complex was abrogated. For a while the members of the *ekklesia* continued to have a place in the *kahal*, but this dual loyalty was a transitional phenomenon. Pentecost was the death-knell of temple, priest, altar, sacrifice, law and ceremony. All disappeared, and in their place came the preaching of the gospel and the sacraments, together bearing witness to the completed work of Christ. "With the coming of the Church, Jerusalem no longer has any function . . . the fall of Jerusalem and the sending out of the apostles into the world—this is the end of the old covenant and the beginning of the new or, if you will, the end of the law and the beginning of the gospel."[10] *At Pentecost a reconstitution of the Church took place which changed the Old Testament sacerdotal kahal into the witnessing ekklesia of the New.* The true worship of the Father would henceforth take place neither in Jerusalem nor on Mt. Gerizim, but it would be exercised in spirit and in truth wherever the gospel is preached and believingly accepted. When the great High Priest had brought His sacrifice on the altar of the cross there was no longer room for the ministry of types and shadows that had foretold His coming. There remained but one task: Witness to His completed work. The veil of the temple had been rent and the middle wall of partition dividing Jew and gentile taken away. The new aeon had come in which there is neither Greek nor Jew, circumcision nor uncircumcision, for all have been baptized into one body, and all were made to drink of one Spirit.[11] The new cultus is not a nationally conditioned one, it is a ministry of the Word, and the sacrifices which are offered are spiritual sacrifices brought by the royal priesthood of believers. The old has passed away; behold, all things are become new. In this renovation there is involved not least the constitution, the structure, of the ecclesiastical organism in which God's people express their new life in the Spirit. "How is the Jew recognized? By the law, by the sabbath, by circumcision. The new congregation has no priest, no altar, no metropolis, no sacred soil any more, no ritual by which one can identify its members."[12] The Church has been reconstituted to correspond to her new character as the Jerusalem that is above, which is our mother, which is at the same time an elect race, a royal priesthood, a holy nation, a people for God's own possession, brought forth to declare the wonderful deeds of Him who called her out of darkness to His wonderful light.

The fact and extent of this reconstitution are emphasized by still another remarkable contrast between *kahal* and *ekklesia*. This contrast relates to the place which the bearer of the prophetic word occupies in the institutional life of the two dispensations. The Old Testament prophets either were not office-bearers in the *kahal* or, if this statement be too strong, their official status was so tenuous that it does not seem capable of definition. In any case, it is not subject to dispute that the office-bearers in the Old Testament religious institute were pre-eminently the priests. They were officially anointed, presided at sacrifice, and taught the people the *Torah*. So completely did the priestly cultus dominate the religious life of Israel that when Ezekiel pictured the messianic age, he did so in terms of a rich and heightened restoration of the cultus. The prophets, on the other hand, did not derive their mandate to speak from any institutional authority, but directly from

God. They were generally lonely men who often found themselves opposed by the representatives of the religious institute. They spoke directly to the nation and depended for the effect of their preaching on the power of their prophetic word, for they were the bearers of the Spirit and the communicators of the divine *dabar*.

In the New Testament the situation is obviously quite different. Not only has the priest as cultic official completely disappeared, but the prophetic office has become the central office in the Church. Jesus ordained the apostles to be under Him the founders of the Church, and after them came prophets, evangelists, pastors and teachers, for the perfecting of the saints, for the work of the ministry, and for the edifying of the body of Christ, Eph. 4: 11, 12. Especially the elders who labor in the word and in teaching must be counted worthy of double honor, 1 Tim. 5: 17. Yet the situation is not simply so that the prophetic office is now the central office in the Church, whereas in the Old Testament this was not the case. The character and function of this office have themselves undergone great changes. The minister of the gospel is not, as was the Old Testament prophet, an individual bearer of the Spirit, nor is he seized by Him on occasion for some specific purpose. He has the Spirit, not occasionally but always, and not alone but in common with all the members of the body of Christ, for the Spirit dwells in the body and informs all its members. He has been called to minister in a very special sense the word of God to men, but he can do so precisely because the body within which he has been set aside for this work is a witnessing body. Moreover *the prophetic office entered upon a new function*. In a certain sense we can speak of a reconstitution also of the prophetic office. Old Testament prophecy is properly called *prophecy* because the central object of its proclamation lay beyond itself, beyond its message, beyond any act of God in the then present. Prophecy in the Old Testament pointed to a *coming* Messiah. The proclamation of the Church of the New

Testament, on the other hand, *witnesses* to an *historical reality*. It witnesses to the fulfilment of cultus and prophecy in the life and work of Christ, the Messiah who *has come*.

It is doubtless for this reason that the verb to prophesy recedes into the background in the New Testament, and prominently on the foreground appear witness, exhort, preach, evangelize. When "witness" is isolated from this complex and attention is focused on its juridical meaning, a coloring is given to it and its related words that hardly allows the full richness of their meaning to come into its own. In the New Testament a witness of Christ or to Christ is one who proclaims the historical fact and the redemptive meaning of the work of Christ with a view to moving men to faith in Him, and who is either an apostle and therefore an eyewitness to the resurrection of Christ, or who in his witnessing was faithful unto death. Although the witness of the Church rests on the eyewitness of the apostles, her witness is, in the nature of the case, not eyewitness. Nor is the Church always called upon to seal her witness with her blood. The element of lasting significance in the New Testament concept of witness is, therefore, that of "a testimony about Christ's being and meaning with a view to moving men to believe in Him".[13] The Church does not announce a salvation still to come, but a salvation that has been accomplished in history, the power of which she has experienced in her life. To this salvation she testifies, she witnesses, that is, she supports her proclamation with the authority of God's word and with her own experience of the truth of that word. The prophetic office is, therefore, the central office in the New Testament Church, it takes its rise from the prophetic character of the Church as a whole, and its function is to witness to the redemption that has been historically realized in Christ with a view to moving men to faith in Christ.

Radical though the reconstitution of the Church at Pentecost was, it must not be thought that Pentecost dropped from the sky without any relationship to existing factors and conditions. It is not the way of God so to work. The fact must strike the careful reader of the New Testament that the witnessing function that devolved upon the Church is nowhere presented as a matter of surprise, or as a strange and peculiar function. It seemed quite natural to witness. How is this to be explained?

We may note, first, that the prophetic tradition had had a long and honorable history in Israel. It was, moreover, a part of the prophetic testimony that in the messianic age *all* would prophesy. One standing so early in Israel's history as Moses had exclaimed, "Would that all God's people were prophets!" Num. 11:29. Isaiah had prophesied that the pouring out of the Lord's Spirit would be followed by confession of the Lord's name, 44:5, and the words that God would put into the mouth of the Messiah's seed and of his seed's seed would not depart from them forever, 59:21. Later Joel had foretold that when in the last days God would pour forth His Spirit, sons and daughters would prophesy, 2:28. The pious Israelite, therefore, lived in the expectation of a general dissemination of the prophetic function.

More especially, however, we wish to call attention to the preparation for Pentecost provided by that significant historical phenomenon, the Diaspora. It had brought into being a widespread religious community in which the *spoken word* was the chief element around which worship centered. The Old Testament and the apocryphal writings had been made available to the entire Greek-speaking world in the Septuagint sometime between 250 and 130 B.C. The publication of the LXX had been followed by a rich apologetic-polemic literature, the chief message of which was that Judaism is the *revealed* religion. This religion was, like Islam later, spread abroad through the zeal of its adherents. They proclaimed the *one* God, His moral law, and the coming judgment. The center of Diaspora worship was the local synagogue, which worship was characterized by absence of sacrifice, by reading from the Law and the

Prophets, followed by free discourses by such as were able to hold them. It was this universal form of worship of which Paul availed himself time and again to present the Christian message to the Jewish world. A striking example of this is given in Acts 13: 15 in connection with the visit of Paul and Barnabas to the synagogue in Antioch of Pisidia: "And after the reading of the law and the prophets the rulers of the synagogue sent unto them, saying, Brethren, if ye have any word of exhortation for the people, say on." Contact between the Diaspora communities and the religious capital, Jerusalem, was maintained through officially commissioned apostles, usually rabbis sent out in pairs, for teaching and fund-collecting purposes. It is therefore clear that the Church, so far as her form as witnessing community was concerned, far from finding herself in a wholly strange situation, found herself in one that was entirely congenial to the expression of her newly received character.

Having seen how prominently the New Testament identifies the Spirit given at Pentecost with the witnessing task of the Church, and that at Pentecost the Church was reconstituted to become a witnessing body, we must now further elaborate the relationship between Pentecost and the witnessing Church by discussing

C. *The Great Commission as Law of the Church's Life*

It will be recalled that in Chapter 1 we concluded that, as far as can be determined, the Great Commission played no conscious role in moving the Church to her witnessing labors. It was also seen that in this respect the primitive Church forms a strong contrast to the Church of modern times in which the Great Commission has explicitly dominated missionary motivation. It will also be recalled that we did not suggest that the Great Commission played no part at all in the witnessing activity of the early Church. On the contrary, we stated, "it has always been, is now, and always will be, the heart and soul

118

of all true missionary labor. But its meaning for and place in the life of the missionary community must, we believe, be differently construed than is customarily done. The Great Commission, as we shall have occasion to see, derives its meaning and power wholly and exclusively from the Pentecost event. It does so in terms of a deeply organic relationship, the nature of which we shall endeavor to set forth in the course of the argument." We have now reached the point in the discussion where we can enter further upon this important question.

The many and varied activities that are attributed to the Spirit must be subsumed, as we have seen, under the one concept—*Life*. We have also seen that it is the kerugmatic proclamation of the Church that transmits the life of the Spirit to the ever-growing community of New Testament believers. It is for this reason that the pre-eminent activity with which the Spirit of Pentecost as the *lifegiving* Spirit is identified, is the *preaching of the gospel*. Whatever further activity the Spirit engages in grows out of the believing acceptance of the Church's witness to her risen and ever-living Lord. The proclamation of the gospel is therefore not one activity among many in which the Church of the New Testament engages, but it is her basic, her essential activity. It is for this reason that the *preaching* office is the *central* office in the Church.

When a given activity is not accidental to the life of an organism, but is an essential manifestation of it, that activity may be said to be the expression of the law of the organism's being. It is an expression of its deepest nature. It is in this way that we must regard the witnessing activity of the Church. The kerugmatic activity of the Church is an expression of the law that governs the discharge of her task in the world. *This law is the Great Commission.* At Pentecost this law went into effect. The Great Commission is a mandate to *witness*, and it is a mandate to witness *universally*. At this point we shall discuss only the first aspect: At Pentecost the Church became a witnessing institute because the coming of the Spirit made Christ's mandate an organic part of her being, an essential expression of her life. This thesis we must now enlarge upon.

It was earlier seen that the function of the Spirit in the new aeon as a conferring of life corresponds wholly to His life-giving function in the realm of nature. In the sphere of creation the Spirit confers and sustains natural life, in the sphere of redemption the Spirit renews this life and elevates it to a higher, an indestructible, an incorruptible level. The Spirit is life-giving in creation as well as in redemption. The operations of the Spirit in nature and in grace are therefore analogous. It may even be said that because redemption envisions the restoration of what was lost in the fall of man from his primal state the work of the Spirit in both spheres is *one work*. Since the task of witnessing entrusted to the new humanity at its inception is its basic, its determinative task, we cannot but ask whether an analogous task was given mankind at the beginning of its history at creation. At every point creation and redemption are interlocked and related. Christ is the Mediator of both creation and redemption; the God who created is also the God who redeems; a humanity was brought into being at creation, a renewed humanity in redemption; the old heavens and the old earth will become the new heavens and the new earth. It is not arbitrary, then, to ask whether mankind was given a task at creation that may be considered analogous to, and therefore may shed light upon, the witnessing task given to the new humanity which is the Church.

We believe that in answering this question serious considera-tion should be given to the command promulgated at the beginning of man's history, "And God blessed them: and God said unto them, Be fruitful and multiply, and replenish the earth, and subdue it; and have dominion over the fish of the sea, and over the birds of the heavens, and over every living thing that moveth upon the earth" Gen. 1: 28. This command was repeated to Noah after the flood when he and his sons became the progenitors of the post-diluvian humanity, although in a form reflecting the condition of sin that had come into being: "Be fruitful, and multiply, and replenish the earth. And the fear of you and the dread of you shall be upon every beast of the earth, and upon every bird of the heavens; with all wherewith the ground teemeth, and all fishes of the sea, into your hands are they delivered" Gen. 9: 1, 2. In comparing this command with the Great Commission we must examine it (*a*) with respect to its form, and (*b*) with respect to its content.

Although we have before us here a command, it is no less plain that we are dealing with more than *simply* a command. It would be better to say that the command we find in Gen. 1 and 9 is a divine and therefore *organic law* which enters into the very fiber of man's being, which penetrates and permeates his entire constitution. It is of the *nature* of man to be reproductive, to subdue the earth, and to rule over the animals that inhabit it. This command is obeyed, the law is observed, by all men everywhere and at all times. Awareness of it is not at all necessary in order to obey it. Men observe this law because their nature, their whole being, drives them to obey it. Not to live in accordance with this law is to deny the human nature with which man was created. Men can rebel against its requirements, they can limit its effectiveness, but essentially they cannot escape it, they cannot not-obey it. Even those who are aware of the primordial promulgation of this law and who willingly observe it, do so not so much consciously as instinctively, spontaneously. It is only when men try to evade or escape the law of their natural being that this law becomes a command for them. Then they must be confronted with the command in order that via obedience to the objective imperative they may be brought again to a normal observance of the law of their life. The difference between command and law in the present discussion is, as we conceive it, that command has objective but no subjective force, whereas law has both. A command comes from the outside and can be obeyed or disobeyed, depending on the attitude of the recipient to it. A divine law, on the other hand, although it has an external origin, carries within itself its own effectuation. It finds its subjective aspect willingly responding to its objective aspect. Understanding command and law in this sense, it may be said that God alone can make laws, and man can give only commands.

The Great Commission as the divine mandate to the Church to be a witnessing Church, is not only a law similar to that which was promulgated at the beginning of human history, but *it is its spiritual counterpart in the new creation.* It is a statement of the task of the renewed humanity as the other is a statement of the task of old humanity. The urge to witness is inborn in the Church, it is given with her nature, with her very being. She cannot not-witness. She has this being because of the Spirit who indwells her. Pentecost made the Church a witnessing Church because at Pentecost the witnessing Spirit identified Himself with the Church and made the Great Commission the law of her life. "This mandate", says Karl Barth, "became effective through the gift of the Holy Spirit."[14] At Pentecost the witnessing Spirit became the Soul of Christ's body, and the mandate of Christ the law of its nature. We draw attention in this connection to two considerations. When Jesus laid upon the apostles and upon the Church of all time the mandate to witness to Him, he availed Himself in Acts 1: 8 of an expression that sums up in a word the nature of the Church as witnessing institute. Jesus said, "You will be my witnesses". Note well, Jesus did not say, You shall witness to me, or, You shall bear witness to me, but, You shall *be* my witnesses. The use of the verb "to be" here has a value which must be taken with full and literal seriousness. The expression "you will be my witnesses" does not merely state what the Church would *do*, but what the Church would *be*. R. Schippers has with fine perception seen that Acts 1: 8 speaks not only of the *witnessing to* of the Church, but emphatically of her *witnessing being*. If "you will be my witnesses" did not stand in the large and eloquent context of the nature of the Church as witnessing community which we have so far discovered, it would doubtless be asking too much of this expression to freight it so heavily as we are now doing. But it states in a word all that scripture clearly teaches about the task of the Church in the interparousia period: The Church of Jesus Christ is, by virtue of the Spirit who indwells her, a witnessing body, being so constituted by the effectuation in her life of the Great Commission at Pentecost.

The organic nature of the Great Commission as manifested in the life of the Church has often been noted. There is a drive in missionary outreach that transcends obedience to an external command. But the theological correlation between the command and its obedience has been too little considered. Robert E. Speer had a sharp eye for this organic character of Christ's mandate. He writes:

> Men who assent to the missionary enterprise on the strength of the last command of Christ alone, or primarily, will give it little support, and their interest in it will soon become as formal as the ground on which it rests. The spirit of Christianity is higher than legalism, and it is of the spirit of legalism to press injunctions of courses of action where the underlying principles of action are unseen or unfelt. The men who have done the work of God in the world are men in whom the Spirit of God was at work, and who would have done God's work even in the absence of expressed legislation as to the nature of the work God wanted done.[15]

In this remarkable testimony to the internal power of Christ's command one thing is to be noted. It is characterized by an under-evaluation of the objectively spoken divine word: "The men who have done the work of God in the world . . . would have done God's work even in the absence of expressed legislation as to the nature of the work God wanted done." It should not be forgotten that the Spirit did not work independently at Pentecost. It was *the command* that was effectuated in the Church by the Spirit. The Spirit does not operate apart from the word of God. He effectuates it. Word and effectuation are one. They are distinguishable but not separable. That the Church is not always *aware* of the objectively spoken word does not mean that she could act as she does had the word according to which her action corresponds not been spoken.

In the second place, the witnessing activity of Christ and of the Spirit, and therefore of the Church, dates from "the beginning". When Peter gave account to the Church at Jerusalem of his baptizing the household of Cornelius, he saw in the speaking with tongues evidence of the descent of the Spirit "even as on us at the beginning" Acts 11: 15. For Peter the descent of the Spirit and its accompanying oral declaration of the great works of God took place, therefore, at "the beginning". Peter does not stand alone in making a use of "beginning" in connection with the inception of the gospel proclamation that is strongly suggestive of the "in the beginning" of Gen. 1: 1 and John 1: 1. John does not write a new commandment to his readers, but an old commandment which they had *from the beginning*, and this commandment is the *word which they had heard*, 1 John 2: 7; they must let that abide in them which they *heard from the beginning*, 2: 24; that we should love one another is the *message* which they had *heard from the beginning*, 3: 11; they *heard* the commandment of love *from the beginning*, that they should walk in it, 2 John 5, 6. The public ministry of Christ is called the *beginning of the gospel*, Mark 1: 1; Heb. 2: 3. Paul regarded his preaching in Macedonia as the *beginning of the gospel* in that area, Phil. 4: 15. In short, the proclamation of or concerning Christ which heralds the introduction of the new aeon is in the New Testament called "the beginning". It is the second beginning which announces the quickening and renewal of the old beginning; it proclaims the last Adam who restores what was lost in the first Adam; it creates a new humanity that shall render the obedience that was refused by the old humanity; it confers upon men for whom the remnants of the old life are a living death the new life of the

Spirit. At the beginning of the new aeon stands the proclamation of the gospel. Always it is the preaching that initiates the new age. The Church as a whole entered the new aeon at Pentecost, it dawned for succeeding generations of men when the gospel was made known to them. Thus, the new age came to central Africa when in the 1850's David Livingstone made known the good news of salvation in that area.

The law to multiply and subdue the earth given to man at the beginning of his history finds its counterpart, therefore, in the law that conditions the life of the Church to witness to the gospel of Christ. So much must be said about the analogous character of these two tasks, these two laws, *formally*.

On the *material* side the analogy is no less striking. The task given mankind at creation was to reproduce and to subdue the earth, that is, to transmit life and to have dominion. Doubtless we must say that this twofold task was not a duality, but must be so conceived: man had to transmit life *in order that* he might have dominion. The transmission of life was not an end in itself, but it envisioned the realization of the purpose of creation, which was man's dominion over all things under God and for God. Moreover mankind was not, like the angels, created singly and simultaneously, but it was created potentially in the one father of the human race. This fact ensured an organic relationship between the members of the human race, on the one hand, and the coming into being of history in the course of which mankind as potentiality would become mankind in actuality, on the other. When we examine the witnessing task of the Church we find all these elements prominently recurring. The thought that the purpose underlying the preaching of the gospel is the transmission of the life of the Spirit is not only made very explicit in the New Testament, as we have shown, but it permeates the New Testament form of expression about the proclamation of the gospel. The gospel is the word of life, Phil. 2: 16; the word of God is an incorruptible seed which lives and abides forever, 1 Peter 1: 23, 25; we must long for the spiritual milk as new-born babes that we may grow thereby to salvation, I Peter 2: 2; Paul was in travail for his little children until Christ was formed in them, Gal. 4: 19; although the Corinthians had ten thousand tutors in Christ, yet had they not many fathers, for in Christ Jesus he had begotten them through the gospel, I Cor. 4: 15. John wrote his gospel that others might believe that Jesus is the Christ, the Son of God, and that believing they might have life in His name, 20: 31, and he addressed his first epistle to his "little children" 2:1, 12, 18. Paul calls the Church "our mother", Gal. 4: 26, an expression taken over by the theologians of the Church who call her the *mater fidelium*, the mother of believers. This Church, which is at once a mother and under the heavenly Father, a family, has, like the human race, come into being gradually, progressively. She has a definite historical aspect through which one generation grows out of and builds upon another, until the family that is the new humanity shall be complete.

But why does this Church exist, why does her proclamation of the gospel transmit the life of the Spirit to ever widening circles of men? The purpose of the Church's existence and labors is to announce and to secure acknowledgment of Christ's dominion. Therefore the earliest confession of the Church and the burden of her preaching was "Jesus Christ is Lord".[16] This lordship must be announced, and this lordship Christ exercises under God and for God until every tongue shall confess that Jesus Christ is Lord to the glory of God the Father, Phil. 2: 10, 11. In the dominion of Christ there is included, however, the dominion of the Church. Her membership constitutes a royal priesthood, I Peter 2: 9, all things are hers, I Cor. 3: 22, she will judge angels, I Cor. 6: 3, already now she exercises with Christ a millennial reign, Rev. 20: 4, that is hidden from the eyes of men; and in the end she shall reign for ever and ever, 22: 5.

In closing this part of the discussion we wish to call attention to two characteristics of the preaching of the early Church which, in the light of the foregoing, become more intelligible than they may otherwise be. The first characteristic is the overwhelming emphasis on the resurrection of Christ. In the kerugma concerning the resurrection the *life of the new aeon* and the *lordship of Christ* come to unique expression. In the giving of the Great Commission Jesus had Himself laid the basis for the centrality of the resurrection witness. "Then opened he their mind that they might understand the scriptures, and he said unto them, Thus it is written, that Christ should suffer, and rise again from the dead the third day, and that repentance and remission of sins should be preached in his name, beginning from Jerusalem. Ye are witnesses of these things" Luke 24: 45–48. In anticipation of the task that must soon be discharged, Matthias was chosen to take Judas' place, to be with the other apostles a witness to Jesus' resurrection, Acts 1: 22ff. The resurrection of Jesus is the heart of Peter's Pentecost sermon, 2: 24, it is the supreme evidence that God had made Him both Lord and Christ, v. 36, and it is the theme of the witness of the apostles, which witness they gave with great power, 4: 33. Paul preached "Jesus and the resurrection" 17: 18, and in his defense before Jewish and imperial authorities the heart of the issue was "Touching the resurrection of the dead I am called in question before you this day" 24: 21. The "resurrection of the dead" was not for Paul an abstract and general idea of resurrection, but the major premise of the argument that proved Christ's resurrection: "if there be no resurrection of the dead, neither hath Christ been raised" 1 Cor. 15: 13. At Corinth Paul preached "Christ and him crucified" 1 Cor. 2: 2, but the message of the cross is the "power of God" 1: 18, and this power lies in the resurrection, for "if Christ hath not been raised, then is our preaching vain, your faith also is vain" 15: 14. For Paul cross and resurrection stand related as death and overcoming life. "It is Christ Jesus that died, yea rather that was raised from the dead, who is at the right hand of God" Rom. 8: 34. Christ took death from us through the cross, and now as Lord gives us life through His resurrection. Therefore Paul's ethical appeal for the suppression of sin is constantly the fact that we have been crucified and buried with Christ and, conversely, his appeal for perseverance in the new life is equally constantly the fact that we have been raised with Christ. The apostolic kerugma therefore, wholly reflects the sense and import of the Great Commission as the law of the Church's life that impels her to proclaim the new life of the Spirit and the lordship of Christ, which are the central features of the new creation.

Secondly, we must note the *spontaneous character* of the witness of the early Church. The view of the Great Commission which has been set forth in this chapter explains how it played both a tremendous role in the witness of the primitive Church, on the one hand, and why no reference is made to it, on the other. The obedience of the Church to the law of her being was a natural obedience, unreflective, spontaneous. It was the response of a healthy organism to the law of its life. "We cannot but speak the things that we have seen and heard" Acts 4: 20; "necessity is laid upon me; for woe is unto me, if I preach not the gospel" 1 Cor. 9: 16. So spontaneous was the response of the Church to the Spirit-effected law that informs her life that the need of consciously obeying the command of Christ was not felt. We do not wish to suggest that the command of Christ was not at all in the mind of the early Church. So far as we know, however, it formed no part of her motivation. And that is significant. It indicates that in the judgment of God the ideal form of witness is that which takes place through inner compulsion. Witness began not with the receiving of the Great Commission, but with its *internal effectuation* at Pentecost. So also the witness of Paul began "when it pleased God . . . to reveal his Son *in me*, that I might preach him among the gentiles" Gal. 1: 16. It is as unreasonable to ask why we do not read of the Great Commission as motivating the early witness of the Church as to ask why we do not read of the command to multiply and replenish the earth and to subdue it as the motivation for the reproductive and economic activity of man. It is only when man's disregard of his nature and duty leads him to violate this law of his being that it again comes to the fore. This is evident in some of Paul's exhortations. Since some had turned aside after Satan to lead an irresponsible life, Paul desired that the younger women marry, bear children, rule their household that by so doing they might give no occasion to the adversary for reviling, 1 Tim. 5: 14, 15. He scores those who forbid to marry, 1 Tim. 4: 3, 4. Who does not provide for his own, especially his own household, is worse than an unbeliever and has denied the faith, 5: 8. When Paul discovered that there were among the Thessalonians men who were disorderly, and worked not at all but were busybodies, he wrote that if any would not work he should not eat either, but that they should study to be quiet, do their own business, work with their hands, and eat their own bread, 2 Thess. 3: 10–12; 1 Thess. 4: 11. The prominence of the Great Commission in the modern period of the Church's history is a sign of vigor and health in so far as it was put forward by men burdened by the undischarged task of the Church; it is a sign of spiritual decadence in so far as emphasis on the binding character of the Great Commission was made necessary by the indifference of the Church to her calling, and by her blindness to the responsibilities which the law of her being placed upon her.

Pentecost made the Church a *witnessing* Church. Her witness was spontaneous, immediate. She did not need a basis in reflection for the discharge of her kerugmatic task, for she had been naturally constituted to be a kerugmatic community. What required reflection was the *extent* of her witness. That gentiles as well as Jews were to be the recipients of the good news of the gospel was not immediately apparent to her. This is understandable. There was an age-old history of pride and national exclusiveness to overcome. This prejudice was not removed by the words of the Great Commission that reached the ears of the apostles. It was not even immediately removed by the reconstitution of the Church at Pentecost. Its removal required elaboration of the basic revelation concerning the universalism of the gospel given at Pentecost. In the revelations of the Spirit and in the concrete circumstances into which the Church was led this elaboration was given. It is clear that once the intent of the Spirit became clear to the Church she hurdled the national and racial barriers and sent the gospel even during the lifetime of the first generation of Christians to the limits of the empire. There is in the entire history of the Church no example of active submission to the Spirit comparable to the self-abnegation and aggressive obedience that comes to expression in the earliest expansion of the Church from its Jewish nucleus to the whole Jewish and gentile world. In the following chapter we shall discuss the backgrounds of and the manner in which this universal expansion was effected.

D. *The Reticent Spirit*

We could rest the case for this part of the argument at this point were it not for one question that constantly recurs in studying the Holy Spirit in His witnessing character. One cannot but ask why the Church has been so little *aware* of the Spirit as the source and bearer of her witness to men. This question may, in fact, be asked concerning the Spirit with respect to all His work. The Father and the Son stand much more prominently before the mind of the Church than does the Spirit. There is an extensive Theology and Christology, but there is no unified and clearly circumscribed Pneumatology. Herman Bavinck has commented on the want of clarity with which the Church regards the Spirit from several points of view. The person and deity of the Spirit do not stand so objectively before us as do those of the Father and of the Son. The sanctifying work of the Spirit does not appear so clearly to our consciousness as do the works of the Father and the Son in creation, incarnation and atonement. Our prayer is less directed to Him than to the Father and the Mediator. He is more the author of prayer than the object of prayer. There was for long a question in the Church as to the person and deity of the Spirit. Not least in theological reflection, therefore, the Spirit has, relative to the other Persons of the Trinity, remained in the background. Whence this want of concreteness in the Church's thinking about the Holy Spirit?

Before suggesting an answer to this question we must note one aspect of the Spirit's nature to which no reference has yet been made. It has been emphasized that the Spirit is the Spirit of *life* and that He transmits this life through the *witness* of the Church. We must now further observe that the Spirit is also the Spirit of *love*. We shall not enter into the difficult question whether the Spirit is to be understood as the personal love element in the Trinity that unites the Father and the Son. St. Jerome has given classic expression to this thought: "The Holy Spirit is neither the Father nor the Son, but the love which the Father has in the Son, and the Son in the Father. Whence Paul the apostle says: Because the love of God is diffused in our hearts through the Holy Spirit who has been given to us."[17] We wish at this point only to indicate the profound association that scripture establishes between the divine love and the divine Spirit.

Of all the attributes that scripture ascribes to God two are prominently *identified* with God. God is love. "He that loveth not knoweth not God, for God is love" 1 John 4: 8, and "God is love; and he that abideth in love abideth in God, and God abideth in him" 4: 16. God is also said to be spirit. "God is a spirit, and they who worship him must worship him in spirit and in truth" John 4: 24. The spirit-character of God is emphasized here by the placing of "spirit" first in the Greek word order "spirit is God". Since God cannot be identified with spirit in general, there is here predicated a relationship of identity between God and the uncreated Spirit. The Spirit as quality rather than as person stands on the foreground, however, because the purpose of Jesus' conversation with the

Samaritan woman is to present God's spiritual nature to which must correspond the character of man's worship.

Love, therefore, lies at the heart of the life of God, and God, whose being is love, is spirit. The correlation between love and the Spirit that is here suggested is made explicit in other places in the New Testament. Immediately after giving the first promise of the Paraclete, John 14: 16, 17, Jesus continues, "He that hath my commandments and keepeth them, he it is that loveth me; and he that loveth me shall be loved of my Father, and I will love him and manifest myself to him" vv. 18–21. Since Jesus comes to us only in the Paraclete, the inextricable union of love between the believer, the exalted Christ and the Father in the bond of Spirit is here plainly set forth. Similar expressions, made directly or indirectly in connection with the coming of the Paraclete, are found in 14: 23, 24; 15: 9, 10 and 17: 26. In 1 John 4: 7–14 the centrality of the Spirit in the believer's love for God and for others is clearly indicated. "Beloved, let us love one another: for love is of God; and every one that loveth is begotten of God, and knoweth God. He that loveth not knoweth not God, for God is love." The specific function of the Spirit is to beget the new life in men, John 3: 5–8, and this life is manifested in love. With this love is also associated the knowledge of God and the believer's dwelling in God, both of which are specifically related to the Spirit by John. "No man hath beheld God at any time: if we love one another, God abideth in us, and his love is perfected in us: hereby we know that we abide in him and he in us, because he hath given us of his Spirit." The entire exposition of Christian love and its requirements in John's first epistle rests on this central thesis, "God is love". And this God of love, says the same writer in the Gospel, is spirit. Paul also conceives of a most intimate relationship between love and the Spirit. "The love of God", he writes, "hath been shed abroad in our hearts through the Holy Spirit which was given unto us" Rom. 5: 5, and he enjoins his brethren that they strive together with him in their prayers to God for him, and that they do so "by our Lord Jesus Christ, and by the love of the Spirit" 15: 30. The love of the Colossian Christians is "love in the Spirit" Col. 1: 8. All the gifts and graces that are in the Church are gifts of the Spirit, 1 Cor. 12: 4ff., and the greatest of these is love, 1 Cor. 12: 31–13: 13.

The Holy Spirit, then, is *loving* Spirit, *life-giving* Spirit, and *witnessing* Spirit. Disparate though love, life and witness at first glance seem to be, they appear on reflection to have one prominent characteristic in common. This characteristic is that all three direct attention *away* from themselves to the loved object, to the activities and expressions of life, to the content of the witness. So it is that the loving, life-giving, witnessing Spirit does not press Himself on the attention of the Church. He is a reticent Spirit. He remains in the background. He is content to see His love exercised, His life expressed, His witness borne forward without obtruding Himself prominently as the author of these activities. He does not bear witness to Himself but to *Christ*, John 15: 26, He is sent by the Father *in the name* of Christ, and He will bring to remembrance all that *Jesus* has said, 14: 26. He will not speak by his own authority, but what He *hears* He will speak, He will glorify *Christ*, He will take *from Him* and declare it to His disciples, 16: 13–15. The Church is the organ of the Spirit's expression. He is the *power* of her witness, but *men* are the witnesses, Acts 1: 8. The union between the Church and the Spirit, between believers and the Spirit, is so intimate, so organic, that the works of the Spirit are manifest as *their* works, the thought He inspires as *their* thought, and the fruit of the Spirit: love, joy, peace, patience, kindness, goodness, faithfulness, gentleness, self-control, Gal. 5: 22, 23, as the very expression of *their* life. This Paul makes plain when he identifies the varied fruit of the Spirit with the believers themselves in whom this fruit appears, "Against such [men] there is no law" v. 23b.

Wholly in keeping with His retiring and self-effacing character, the Spirit is as a parent who is content to see his care, nurture and sacrifice come to expression solely in the progress and faithfulness of the child. After His dramatic outpouring at Pentecost the Spirit remains in the Church as a powerful reality but overshadowed in the consciousness of the Church by the more concrete figures of the Father and the Son. The witness of the Spirit in the proclamation of the gospel sets *Christ* as central. In Him the Father is revealed and through Him the Spirit is given. The Spirit witnesses to Christ and Christ leads to the Father. Perhaps it is because of the hidden role which the Spirit plays in redemption that He has been given a name which, as contrasted with that of the Father and the Son, allows of no concrete representation or association in our minds.

Chapter 7

As one reads the Pentecost account in Acts 2 the elements of *witness* and *universality* stand so prominently to the fore that it is quite impossible to say that one receives more emphasis than the other. The reason for this is that Pentecost is the declaration that the *gospel* is meant for the *world*. The effect of the coming of the Spirit Luke describes thus:

> And they were all filled with the Holy Spirit, and began to speak with other tongues, as the Spirit gave them utterance. Now there were dwelling at Jerusalem Jews, devout men, from every nation under heaven. And when this sound was heard, the multitude came together, and were confounded, because that every man heard them speaking in his own language. And they were all amazed and marvelled, saying, Behold, are not all these that speak Galileans? And how hear we, every man in his own language wherein we were born? Parthians and Medes and Elamites, and the dwellers in Mesopotamia, in Judea and Cappadocia, in Pontus and Asia, in Phrygia and Pamphylia, in Egypt and the parts of Libya about Cyrene, and sojourners from Rome, both Jews and proselytes, Cretans and Arabians, we hear them speaking in our tongues the mighty works of God. Vv. 4–11.

The consciously expressed linguistic diversity and the geographic spread of the audience whom the disciples addressed emphasize the interest of the author in placing the witness that was spoken in a framework of *universal* reference. Pentecost envisioned the proclamation of the gospel to "every nation under heaven". It may be repeated here again that Luke has no interest whatever in acquainting us with the nature of the "speaking with other tongues", or in telling us whether the miracle was a "hearing" or a "speaking" miracle. These questions, to which so much attention has been given, do not even lie at the periphery of his interest. It is therefore refreshing in the extreme to read how Roland Allen cuts through the gordian knot of fruitless exegesis to set forth in simple language the meaning of the "speaking with other tongues":

> When the Holy Spirit descended upon the Apostles His first gift was the gift of Tongues. Men, gathered from every nation under heaven, marvelled to hear the Apostles speak in their tongues the wonderful works of God. Much learned ingenuity has been spent in attempts to explain what exactly happened. Into this controversy I do not propose to enter. To me, I confess, these discussions seem curiously interesting and unprofitable, and their conclusions equally dubious and barren. They tend rather to divert the mind, and to lead it away from the point of real significance and importance. From these learned disquisitions we gain little insight into the nature and work of the Holy Spirit given at Pentecost; but from the fact that a gift of tongues was given we ought to learn much, and what we learn must affect profoundly our life and conduct; because that fact must affect profoundly our conception of the Spirit which is given to us of God. The fact, clear and unmistakable, is that the Apostles, when the Holy Spirit descended upon them, began at once to address themselves to men out of every nation and language, and that the Spirit enabled them so to speak that men understood. Thus, at His first coming, the Holy Spirit revealed His nature and His work as world-wide, all-embracing. He revealed His nature as a Spirit who desired the salvation of all men of every nation; He revealed His work as enabling those to whom He came to preach Christ to men of every nation.
>
> The Holy Ghost was given: forthwith the Apostles began to preach Christ. They began to preach Christ to those who did not believe. There is in the Acts only one speech after Pentecost addressed to believers: it is the farewell speech of St. Paul to the Ephesian elders. As for the rest, all are missionary sermons.[1]

Allen does not here bring us to the heart of the meaning of Pentecost. That, as we have seen, goes further. But he does lay bare one of the most significant aspects of Pentecost. This aspect is that God, in the gospel, is for the world. The good news, the *euangelion* is good news for all the nations of mankind.

If Pentecost means the gospel for the world it means this, specifically, as the gospel for the *reuniting* of the world in the new fellowship of the Spirit. Pentecost means the divine restoration of the unity of mankind that was forfeited and lost at Babel by the sin of pride. The last act of mankind undivided by language was the erection of a city and of a tower that was to replace God as the integrating center of its life, Gen. 11: 1–9. This effort God frustrated by a radical intervention. The unity of mankind that came to expression in a society welded together by a common language was destroyed by an act of divine judgment. Mankind, created in and for unity, became diverse in its social, political, cultural and religious manifestations. This diversity was not born of the rich potentialities given man at his creation. It was a diversity born of judgment, and therefore an unnatural diversity. The chief unifying factor within the families, tribes and nations in which men lived or began to live, and the chief divisive factor between these units, became a linguistic one.

It did not lie in the divine intention to permit human history to continue conditioned only by judgment, however. Mercy rejoiced against judgment. Wrath was soon followed by a divine action that envisioned mercy alone and that was intended to overcome the judgment. Immediately after the words, "Therefore was the name of it called Babel; because Jehovah did there confound the language of all the earth: and from thence did Jehovah scatter them abroad upon the face of the earth", we read, "These are the generations of Shem", and there follows the genealogy of the redemptive line which proceeds through Arpachshad, Shelah, Eber, Peleg, etc., to Abram who becomes the father of the nation from which shall arise the universal Messiah, the *Son of Man*. The Spirit of this Messiah shall bring into being a new humanity welded together into one fellowship of love and understanding by the universal language of the gospel. Therefore at Pentecost a new language was spoken, the language of redemption, that unites through all the barriers of race and nation and class the sin-disrupted humanity.

At Babel the *goiim* (the nations) came into being, the *goiim* in their religious alienation from God, in all their earthly power and achievement, and in all their ultimate moral and spiritual powerlessness. At Pentecost they began to be resolved into the "people of God" as the message of the gospel was addressed to the Jewish representatives of the nations of the world. Throughout the Old Testament history the *goiim* hovered at the fringes of Israel's existence, a sort of "people of the periphery", as Barth calls them, always within spiritual sight but beyond spiritual reach. At Pentecost they began to enter into the fellowship of the new Israel. At Pentecost the Babel that was destroyed was replaced by the revelation of the new *polis*, the city that hath foundations, whose builder and maker is God, Heb. 11:10.

It is customary to speak of the period lying between the call of Abraham and Pentecost as the period of "particularism". As contrasted with the pre-Abrahamic and the post-Pentecostal periods, Israel alone was the recipient of redemptive revelation. The word "particularism" may be used as a convenient description of the restricted operations of redemptive grace during this time. It must be remembered, however, that the expressions "particularism" as applied to this period, and "universalism" as applied to the periods before and after it, do not, in an important respect, express a true antithesis. The calling of Abraham and the separate existence of Israel among the nations envisioned the redemption of mankind. They were integral and essential parts of the divine plan to redeem *the world*. Pentecost was the revelation of the mystery that the dispersion of mankind at Babel and the separation of Israel to a peculiar service among the nations were but steps on the way to a larger purpose.

We wish in this chapter to discuss how the universality of the gospel lies rooted in the resurrection of Christ and extends to the end of time. We consider:

A. *Pentecost and the Promulgation of the Great Commission*
B. *Missions as an Eschatological Reality*

reserving for the next chapter a review of how this universality manifested itself in the witness of the early Church.

A. *Pentecost and the Promulgation of the Great Commission*

Wilhelm Michaelis has pointed out as highly significant and suggestive the fact that Jesus, in each recorded instance of the promulgation of the Great Commission, gave His command to disciple the nations *after* His resurrection. Michaelis saw two dangers attending any effort to relate the missionary activity of the Church to the missionary consciousness of Jesus. He suggests that the post-resurrection character of the Great Commission should help us avoid these dangers. The first danger is that of seeing only a disjunction between Jesus and the missionary witness of the Church. Into this danger Harnack clearly fell when he denied that Jesus had had a vision of the universal expansion of the gospel, and attributed the expansion that took place to the inherent universalism of Jesus' teachings. The other and perhaps larger danger is that no disjunction will be seen at all.[2] A striking example of this is provided by Gustav Warneck. For him the giving of the Great Commission is simply the natural and unavoidable climax of Old Testament universalism and of Jesus' teaching concerning the kingdom of God. In the same manner, the missionary witness of the Church flows from the natural and unavoidable obedience of the disciples to the Great Commission. We have seen that the Church immediately after Pentecost manifested no awareness of the Great Commission, that her witness did not arise from conscious obedience to it, but that her witness can be understood only in terms of Pentecost. We wish now to examine the circumstances attending the *giving*, that is, the *promulgation* of the Great Commission. What is the significance of the fact that Jesus promulgated it *exclusively after* His resurrection from the dead? We shall introduce this discussion by briefly reviewing Warneck's conception of the manner in which the command of Jesus came into being.

It is an appealing and imposing conception that Warneck sets forth. The universalism of the gospel has its roots in the fact that the God of Israel is the almighty Creator of heaven and earth who has made a universal covenant with man. He is the Lord of the whole world, not only of nature, but also of the nations of mankind. The human race is an organism descended from one pair of parents and therefore no amount of racial or national division can obliterate the indelible fact of the unity of the race. As mankind is one in its origin, so it is one in its sin, one in its guilt before the holy Creator-God, one in its need of redemption. This need God met by giving a universal promise of redemption which shone as the morning star of hope in the night of banishment from Paradise. After the judgment of the flood God renewed His promise. Only when man spurned the divine mercy did God elect Israel to be the bearer of the redemptive process. But Israel's separation from the other nations has, in fact, the other nations in view and intends their salvation. She has the mandate to be the mediator of God's salvation to the gentiles. Although Israel frequently regarded God as her God alone, the prophets reached back to the original universalism of God's dealings with mankind and prophesied a time of universal grace for the *goiim*. The diffusion of this grace among the nations will be effected by the servant of Jehovah. While it is at first expected that the *goiim* will of themselves come to participate in the universal kingdom of Jehovah that is to be established, there are many indications, especially in the Psalms, that the grace that is to be manifested will be proclaimed to the nations. These developments in the Old Testament revelation represent the preparatory stages for the New Testament execution of the world mission.

The Old Testament revelation of the universal diffusion of grace is the basis on which Jesus builds. The climax of the universalism that He proclaimed is the Great Commission. The central doctrine in the teaching of Jesus is the doctrine of the kingdom of Heaven. This kingdom is a universal kingdom and the area in which it is realized is the world. In keeping with the universal character of Jesus' teaching He requires worship in spirit and in truth that shall be congenial to the nature of man as man, and be independent of local forms of worship. Therefore, also, repentance and faith, as conditions for entering the kingdom, are conditions that are not circumscribed by territorial, national or ethnic limitations, but are within the reach of all men. It was therefore wholly natural and in keeping with the universal character of Jesus' religion that He should constantly refer to Himself as the "Son of Man" and avoid the use of the title "Son of David" as a self-designation. The idea of universal salvation therefore lies at the root of Jesus' teaching. If this is true, then the necessity of a general offer of salvation to all men, and with it the necessity of a *sending out*, is also given as a law of nature. On such a foundation a universal kingdom *must* be erected and this can only be done by universal proclamation. This result would have been inevitable even if Jesus had not given a direct missionary command.

There is for Warneck, therefore, a "necessity" of a general offer of the gospel, and this necessity is a "law of nature", as a result of which a universal kingdom of God "must" come into being.[3] There exists for Warneck therefore an organically unbroken line from Jesus' activity within the confines of Israel to the universal missionary command. There is no break anywhere. The Great Commission does not bring anything qualitatively new into being.

Strange as it may seem, Harnack and Warneck, far apart though they stand religiously and theologically, and keen though Warneck's criticism of Harnack has been, hold to formally similar conceptions. Harnack sees the missionary witness of the Church arising by internal necessity out of the teachings of Jesus, Warneck sees it arising by internal necessity out of the pattern of universal redemption announced in the Old Testament and in the proclamation of the kingdom of God by Jesus. Harnack does not believe that Jesus ever spoke the Great Commission; for Warneck it is essentially immaterial whether He did or not. The missionary witness of the Church would have come into being "even if Jesus had not given a direct missionary command". Although Warneck stands wholly within the evangelical tradition, while Harnack stands in the liberal tradition, his view, persuasive though it appears to be, does not square with the biblical data. Something happened to bring the missionary witness of the Church into being that is not explainable in terms of "natural" development. As Dürr writes,

> The early Christian mission, as over against the situation in the gospels and as over against the relationship of Jesus to the gentiles, is indeed something *new* and does not represent simply a gradual progression.[4]

If the promulgation of the Great Commission is not in first order to be related to the universalism of the Old Testament and to the teachings of Jesus in His earthly existence, if it is not simply the climax of preceding universalistic indications, what then is its place in the history of redemption? The promulgation of the Great Commission belongs to a complex of redemptive activity which, while of course most intimately related to the universalism of the Old Testament and of the teachings of Jesus, must be clearly distinguished from them. *This complex is the exaltation and lordship of Christ and the ensuing effusion of the Spirit.* It is because Jesus' command to disciple the nations is in first order related to *this* complex of redemptive activity that its meaning for us is so wholly dependent upon Pentecost. It is not the long historical development that makes it possible for us to appreciate and obey the Great Commission. If this were so, why did the apostles have to await the coming of the Spirit in Jerusalem? And why were they so completely inactive missionarily until that Spirit came? We must therefore inquire into the meaning of Christ's lordship for the promulgation of the Great Commission, and the relationship in which Pentecost stands to both the lordship of Christ and the promulgation which He effected.

The intimate and indissoluble connection between the exaltation of Christ and the outpouring of the Holy Spirit is made plain in Acts 2: 33–36:

> Being therefore by [or at] the right hand of God exalted, and having received of the Father the promise of the Holy Spirit, he hath poured forth this which ye see and hear. For David ascended not into the heavens, but he saith himself, The Lord said unto my Lord, Sit thou on my right hand, till I make thine enemies the footstool of thy feet. Let all the house of Israel therefore know assuredly that God hath made him both Lord and Christ, this Jesus whom ye crucified.

The Spirit was poured out, therefore, because Christ had been exalted and had received the promise of the Spirit. Consequently, Pentecost is the manifestation of a reality that existed *before Pentecost took place*. This reality is a twofold one: Christ is Lord and He has received the Spirit. Whether Christ is Lord because He received the Spirit or bearer of the Spirit because He is Lord is a question that is probably fruitless to discuss. The two are one and inseparable. Christ is the Spirit-conditioned Lord, the sovereign Pneumatophoros. That is the reality we must fully appreciate. This Spirit-conditioned lordship was conferred on Christ *at His resurrection*. There had been flashes of the power which Jesus as the incarnate Son of God had had in the days of His flesh. He had stilled the wind and the sea, Luke 8: 22–25, He had forgiven sins, Mark 2: 5; Luke 7: 48, He had power to call more than twelve legions of angels to His assistance, Matt. 26: 53, He had exercised His control over nature to heal men of their afflictions. But He had used this power only occasionally and in subordination to the purposes of His ministry. Time and again He commanded that the great things He had done should not be made known, Mark 1: 44 5: 43, 7: 36. Moreover, He had resisted the temptation to enter upon the exercise of the power that was rightly His when the way to power would have meant the rejection of the path of suffering. He had rejected the efforts of the people to make him king, John 6: 16. But now that His suffering was finished the exercise of universal power was no longer in conflict with His Messiahship but rather the expression of it.

The great theme of the apostolic kerugma is that Jesus Christ is Lord, and the indisputable proof of His lordship is His resurrection from the dead. Paul has formulated the primitive confession of faith classically:

> If thou shalt confess with thy mouth Jesus Christ as Lord, and shalt believe in thy heart that God raised him from the dead, thou shalt be saved, Rom. 10: 9.

The centrality of the confession that Jesus Christ is Lord in the earliest Christian faith has been set forth by Oscar Cullmann in his study *Die ersten christlichen Glaubensbekenntnisse*, the heart of which is given in the following sentences:

> The *here-and-now lordship* of Christ upon which He entered at His resurrection and His ascension to the right hand of God stands at the center of the faith of the primitive Church. The declarations about the present character of the lordship of Christ and about the authority conferred upon Him in heaven and on earth constitute the historical and dogmatic center of the Christian confession. . . . Its simplest expression is the formula *Christ is Lord*.[5]

The lordship of Christ is everywhere in the New Testament associated with the *resurrection* of Christ. By His great might God

> raised him from the dead and made him to sit at his right hand in heavenly places, far above all rule, and authority, and power, and every name that is named, not only in this world, but also in that which is to come, Eph. 1: 20, 21.

Christ's ascension and His session at the right hand of God are the completion of his exaltation begun at the resurrection and the crowning and public manifestation in the heavenly regions of His universal lordship. The fundamental declaration of Christ's lordship is to be found, however, in the resurrection. When in the promulgation of the Great Commission, therefore, Jesus said, "All authority has been given unto me in heaven and on earth. Go ye *therefore* and make disciples of all nations . . ." Matt. 28: 18f., he spoke consciously as Lord of lords and King of kings under whose aegis His subjects would herald the new reign that had been inaugurated.

To the fact that the command to disciple the nations was given by the *Risen One* must now be added the further consideration that Christ gave this command *in full possession of the Spirit*. It may appear from Acts 2: 33, "Being therefore by the right hand of God exalted, and having received of the Father the promise of the Holy Spirit, he hath poured forth this which ye see and hear", that the Spirit was conferred on Christ *after* His reception into heaven. Care must here be exercised not to conclude from the order of statement to the order of occurrence. Peter states two chronologically unrelated facts concerning Christ's lordship: Jesus is at the right hand of God, and He has received the promised Spirit. When, then, did Jesus receive the Spirit? The New Testament hardly leaves another understanding open to us than that Jesus' resurrection and His receiving of the Spirit occurred simultaneously. Christ was "declared to be the Son of God with power, according to the Spirit of holiness by his resurrection from the dead" Rom. 1: 4. The Spirit that dwells in Christians is "the Spirit of him that raised up Jesus from the dead" Rom. 8: 10–11. In His post-resurrection appearances Jesus had shown Himself to transcend the natural laws governing the mobility of mortal flesh. His body was "spiritual" 1 Cor. 15: 44, and therefore subject to the laws of that sphere of reality that stands wholly under the governance of the Spirit. But most importantly of all, Jesus conferred the Holy Spirit on the disciples on the day of His resurrection when He "breathed on them, and saith unto them, Receive ye the Holy Spirit" John 20: 22. Whether we regard the transmission of the Spirit here as actual or as a symbolic anticipation of the gift to be bestowed at Pentecost is not here of great significance. This action of the Lord, however understood, clearly presupposes His possession of the Spirit and of the authority to transmit Him to others. Resurrection, lordship, the receiving of the Spirit—these are one and inseparable. They are all united in the one act of God when He raised Christ from the dead and gave him glory, 1 Peter 1: 21. To the conclusion that Jesus gave the command to disciple the nations *as Lord* we must, therefore, add the further conclusion that He gave this command *in the Spirit*.

At Pentecost the power of Christ's resurrection, the Spirit which He received at His resurrection, and the task of proclaiming Christ's lordship were given to the Church in the outpouring of the Spirit. Pentecost concludes the complex of redemptive activities that was immediately initiated by the resurrection. It is the last act in the majestic fourfold movement of Resurrection, Ascension, Exaltation at the right hand of God, Pentecost. It mediates to the Church the benefits of the others. The Great Commission was given by Christ in the power of His resurrection lordship. It is the supreme expression of His lordship. By virtue of the giving of the Great Commission Christ is the Rider on the white horse who goes forth conquering and to conquer, on whose garments is written King of kings and Lord of lords, whose name is called The Word of God, Rev. 6: 2 and 19: 13–16. Central in the period between resurrection and ascension stands the promulgation of the Great Commission. It is not one act among many of the risen Lord, it is the essential expression of the lordship that was conferred on Him at His resurrection. The execution of the Great Commission is the central task of the Church, for by means of it the Spirit transmits to men the life that shall make possible the recognition of the lordship that is Christ's. For these reasons the Great Commission was given *after the resurrection*, began to function actively in the life of the Church only *at Pentecost*, and will determine the nature of the Church as witnessing community until every tongue shall confess that Jesus Christ is Lord, to the glory of God the Father, Phil. 2: 11.

The fact that the command of Christ was given by the resurrected One stamped the apostolic witness with its peculiar character. The apostles preached the resurrection and the lordship of Christ. They also preached the crucified One, but the crucified One who was "raised for our justification" Rom. 4: 25. The cross is always seen in the light of the resurrection. In this kerugma which arises from the resurrection of Christ the unity of the whole redemptive process is set forth. The resurrection and the lordship of Christ are *fulfilment* of Old Testament prophecy. The note sounded by Christ, "And beginning from Moses and all the prophets, he interpreted to them in all the scriptures the things concerning himself" Luke 24: 27, is continually echoed in the witness of the apostles. The execution of the Great Commission takes place in this context of *fulfilment*. When the Great Commission became at Pentecost the law of the life of the Church it effected at the same time the realization of the pre-Pentecostal hopes of universal salvation spoken by the prophets and even more clearly by Jesus. But regarding the Great Commission in the light of fulfilment is something quite other than viewing it as the climax of a "natural" development. When the Great Commission is seen as a "necessity" that "must" be promulgated, that stands under the compulsion of a sort of "law of nature", the divine good pleasure that it reflects and the sovereign gift and mandate that come to expression in it cannot be adequately appreciated. Still less will it be possible to appreciate in its profound sense the fact that the preaching of the gospel is the declaration of a *mystery* that has been hid for ages and generations but that has *now* been revealed to His holy apostles and prophets in the Spirit. There is, indeed, development in redemptive history. There is even a strong compulsive element: "Was it not *necessary* that Christ should suffer these things and enter into his glory?" Luke 24: 26, and "delivered up by the *determinate counsel* and foreknowledge of God" Acts 2: 23. But this is not the compulsion of a necessity arising from previous revelation. It is the compulsion of the divine plan unfolding under the pressure of divine love which leads the revelation that has already been given to its intended climax. In this process every step in the drama of redemption comes to us as a wonderful surprise and as a new and unlooked-for happening. Such a new development was also the promulgation of the Great Commission, partaking as it did of the glorious newness of Christ's resurrection and the receiving of His Spirit. The idea of fulfilment in its application to the command of Christ to disciple the nations does justice to the continuity that exists between prophecy and historical realization, while safeguarding the mandate as a commission to the Church that can be understood only in the light of Christ's resurrection from the dead and His coming to the Church in the Spirit.

B. *Missions as an Eschatological Reality*

The universalism of the gospel is an inseparable aspect of the eschatological emphasis in the New Testament. This universalism embraces the whole of mankind and is geographically without bounds. The correlation between universal witness and *eschatos* (end) comes most prominently to expression in a prophetic word of Jesus, in the giving of the Great Commission, and at Pentecost. This gospel of the kingdom, says Jesus, shall be preached in the *whole world* for a testimony unto *all nations*; and *then* shall the *end* come, Matt. 24: 14. To Jesus has been given all authority *in heaven and on earth*; *therefore* the disciples can go out to gain *all the nations* and the Lord will be with them *unto the end of the world*, Matt. 28: 19, 20. When the disciples shall have received the power of the Holy Spirit they shall be

Christ's witnesses in Jerusalem, Samaria, and unto *the uttermost part of the earth*. This power and task they receive *in the last days* when the Holy Spirit is poured out, Acts 1: 8, 2: 17. Here the end of time, the ends of the earth, and the whole of humanity are related to each other, and cosmic contexts are indicated. The whole world is taken up into the *eschatos* concept.

Explicit though these statements are, we are not dependent on them for knowledge of the matter which they teach. Rather, they dramatically illustrate the teaching that runs as a theme throughout the New Testament. At Pentecost the new aeon became a reality in the life of the Church. It was then that the *still here* of the old age became conjoined with the *already here* of the new age to bring into being the New Testament *now*, the "time between the times". At Pentecost the Great Commission became the law of the Church's life, at Pentecost Christ began to call men to the acknowledgment of His universal lordship as the Church addressed to men from "every nation under heaven" the wonderful works of God. What we have set forth earlier at greater length may be summarized in the words of R. A. Nelson:

> Everywhere in the New Testament the Holy Spirit is spoken of in eschatological terms. Pentecost, like Cross and Resurrection, was an eschatological event. The Holy Spirit was the first-fruits of the new age, the first instalment which guarantees the rest. The New Testament Church was certain of the new age not only because Christ was risen and ascended but because the Holy Spirit was given. The Holy Spirit was the first instalment of the Age which was to come, and through it the powers of the Age to come were at work, in the healing of disease, the overthrow of demons, the patterns of community life, and the striking phenomenon of the Pentecost event itself, where the different language groups were able to understand the Christian proclamation, thus symbolizing, as an accomplished fact, the preaching of the gospel to all nations which, as we have seen, was one of the eschatological signs.[6]

We must now enlarge upon the missionary significance of Pentecost from two other points of view.

1. The awareness of a close relationship between missions and the End that has come to expression in recent theological thinking is not in itself the result of a new insight. Rather, it is the deepening of an already existing awareness. The difference between earlier and contemporary reflection on the relationship between missions and the End can perhaps be best put thus: earlier theological reflection saw missions as a *condition* for the revelation of the End; contemporary theological thought, particularly in Europe, views missions as not only a *condition* for the revelation of the End, but also as being a *characteristic* of the *already existing End*. The missionary proclamation of the Church is therefore regarded as both a necessary *precursor* of the End and as itself *partaking* of the End. This newer emphasis is made possible by an enlargement of the *eschatos* concept. The End is increasingly being viewed as not only a particular *point* in time, but also as a *period* of time, that period, namely, which extends between the first and the second coming of Christ.

The great step forward which this emphasis makes lies in the possibility that it so opened for doing greater justice to a number of New Testament data than was possible on the basis of the older view, and in distancing Christian eschatology more completely from the Jewish doctrine of the End. Inherent in these gains lies a clarification of the eschatological aspect of the missionary proclamation. By dwelling a moment on the difference between Jewish and Christian eschatology this will become more evident.

In rabbinic eschatological thought the End, that is, the beginning of the time of the Messiah, would be revealed when Israel's fortunes should have fallen to their lowest ebb. The signs that announce the coming of this time are signs of woe: unrest and war, pestilence and famine, crop-failure and dearth, apostasy from God and the *Torah*, rejection of all moral laws, the dissolution even of the laws of nature. The coming of the Messiah will mark the end of the present aeon, Israel will be restored, and after the Messiah has reigned for a period of time the age of unending bliss will begin. To this view corresponds the Christian conception of "the last things" when the End is identified simply with the return of Christ to judge the living and the dead. In both instances the End is a point in time which is preceded by catastrophic events in the heavens and on the earth. In Christian thought there has been an additional precursor of the End that is wanting in Jewish thought: the gospel must be universally proclaimed before Christ returns. Even so, it remains a precursor, a condition. It stands, like the catastrophes, before the End and points to the End. Christian eschatological thought has therefore had this formal characteristic in common with the Jewish conception of the End: the End will come at that point in time when the Messiah shall be revealed.

In the more recent eschatological thought to which we called attention in Chapter 3 this view remains wholly intact but it is enlarged and deepened. The universal proclamation of the gospel is not only a sign of the End that is to come, but it is also an evidence of the End *that has come*. The old aeon and the new aeon are conjoined and locked in a death struggle. The woes and catastrophes that take place are the final unleashing of the power of the old age. The universal proclamation of the gospel through which the life of the Spirit is imparted manifests in the last days the power of the eschatological glory in which Christ now dwells. During this period the Rider on the white horse goes forth conquering and to conquer, but there follow him the riders on the red horse of war, the black horse of famine, and the pale horse of death, Rev. 6: 1–8. The End has come but it has not yet worked out its full implications; it is here, but it awaits consummation.

Graphs are not wholly satisfactory means of depicting time schemes, but the use that has been made of them by two authorities[7] may justify an adaptation of their presentations at this point. The first graph represents the older eschatological conception, the second the more recent:

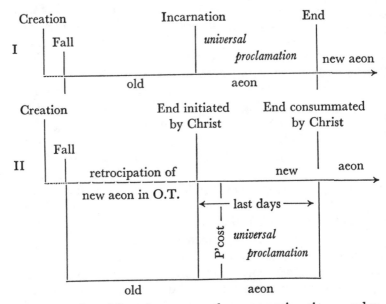

These graphs, although no more than approximations, underscore the difference in eschatological thinking. In the second,
the conjunction of old aeon, new aeon and universal proclamation in the last days emphasizes, more than can be possible
in terms of the first, the eschatological character of the missionary task. It not only precedes the End, but it is taken up *in
the End.* In other words, missions as an eschatological reality
point both to the End that has come and to the End that is
coming. The missionary witness takes place "between the
times". The terminus *a quo* is no less important than the
terminus *ad quem* for the determination of its eschatological
character. The resurrection of Christ, His ascension, His
session at the right hand of God, His lordship, and the giving
of the Great Commission are all eschatological realities that
condition the life of the Church. Through Pentecost the life of
the Church is derived from Christ who dwells in the eschatological glory. It is from this Spirit-mediated power of the new

aeon that the missionary witness of the Church flows, and it is to the full revelation of this power that the witness of the Church tends. What Barth says about the origin and movement of the Church is equally true of her universal witness:

> The Church exists between His coming as the Risen One then and this His last coming. Therefore her time is a time between the times. The Church derives from His being directly visible, and she goes to meet Him as the One who shall be seen . . . she comes from Him as the First One and she looks forward to and goes to meet Him as the Last One.[8]

This conception is of importance in considering the next point to which we wish to call attention, namely Paul's understanding of the mystery of Christ.

2. The intriguing and perplexing conception of the "mystery" that Paul alludes to a number of times invites attention at this place because of its pronounced eschatological and universalistic reference. Before engaging ourselves with the question of its relationship to missions and to Pentecost it will be well to note three major emphases that condition the mystery concept in nearly all its expressions. These emphases are: its eschatological setting, its Christ-centeredness, and its universalistic reference. These become strikingly evident in the division of the following passages. On the left hand appear those portions of the text in which the Christ reference is dominant, and on the right hand the portions in which the universal element predominates. In both, the eschatological "now", which is Paul's favorite designation for the "last days", is italicized, as are also two other eschatological expressions, the fullness of the gentiles and the fullness of the times.

CHRIST	UNIVERSALISM
Rom. 11: 25, 26	For I would not, brethren, have you ignorant of this mystery . . . that a hardening in part hath befallen Israel, until the *fullness of the Gentiles* be come in; and

so all Israel shall be saved: even as it is written,

There shall come out of Zion the Deliverer; he shall turn away ungodliness from Jacob.

Rom. 16: 25, 26

the revelation of the mystery which hath been kept in silence through times eternal, but *now is manifested* and is made known unto all nations unto obedience of faith

Eph. 1: 9, 10, making known unto us the mystery of his will, according to his good pleasure which he purposed in him unto a dispensation of *the fullness of the times* to sum up all things in Christ,

the things in the heavens, and the things upon the earth

Eph. 3: 3–6 how that by revelation was made known unto me the mystery, as I wrote before in a few words, whereby . . . ye can perceive my understanding in the mystery of Christ; which in other generations was not made known unto the sons of men, as it hath *now been revealed* unto his holy apostles and prophets in the Spirit;

to wit, that the Gentiles are fellow-heirs, and fellow-members of the body, and fellow-partakers of the promise in Christ Jesus through the gospel

Eph. 3: 8–11

Unto me . . . was this grace given, to preach unto the gentiles the unsearchable riches of Christ; and to make all men see what is the dispensation of the mystery which for ages hath been hid in God who created all things; to the intent that unto the principalities and the powers in the heavenly places might *now be made known* through the Church the manifold wisdom of God,

according to the eternal purpose which he purposed in Christ Jesus our Lord.

Eph. 5: 32 This mystery is great, but I speak in regard of Christ and of the Church.

Col. 1: 26, 27 the mystery which hath been hid for ages and generations: but *now hath it been manifested* to his saints, to whom God was pleased to make known what is the riches of the glory of this mystery among the gentiles,

which is Christ in you, the hope of glory.

1 Tim. 3: 16 And without controversy, great is the mystery of godliness; He who was manifested in the flesh,
Justified in the Spirit,
Seen of angels,

Preached among the nations,
Believed on in the world,
Received up in glory.

The word "now" is Paul's favorite designation for the period of the last days, in which the Christian has come to live. It is the time that was initiated by the coming of Christ and into which the Church entered at Pentecost. When the Spirit was poured out the new aeon became a reality for the Church that would never die, while the old aeon remained a reality whose duration was marked. Paul uses "now" sometimes in one sense, then in another, sometimes in both, whereby the twofold character of the last days is indicated. Believers were *once* darkness, but are *now* light in the Lord, Eph. 5: 8. They *once* walked in the evil desires that bring the wrath of God on the children of men, but *now* they must put them all away, seeing they have put off the *old man* with his doings, and have put on the *new man*, Col. 3: 5–10. The contrast that Paul makes here between what once was and now is we find even more emphatically in 2 Cor. 5: 16, 17, "even though we have known Christ after the flesh, yet *now* know we him so *no more*. Wherefore if any man is in Christ he is a *new creation: old things* are passed away, behold, *they are become new*." Parallel to the "now" of the new aeon runs the "now" of the old. Paradoxically, the "once" is still a "now", but it is a present reality that has been overcome and will one day fall into the absolute past. The whole creation groans *until now*, and we who have the first-fruits of the Spirit participate in this groaning, waiting for the redemption of the body, Rom. 8: 22, 23. Although our salvation is now nearer than when we first believed and the day is at hand, yet the night is *not yet wholly spent*, Rom. 13: 11, 12. In this "now" our knowledge is partial. For *now* we see in a glass darkly, but *then* face to face, *now* I know in part, but *then* shall I know fully, even as also I was fully known, 1 Cor. 13: 12. Here the "seeing", but "darkly", and the "knowing", but "in part", emphasize the conjunction of the two aeons in the interparousia period. At the same time, the contrast between "now" and "then" underscores the fact that this conjunction is a passing phenomenon. The time will come when the new aeon will exist unburdened and unchallenged by the old.

In this "time between the times", then, the mystery is revealed. But what is this mystery? Obviously, it cannot consist simply in this, that salvation has come to the gentiles. That this would happen had been plainly foretold in the Old

Testament. It was part of Israel's eschatological expectation that the gentiles would enter upon the salvation promised the covenant people. In the latter days it would come to pass that the mountain of Jehovah's house should be established on the top of the mountains, and would be exalted above the hills, and all nations would flow unto it, Isa. 2: 2. This theme lies in the eschatological vision of the whole Old Testament. Nor can the mystery consist in the revelation of Christ alone, whether we understand this revelation in the narrower sense of His appearance in the flesh or in the wider sense of His work from incarnation to ascension. While His concrete appearance and work on earth presented many new and unlooked for aspects, yet the revelation of Christ in the flesh was also clearly a part of Old Testament prophecy. Therefore Jesus was able to chide His disciples for not understanding the meaning of His death and resurrection. "And he said unto them, O foolish men, and slow of heart to believe in all that the prophets have spoken! Behoved it not the Christ to suffer these things, and to enter into his glory? And beginning from Moses and all the prophets, he interpreted to them in all the scriptures the things concerning himself" Luke 24: 25–27. Certainly it cannot be said of either the extension of salvation to the gentiles or the appearance of the Christ among men that it "has been kept in silence through times eternal", or that it "has been hid for ages and generations", and that "in other generations [it] was not made known unto the sons of men". Nor can the mystery lie in the manifestation of both of these phenomena in the last days. That the Messiah would be revealed and that salvation would be granted to the gentiles were definitely Old Testament *eschatological expectations*. Neither of the former possibilities, nor their combination in an eschatological revelation, brings into being the comprehensive and unified conception that the mystery evidently is. Yet it is also clear that the mystery must be resolved in terms of the eschatological, the Christological, and the universal elements. The emphases that run through the texts that have been cited allow no other possibility. The nature of the mystery becomes clearer when we see these three elements not separately, nor collectively, but in the unity which their mutual relationships reveal. *The mystery is the eschatological union of Christ with Israel and the gentiles in his Body which is the universal Church.* That *this* union could take place, that Christ, Jew and gentile could be welded into one spiritual organism called the *Ekklesia*, the Church, and that this union should have significance for the restoration of the whole of cosmic reality—that is the great mystery that eye saw not and ear heard not, and which entered not into the heart of man, 1 Cor. 2: 9. The fact of the Church—not merely the fact of her empirical existence, but the fact of her existence as a body organically related to Christ her exalted Head, and cosmic in her significance—this is the mystery that has been revealed. It is to be emphasized that although the mystery has been *revealed* it has not been *resolved*. The mystery even after its revelation remains a mystery. The riches of Christ are unsearchable. Like the work of the Spirit it is evident but not comprehensible. "This is the *Lord's* doing; it is *marvelous* in our eyes" Ps. 118: 23.

It is not the cosmic aspect of the mystery, however, that stands on the foreground. The emphasis in most of the passages and in other references lies on Christ's relationship to men. The mystery is that of "Christ and of the Church" Eph. 5: 32, it is the gospel, Eph. 6: 19, it is "Christ in you" Col. 1: 27, it is the breaking down of the middle wall of partition between Jew and gentile, Eph. 2: 14, into which Paul has insight enabling him to make the mystery known, 3: 1–9, it is that the gentiles are fellow heirs with Israel and fellow members of the body, 3: 6. This mystery has been revealed to be proclaimed and it is proclaimed to be believed. It is both the subject of proclamation and the object of faith: "I believe a holy, catholic Church." Therefore the mystery stands everywhere in a kerugmatic context. It is made known unto all nations unto the obedience of faith, Rom. 16: 26, it is the unsearchable riches of Christ that is preached to the gentiles, Eph. 3: 8, it is preached among the nations, believed on in the world, 1 Tim. 3: 16; Paul asks the Ephesians to pray for him that utterance may be given to him in opening his mouth to make known with boldness the mystery of the gospel, Eph. 6: 19. The mystery is therefore of the greatest *missionary* significance, and because it is of great missionary significance it is specifically related to Pentecost. The following conclusions with respect to the bearing of Pentecost on the understanding of the mystery concept would seem to be warranted:

a. The revelation of the mystery means the end of the distinction between *'am* and *goiim.* Although the distinction between the people of God and the children of the world remains, this distinction can be overcome in the sense that the children of the world can by faith in Christ become the people of God. God will call that His people which was not His people, and her beloved who was not beloved, Rom. 9: 25. The revelation of the mystery, therefore, means the undoing of the separation between men brought about at Babel. The removal of the "middle wall of partition" was both symbolized and effected in history at Pentecost. There men "from every nation under heaven" heard and believed the gospel, and received the sacrament of baptism which is the sign of their incorporation in the Body of Christ. *It is at Pentecost that the revelation of the mystery first took place.* Later revelations of it were only explications of this fundamental revelation.

b. The mystery is revealed and proclaimed in the eschatological "now" of the New Testament last days into which the Church entered at Pentecost. Its revelation and proclamation therefore stem from the Pentecost event.

c. "Mystery" is the comprehensive term designating the subject matter of the kerugma of the Church from the view-point of its ineffableness and human thought transcending character. To it corresponds the wholly mysterious and incomprehensible character of the Pentecost event with its prophecy of cosmic consummation. The form which the revelation of the mystery took at Pentecost not only befitted but itself expressed the nature of the wonderful matter that was being disclosed.

d. There is a close connection discernible between the revelation and proclamation of this mystery and the work of the Paraclete. The activity of the Paraclete is described with the words teach, remind, guide, declare, convince, witness. Corresponding to these activities is the disclosure of the universal announcement of the mystery by the Spirit. The mystery was revealed to the holy apostles and prophets by the Spirit, Eph. 3: 5. In 1 Cor. 2 it is called the wisdom that has been hidden, which God foreordained before the worlds to our glory, and which God reveals through the Spirit, v. 10. This wisdom, the mystery, says Paul, we speak not in words which man's wisdom teaches, but in teachings of the Spirit, 2: 13. He asks believers to pray for him that he may be able to proclaim the mystery of the gospel boldly, Eph. 6: 19, and to speak the mystery of Christ, Col. 4: 3. Grace was given him to preach to the gentiles the unsearchable riches of Christ and to make all men see the dispensation of the mystery hidden for ages in God, Eph. 3: 8, 9. This mystery is the burden of his proclamation which includes admonition and teaching, Col. 1: 28. The mystery is therefore revealed through the Spirit and preached and taught in the Spirit. In the center of the mystery concept stands the promised Paraclete in His revealing and teaching functions.

The mystery of Christ is therefore a revelation that is disclosed in the last days; it became at Pentecost the central revelation of the will of God for the reunion of men in the new humanity which is the Church, the body of Christ. The mystery was dramatically illustrated at Pentecost, and through the Paraclete who at Pentecost began to indwell the Church is now declared to men everywhere in the outreach of the missionary witness from Jerusalem to the ends of the earth as a necessary prelude to the consummation of all things at the End of time.

Chapter 8

THE book of Acts is the only historical book in the New Testament that deals with the life of the Church. What it has to say about that life may therefore be presumed to be of great importance. This importance, obviously, does not lie in a description of relations between Church and State, of the deliverances of synods and councils, or of the adjudication of theological disputes in the Church. It is these matters that occupy the largest space in the usual "Church histories". Nor is Acts much concerned to describe the internal life of the Church—her organization, her ministry, the relations obtaining between the several sections of the Church, her spiritual life. While all of these, and other subjects like them, are not wanting, they stand on the background and subserve a larger purpose. Acts is governed by one dominant, overriding and all-controlling motif. This motif is the expansion of the faith through missionary witness in the power of the Spirit. So strong, so central, is this motif, so graphically is it portrayed, and so completely is the witness that it sets forth integrated with the life of the Church, that its very centrality obscures it for us, children of the "organized Church". One hardly knows where in Acts to look for a distinction between Church and missions. Restlessly the Spirit drives the Church to witness, and continually churches rise out of the witness. The Church is missionary Church. She is not missionary Church in the sense that she is "very much interested" in missions, or that she "does a great deal" for missions. In Acts missions is not a hobby of an "evangelical section" of the Church. The Church as a whole is missionary in all her relationships. Johannes Dürr has spoken a strong word here.

> The origin of missions coincides wholly with the founding of the Church. Therefore the New Testament does not know the word "missions", since the matter which it signifies is identical with what is understood by Church.[1]

If the missionary witness of Acts is inseparable from the Church, it is equally inseparable from the Spirit. The Holy Spirit launched the witness of the Church at Pentecost and He continues to carry and qualify it in all its manifestations. Roland Allen has rightly rebuked the effort to press Acts into the service of justifying one or other theory of Church government while the sweep of its missionary reach and the power of the Spirit manifested in that outreach are all but overlooked:

> In our day this revelation of the Holy Spirit in "Acts" has been strangely overlooked. We have been content to read "Acts" as the external history of the Church: we have used it as a happy hunting ground for arguments on behalf of different theories of Church government. For each of these theories we have sometimes claimed the authority of the Holy Spirit on the strength of one or two isolated sentences or even of a single word introduced incidentally by St. Luke. . . . But in tithing the mint and rue of the "Acts" we have passed over mercy and the love of God. The great, fundamental, unmistakable teaching of the book has been lost. . . . Our conception of the work of the Holy Spirit has been almost confined to the revelation of Truth, of Holiness, of Church government and Order. Missionary work as an expression of the Holy Spirit has received such slight and casual attention that it might almost escape the notice of the hasty reader. . . .
> For it is in the revelation of the Holy Spirit as a missionary Spirit that the "Acts" stands alone in the New Testament . . . it is the one prominent feature. It is asserted, it is taken for granted, from the first page to the last. Directly and indirectly it is made all-important. To treat it as secondary destroys the whole character and purpose of the book. It is necessary to any true apprehension of the Holy Spirit and His Work that we should

understand it and realize it. This revelation embraces one whole hemisphere of the Spirit.[2]

The sweep and driving power of the universal gospel proclamation that Acts sets forth are *massive*. The preaching began when the Spirit under portentous signs descended to indwell the Church. At the first proclamation by Peter three thousand men and women believed. The movement that began in Jerusalem, the capital of the people of God, spread through the countryside, into Samaria and northward into Syria and Asia Minor. It spilled over into Europe, traversed Greece and reached Rome, the capital of the nations of the world. Between Jerusalem and Rome the great drama unfolded, and the spiritual world that lay in between them was literally "turned upside down" by the message that was preached, Acts 17: 6. Paralleling the extent of the spread in the geographic areas is the massive human area that was gained for the Church. Acts is pre-eminently a book describing *group approach* in missions. It speaks of missionary approach and of conversions to the faith in terms of three thousand, five thousand, multitudes, many, cities, great numbers, households. That is how the faith spread. Acts speaks a missionary language that is hardly congenial to the individualism characteristic of so much European, Anglo-Saxon and American Christianity. Perhaps that is the reason why the missionary value of Acts has so long gone unnoticed. But if the scriptures were written for our learning we should pay large attention to this heavy emphasis in Acts. For as the "speaking with other tongues" symbolized the fact of witness that Pentecost brought into being, *so the first large response to the witness on the day of Pentecost established the pattern for the manner in which future ingatherings recorded in Acts were to take place.*

At Peter's preaching on the day of Pentecost "about *three thousand souls*" were converted, 2: 41, and in a short time this number grew so rapidly that there were *five thousand* men alone, 4: 4. Through the witness of the apostles "believers were the more added to the Lord, *multitudes*, both of men and women"

5: 14. The word of God continued to increase "and the number of the disciples *multiplied* in Jerusalem *exceedingly*, and a *great company* of the priests were obedient to the faith" 6: 7. When persecution scattered the Church, Philip went to Samaria to preach "and the *multitudes* gave heed with one accord unto the things that were spoken by Philip" 8: 6, so much so, that the report came to the apostles at Jerusalem "that *Samaria* had received the word of God" 8: 14. On their way back from their inspection of the work in Samaria Peter and John preached the gospel not *in* but "*to many villages* of the Samaritans" 8: 25. Similarly, Philip, after being caught away from his meeting with the Ethiopian eunuch, evangelized *all the cities* till he came to Caesarea, 8: 40. In the course of his evangelistic itineration Peter "went throughout *all parts*" 9: 32, and when he came to Lydda "*all that dwelt in Lydda and Sharon* saw him, and they turned to the Lord" 9: 35. In Joppa "*many* believed" 9: 42. The preaching of proselytes from Cyprus and Cyrene in Antioch brought it about that "a *great number* of them that believed turned unto the Lord" 11: 21, and as this work progressed "*much people* was added unto the Lord" 11: 24. In Antioch of Pisidia "almost the *whole city*" gathered to hear Paul's testimony, 13: 44, and as a result of this witness "the word of the Lord was spread abroad *throughout all the region*" 13: 49. At Derbe Paul preached the gospel "to that city" and "made *many* disciples" 14: 21. In Thessalonica a few Jews were persuaded, but "of the devout Greeks a *great multitude*, and of the chief women *not a few*" 17: 4. The uniformity of the pattern of group conversion is underscored by the disappointment the reader instinctively feels when Luke acquaints him with the poor and individualistic response given to Paul's witness in Athens: "Thus Paul went out from among them. But certain men clave to him, and believed: among whom was Dionysius the Areopagite, and a woman named Damaris, and others with them" 17: 33, 34.

It is very evident, therefore, that although faith is always an individual commitment the conversions which Acts records took place within large social contexts. The healthy *social* character of the Christianity that came into being immediately after Pentecost is emphasized by the frequent references in Acts, as also in other parts of the New Testament, to the conversion of *families* or *households*. The Church was not built up of so many individual Christians but of *basic social units*, of *organic wholes*, and these units, these wholes, were the fundamental cells of society, namely *families*. When Peter came to Caesarea he found Cornelius waiting for him "having called together his kinsmen and his near friends" 10: 24, and while Peter was preaching to them "the Holy Spirit fell on all them that heard the word" 10: 44. At Philippi Lydia was baptized "and her household" 16: 15. How much the effort to effect the conversion and baptism of families was a part of the apostolic method is emphasized by the account of the conversion of the Philippian jailer with its repeated reference to his "house":

> And he called for lights and sprang in, and, trembling for fear, fell down before Paul and Silas, and brought them out and said, Sirs, what must I do to be saved? And they said, Believe on the Lord Jesus, and thou shalt be saved, thou *and thy house*. And they spake the word of the Lord unto him, *with all that were in his house*. And he took them the same hour of the night, and washed their stripes; and was baptized, he *and all his*, immediately. And he brought them up into his house, and set food before them, and rejoiced greatly, *with all his house*, having believed in God, 16: 29–34.

In the same way Crispus, the ruler of the synagogue at Corinth, "believed in the Lord with all his house" 18: 8, and Paul writes in 1 Cor. 1: 16 that he had "baptized the household of Stephanas".

It is in the light of these passages that we must read and understand the frequent reference in the New Testament to the Christian "house". The apostles taught Jesus as the Christ "in the temple and at home" 5: 42. Paul said that he had not shrunk from declaring to the Ephesians everything that was profitable, teaching them publicly "and from house to house" 20: 20. In 2 Tim. 1: 16 and 4: 19 Paul speaks of the "house of Onesiphorus". As men are gained by houses so they are lost by houses: unruly and deceiving men, Paul writes in Titus 1: 11, must have their mouths stopped because they "overthrow whole houses". Because of the central place which the family took in the constitution of the Church Paul emphasized in his pastoral counsel the need of maintaining the integrity of the family, and he regarded this integrity as a standard for evaluating Christian character, 1 Tim. 3: 4, 12, 5: 4, 8, 14; Titus 2: 4, 5.

We must now note that this conversion of larger and smaller groups, in which the family stands out prominently, *was wholly carried by the Spirit*. We meet Him by direct mention at nearly every turn in the development which Acts sets forth. Indeed, it may be said that the many references to the Holy Spirit in Acts are almost entirely associated with the missionary witness of the Church. Not only with respect to the geographic expansion of the faith, but also with respect to the power of the Spirit, Acts unfolds faithfully and plays in all conceivable variations the theme laid down in Acts 1: 8, "But ye shall receive power, when the Holy Spirit is come upon you: and you shall be my witnesses both in Jerusalem and in all Judea and in Samaria, and unto the uttermost part of the earth". The Spirit powerfully launched the witness of the Church at Pentecost, 2: 1–12. He was promised to those who repent and are baptized, 2: 38. When Peter and John were called to account for healing a lame man in the name of Christ, Peter, filled with the Holy Spirit, answered boldly and proclaimed the risen Christ, 4: 8ff. The disciples to whom they returned met with them for prayer and when they had prayed, the whole place in which they met was shaken "and they were all filled with the Spirit, and they spoke the word of God with boldness" 4: 31. The Holy Spirit witnessed with the apostles to the truth of the gospel, 5: 32. The Jewish leaders in refusing to heed this witness resisted the Holy Spirit, 7: 51. The people of Samaria, having believed the preaching of Philip about the good news of the kingdom of God, received the Holy Spirit when the apostles laid their hands on them, 8: 17. The Spirit called Philip from Samaria to meet the Ethiopian eunuch, 8: 29, and caught him away when his task had been done, after which he preached the gospel in all the cities between Azotus and Caesarea, 8: 39–40. After a period of persecution the Church in Judea, Galilee and Samaria had rest, being edified, and "walking in the fear of the Lord and in the comfort of the Holy Spirit, was multiplied" 9: 31. Upon receiving the Spirit in Damascus Paul spent a few days with the disciples and then "straightway in the synagogues he proclaimed Jesus, that he is the Son of God" 9: 17ff. The conversion of the first gentiles stands wholly under the guidance and in the power of the Spirit, 10: 1–11: 16. Paul and Barnabas were called to their momentous mission among the gentiles by the Spirit, 13: 2. Twice the Spirit forbade them to enter fields to which they were seeking to go, 16: 6, 7, and then called them to enter Macedonia, 16: 9. At the Jerusalem council which dealt with the question of gentile Christians and the keeping of the ceremonial law—the question with which the mission to the gentiles stood or fell—Peter contributed to the solution by relating how at the conversion of Cornelius and his house God had given to them the Holy Spirit as He had to Jewish believers at the beginning, 15: 8, 9. The same council sent instructions to the gentile Christians that "seemed good to the Holy Spirit and to us" 15: 28. Time and again we read in direct connection with the preaching of the gospel that the apostles or disciples "received the Holy Spirit" or were "filled with the Holy Spirit" 2: 17, 38, 4: 8, 31, 7: 55, 13: 9, 52, 19: 6.

This brief review of the expansion of the faith as recorded particularly in Acts reveals a number of significant facts. It shows (a) that the witness was *universal* in extent in the sense that it recognized neither geographical nor human boundaries, (*b*) that large *groups* of people were converted, (*c*) that the one social unit within these groups that is repeatedly mentioned as being converted *as a whole* is the *family*, (*d*) that this massive movement was *wholly borne by the Spirit* poured out at Pentecost. Such is the manner in which the Church began to make disciples of all nations.

It will be rewarding to pursue these thoughts further in the context of important recent and contemporary missionary thought. The idea that particularly invites further attention as a concrete center around which to concentrate a discussion about the expansion of the faith in the power of the Holy Spirit is the "house" concept that is so prominent in Acts. It has received a particular coloring in German missionary thought, and a considerable enlargement in J. C. Hoekendijk's alternative to the German ethnic emphasis in the form of a missionary ecology. The exposition of these views will serve to illumine the New Testament conception by way of contrast. Finally, we shall observe the fruitful use that D. A. McGavran makes of the concept in his stimulating study about People Movements. This inquiry into the place of the family in missionary practice is not the discussion of an interesting tangent, but is an effort to understand an important aspect of the missionary method of the apostles and to expose a major channel through which the Spirit imparted Himself to ever larger circles.

It is significant that while we read much in Acts about groups of believers that enter the Church, about families that are baptized as a unit, about the right of Jews to remain Jews and of gentiles to remain gentiles, we read nothing about the significance of *ethnic characteristics* for the ingathering of the Church. On the contrary, Paul, the great missionary to the gentiles, to the description of whose work so much space is devoted in Acts, states specifically that in the Church ethnic characteristics fall away. There is in the Church neither Greek nor Jew, barbarian nor Scythian, Col. 3: 11. When the nations are discipled they enter through the sacrament of baptism into a communion in which ethnic characteristics may play no determinative role. Nevertheless, in Germany ethnic considerations have intensively conditioned missionary thinking. If we would understand the German conception of "house" we must first understand the significance which the *ethnic factor* has been conceived to have for missions.

Who are the nations, "die Völker", who must be discipled? How are we to conceive of the "nations" to whom the Pentecostal Spirit would have the Church address her witness? Nowhere has this subject been more exhaustively discussed than in the German missionary literature of the past one hundred years. The central role which it has played in German missionary thought has been convincingly demonstrated by J. C. Hoekendijk in his comprehensive and illuminating dissertation, *Kerk En Volk In De Duitse Zendingswetenschap.*[3] The Germans, as no other western nation, are enamored of the concept "Volk". It is a romantic, race-conscious, emotionally laden term with religious overtones and is quite untranslatable. Central in the concept is the idea of the socially unifying and integrating power that arises out of the bonds of common blood and common soil. To turn this power to the advantage of the missionary task has been the effort in one form or another of many of the most leading figures in German missionary thought. Some idea of the magic fascination that the Volk concept exercises over the German missionary mind may be obtained by considering the well-nigh endless variations and connections in which one meets it in the literature: Völker, volkstümlich, volklich, Volksboden, Volksgemeinschaft, Volkschristianisierung, Volkskirche, Volksgeist, volksorganisch, Volksganzen, Volksatmosphäre, Volkstum, Volksaufbau, Volksart, Volksnomos, etc. In the brief space in which we can here allude to German thought we can do no better than turn again to Gustav Warneck. In the discussion of this question, too, he towers above his contemporaries and his predecessors and continues to project himself into his after-time. Majestically he walks the *via media* between Zinzendorff's ideal of individual conversion and the radical form of German ethnic missionary thinking that was later to find expression in Bruno Gutmann's "primordial relationships".[4] Warneck, perhaps more than any other, undertook to effect a persuasive synthesis of scripture, history and the German spirit.

Warneck correctly saw that when Jesus commanded to disciple all nations He did not necessarily have in mind nations in the sense of ethnic social units. He could very well have understood, and probably did understand, the word religiously, i.e. mankind that was not Israel, mankind in its separation from the Creator and Redeemer God. An exegesis of other New Testament passages in which the word nations (or gentiles) appears confirms the thought that it bears the latter meaning:

> According to this objective exegetical investigation, it will not be possible to avoid the conclusion that the object referred to in the Great Commission as *ethne* (nations, gentiles) is to be understood as non-Israelites, people from among the gentiles. It is therefore to be regarded as a religious conception.

Jesus' command, therefore, gives no indication that the gentiles are to be approached and discipled in their quality of organic ethnic social wholes. However, the individuals who constitute the "people from among the gentiles" are at the same time

> Members of *volklichen* natural relationships standing under the influence of various *Volks*characteristics, *Volks*languages, *Volks*-conceptions, *Volks*customs, *Volks*laws, and whose thinking and acting is determined through the external and internal ties that bind them to the *Volk* to which they belong.

It is apparent that for Warneck the correct exegesis of nations in Matt. 28: 19 does not exclude large room in missionary practice for acknowledging the native *Volk*spirit. With this, of course, we must agree. But soon the caution with which exegesis ought to surround the use of the *Volk* concept begins to recede into the background. What Warneck aims at is the influencing of the entire life of the *Volk*, so that what actually takes place is *Volk*christianization. And this *Volk*christianization in turn leads to a virtual identification of Church and *Volk* as an ethnic unit. As opposed to individual conversion it must be the purpose of the missionary

> to lead if not the entire, yet the largest possible part of the *Volks*-community into the Church.

How is such a *Volk*christianization to take place? It is for Warneck of the greatest significance that the apostles did not baptize individual believers only but "entire families". The central unit of the Christian *Volks*community is, in Warneck's view, the family:

> Through the creation of "house-congregations" in which at first only the head of the family was a Christian, and through their acceptance as wholes in the Christian Church, the apostles go beyond individual conversion and lay the first foundation-stone for a Christian *Volks*community. *Volk*christianization is in principle the same as family-christianization. If the latter stands canonized, then the former is its theoretical as well as its practical consequence: it is no more than an enlarged family-christianization.

And so we have travelled the road that leads from legitimate respect and regard for "*volklichen* natural ties", via the family, to a situation in which Church and *Volk* pretty much cover each other: "for is not a christianized *Volks*community the Church?" This close association, almost identification, of Church and *Volk*, while admittedly without direct scriptural support, is not without divine sanction. History shows that everywhere the result of missionary witness, whether in apostolic times, in the Middle Ages, or in the modern period, is *Volk*christianization. It is in this connection that Warneck spoke his famous dictum, "The facts of history are also an exegesis of the Bible". By means of a wonderful jump that wholly overlooks the difference between the perfection of the divine command and the imperfect result that flows from man's obedience to it, Warneck concludes that the *result* of mission work must also be the *task* of mission work.

We have cited Warneck at some length[5] to illustrate the danger that lies in giving "nations" an ethnic rather than a predominantly religious connotation. The danger is plainly this, that the foundations of the Church are sought as much in anthropological as in soteriological considerations, and in the end the anthropological elements crowd the soteriological into a corner. Still more specifically, the Christian family is threatened with the loss of its covenantal character and tends to be viewed as a *Volk* in microcosm. The New Testament clearly does not extend the believing social unit beyond the family. It is at that point that unit baptism stops. Warneck has correctly seen the important fact that in the New Testament the conversion of families is "canonized". At any rate, the heavy emphasis that Acts places on the conversion of families as units requires the closest attention of the student of missionary principles and practice. Warneck is quite in error, however, when he claims that only the heads of families were believers and clearly implies that other members of the "house-congregation" were not or may not have been. This may fit in with the idea of a Christian *Volk*scommunity brought about by incorporating the greatest possible number of a *Volk* into the Church, but it has no basis in the New Testament. It is hardly conceivable that when the Holy Spirit descended on the household of Cornelius those who received the Spirit remained unbelievers. Baptism follows upon repentance, Acts 2: 38, and there are no instances in the New Testament of the administration of baptism to those who had not met this condition. Before the household of the Philippian jailer was baptized Paul and Silas "spake the word of the Lord unto him, with all that were in his house" and the reason that is given for the rejoicing of the jailer with all his house is that he had "believed in God" Acts 16: 31–34. Here as elsewhere the faith of the head of the house is referred to in the sense of *pars pro toto*.

If there is any instance in which *Volk* and Church covered each other it was in the case of the Old Testament people of Israel. Here Church and State were one. Here every member of the divinely erected covenant community was also a member of the Jewish nation. Yet no one will seriously question that even here the ethnic element wholly recedes into the background and the religious, the covenantal, aspect predominates. In the missionary witness that went forth from Pentecost, and in the Church that was founded by that witness, there is even less regard for the ethnic element. The Church is a new creation, a royal priesthood, in which Jew and gentile, barbarian and Scythian have no place as Jew or gentile, barbarian or Scythian. The foundation of the Church and therefore of her missionary witness and her membership lies in the eschatological fact of the outpouring of the Holy Spirit. *That* is what determines the nature of the Church and the nature of her witness and those who constitute her membership. The Church and her universal witness is the expression of the new humanity living in the new aeon ushered in by the Spirit. When German missionary thought attempts to make the *Volk* concept an essential part of the Church concept it does violence to the discontinuity that the eschatological event of Pentecost has effected between the fellowship of the new people of God and the natural relationships existing among the peoples of the world. And when it further, in consequence of its *Volk* concept, regards the Christian family as an ethnic rather than as a covenantal unit it devaluates that specific character which the scriptures ascribe to it, namely that it is the fundamental social cell of the Church, the natural but divinely ordained bedding through which the life of the Church is transmitted from generation to generation.

While fully holding to these reservations with respect to the German effort to canonize ethnic ties of race and nation and family in their significance for missionary witness, it cannot be denied that the men and women who are to be gained by the witness of the Church are people of flesh and blood who stand in very concrete relationships to each other and to their environment. The converted gentile or the gentile to be converted did not become a relationless abstraction. It is therefore with interest that we note the alternative which Hoekendijk offers to the German conception, the more so because the name he gives it is derived from the same word whose significant use and frequent recurrence we have noted in the New Testament, namely *oikos*, i.e. house. For the German view of theologically sanctioned natural relationships or orders Hoekendijk wishes to substitute a sociologically oriented ecology.

As a missionary discipline, ecology, in Hoekendijk's view, attempts no more than to effect an accurate description of the concrete environment (*oikos*) in which the individual and the community find themselves. The term "ecology" as applied to missions is new, says Hoekendijk, the matter which it represents is not. Kraemer has discussed "The relation of the Christian mission to its environment", and Merle Davis has given much attention to the relationships in which the younger churches stand to their social and economic environment.[6] In these writings we see coming into being a "missionary or ecclesiological ecology". The purpose of ecological analysis is to give a clear and convincing description of existing community structures. The idea is not to identify or to legitimize particular social structures as having creational sanction. Ecology has no interest in this. Indeed, it disowns any theological interest. It is simply concerned with existing social realities. It is possible that the social space of an individual penetrates into all manner of social complexes. The same is true of a given community. In ecology there is no room for schematization, for any effort to reduce existing social structures to a few basic created or otherwise qualified orders. This would mean losing reality as it concretely exists for the sake of experimenting with a theological construction. When ecology has performed its task the task of Church and mission in a given social milieu will have become clear. For then we shall see lying before us not an amorphous mass called *Volk*, but we shall see the "concrete communities" and the functions which they play in the whole of society.

Clearly Hoekendijk's conception of *oikos* bears but faint resemblance to the concept that we find in the New Testament. Hoekendijk's ecological vision is closely related to his sympathy for the "Comprehensive Approach" in missions. We shall return to this subject in the final chapter. In the present discussion, and on the background of the foregoing, we wish to fix attention more particularly on the conception that we have met in the New Testament, especially in Acts.

In considering the place of the Church in and her message for the world it would, of course, be folly not to take seriously the social, political, economic, cultural and religious milieu in which the Church in a given situation or with a given missionary task finds herself. The people whom the Church addresses live in that milieu, are affected by it, in turn affect it, and are called to live the Christian life in the relationships in which they concretely stand. To these concrete, flesh and blood, living-in-various-relationships men and women the Church must speak the gospel in such a manner that she will help them to be the salt of the earth at that time and place in which they find themselves. And there can be no objection to designating as ecology the analysis of the milieu that will facilitate an effective presentation of the gospel.

It is open to serious question, however, whether Hoekendijk, in giving so broad an extension to the word *oikos*, and in disavowing any theological interest in ecological analysis, has not overlooked as theologically and missionarily fruitful the *oikos* conception that we meet in Acts and in other parts of the New Testament. It is very true that social structures are constantly changing. Nowhere is this more true than in many mission areas where, as Hoekendijk has sharply observed, the transition from primitive social patterns to the levelling

"Great Society" brings into being social complexes that fit neither in the old structures that are passing nor in the new situation that is coming into being. There is one social unit, however, that remains constant. It is the family. It is subject to fluctuation on the score of parental authority, filial freedom, internal cohesion, relationship to the community. For this reason it is perhaps better to say that it remains intact than that it remains constant. However we may wish to describe the permanence amid the flux, the family is a social structure that is met at all times and among all peoples. Clans, tribes, castes, and other forms of society may come and go, but the family abides. The reason for this is that the family is a divinely instituted social unit. It is, in fact, the *only* divinely instituted natural social unit. It is an indestructible created social reality. The larger structures in which families and the individuals that constitute them come to live are creations of history. The family itself is not, however much historical factors and the forces they unleash may modify its character. Abiding, too, because given with the family, are *family relationships* through marriage and descent. These relationships may find organized expression in a clan, they may cease to find organized expression, or they may express themselves in a more or less extended family. However this may come to manifestation in a given society, the family and the relationships which it necessarily calls into being are abiding and cannot be destroyed.

It is clearly around this divinely given social unit that the churches founded by the apostolic witness were built. Families entered the Church as units and their integrity was guarded by expressed apostolic concern. The nature of the family as a divinely instituted social unit and the large attention that is given the family as the only "natural unit" in the Church forbid us to eliminate it from specifically theological and missionary reflection.

We must next recall that the witness that gathered the Church so largely in terms of families was borne by the Holy

Spirit. The Spirit that gave life to the humanity that came forth from the hands of the Creator is the Spirit who brings into being the humanity of the new creation. In doing so he is not unmindful of the one social unit that has creational sanction. The Spirit who reunites the disjoined members of the human race in the fellowship of the Body of Christ therefore makes large use of the family in constituting that Body in its earthly expression. It is an unbiblical spirituality that would sanction and construct a fellowship in the realm of grace which ignores that form of fellowship which God Himself instituted in the realm of the natural. The baptism of children in the communion of the Church is constant testimony to the central place which the family occupies in the realization of the Church throughout the ages of her history. It is especially the family through which the blessings of the covenant of grace are transmitted from generation to generation. Therefore Pentecost prominently envisions the family in the shedding abroad of the grace that has been revealed, and through Peter declares "to you is the promise, and to your children" Acts 2: 39.

The question must at this point be raised: How broadly is the word "house" to be understood? Some understand it to include, in the New Testament, servants and relatives living in the house besides the head of the house and his wife and children.[7] Theologically, this raises the question: can slaves who sustain no blood relationship to the head of the house, and those who are not by birth related to him, be regarded as standing within the sphere of the covenant of grace as this is, in the areas where the Church is established, perpetuated from generation to generation along the lines of procreation? In this connection two observations must be made:

a. Although the conception "family" is an elastic one and does not therefore have at all times and places the same meaning, it does have, as a significant constant factor, the element of paternal authority. This authority may have the narrow scope of being exercised over wife and children, it may also bear the patriarchal character of being exercised over the family more broadly understood, including relatives and slaves or servants. Such a family was Abraham's, all of whose members were circumcised when God sealed his covenant with Abraham. This circumcision is therefore appealed to, and with good grounds, by those who hold to the legitimacy of the baptism of adopted children. In the same manner, the missionary, in analysing the relationships obtaining in a given social complex, will not hold to an always constant conception of the family, but will see it in relation to the scope of the authority exercised by the family head.

b. The baptism of "houses" recorded in the New Testament gives us no ground to believe that unbelieving adults were baptized. The question before us, therefore, is not whether unbelieving slaves as well as unbelieving adult members of the immediate family were the recipients of baptism. We saw earlier that there is no reason to believe that such baptisms took place in the early Church. The question is, rather, whether slaves as well as members of the immediate family were included in the evangelistic approach to the family conceived of as a covenantal unity. The scriptural answer to this question would seem to be in the affirmative.

The correlation that has here been suggested between the Spirit of Pentecost and the family within the context of missionary witness is not a correlation that is explicitly made in the New Testament. There we find an association of these two rather than a direct correlation. But the association is so close and so prominent that it would seem to have correlative value. While therefore guarding against dogmatism and schematization on this score, we shall also want to be careful not to eliminate from our theological reflection a constellation of scriptural data that bears so closely on the primitive missionary witness.

That we are not dealing here with a theological nicety but with an idea that can become a powerful missionary instrument

178

is demonstrated in D. A. McGavran's conception of People Movements. We shall conclude this section by examining the view he has set forth.

McGavran breaks a powerful lance for a larger recognition of the significance in mission work of social relationships, particularly the family in the broader sense of the word. Supported as he is by thirty years of missionary experience in India, during which he was closely associated with Bishop J. W. Picket and his investigations in group movements to Christianity,[8] by close study of scripture and broad acquaintance with the history of missions, and by investigations of mission areas outside of India, he is entitled to a careful hearing. McGavran presents a plea for the discipling of *Peoples*. The central question to which his book, *The Bridges of God*, addresses itself is, *How do Peoples become Christian?* By "Peoples" McGavran does not have in mind an anglicized version of the German conception of *Volk*. His view of what a People is, is quite free from the emotional complex surrounding the *Volk* idea:

> Every nation is made up of various layers or strata of society. In many nations each stratum is clearly separated from every other. The individuals in each stratum intermarry chiefly, if not solely, with each other. Their intimate life is therefore limited to their own society, that is, to their own people. . . . Individuals of a stratum other than theirs, possibly close neighbours, may become Christians or Communists without their own stratum being much concerned. But when individuals of their own kind start becoming Christians, that touches their very lives. How do chain reactions in these strata of society begin? How do *Peoples become Christian?*[9]

A People, therefore, is not, in McGavran's view, an a-priorily determined social group as in the case of the German *Volk* conception. In every society that is approached it will have to be determined where the lines that circumscribe the People lie.

In a true people intermarriage and the intimate details of social

intercourse take place within the society. In a true people individuals are bound together not merely by common social
practices and religious beliefs but by common blood. A true
people is a social organism which by virtue of the fact that its
members intermarry very largely within its own confines becomes
a separate race in their minds.[10]

The People conception is therefore a rather fluid one. In
simpler societies it may correspond to clan or caste, in more
complex societies a People will run along the lines of layers or
strata of society. The decisive question in each case is, Where do
the lines of social cohesion lie? It is these lines that the missionary must discover and utilize.

In utilizing the social structure for missionary purposes the
central unit to be labored with is *the family*. This is the refrain
that runs through McGavran's book. The word "family" is
used in a very broad sense. It includes near and more distant
relatives as well as the family in the narrower sense of the word.
Not the least valuable part of the author's contribution lies in
the close manner in which he associates his thought with the
missionary strategy set forth in Acts. The entire third chapter
of the book is devoted to an analysis of the role which the family
as part of an endogamous People played in the early expansion
of the Church. McGavran relates the family-wise expansion of
the Church directly to Pentecost and to the continuing guidance of the Spirit:

> When the Holy Spirit first descended, its most remarkable mani-
> festation was that the little Church without hesitation baptized
> "about three thousand souls" in a single day. . . . There was
> excellent reason for this guidance of the Holy Spirit. A mighty
> People Movement had to start with the simultaneous conversion
> of huge numbers so that each Christian came into the Church
> with some of his kindred, leaders whom he could follow, families
> whose opinions he respected, homes where he felt like one of the
> family, and a public opinion which he respected and a corporate
> worship which thrilled him.[11]

A further great advantage of this large influx into the Church was that no effective ostracism of the converts could take place. Many an incipient movement toward Christ has been nipped in the bud by placing its members outside the social pale. Through ostracism social intercourse is cut off, the means of livelihood endangered or taken away. When a convert becomes ill he is not cared for, when he dies there is no provision for an appropriate funeral.

> Had the movement in Judea not been one of multitudes, all these handicaps would have been loaded on to it from the start. It might well have been seriously weakened. The most successful answer to ostracism is the conversion of chains of families. The lone convert is particularly susceptible to boycott.

McGavran points out that the large number of Jews who became Christian at Pentecost were not isolated individuals from many Peoples: they were relatives from one People. It is therefore difficult to believe that the emphasis on "house" or family in Acts was not from the beginning a salient characteristic in the apostolic evangelism. This would seem to be supported by Luke's testimony concerning the immediate post-Pentecostal Christian community. "And day by day, continuing steadfastly with one accord in the temple, and breaking bread at home, they took their food with gladness and singleness of heart" Acts 2: 46. In respect of family solidarity the Hebrew People undoubtedly stood much closer to the oriental and primitive than to the loose western social consciousness. Therefore Acts is so tremendously instructive at this point.

> With every new accession not only did the numbers of persons with one or two Christian relatives increase, but individual Jews began to find that they had large numbers of Christian relatives. . . . The people which make up the nations of Indonesia, China, India, Japan, and Africa keep track of relatives very much more carefully than do individualistic Westerners. Relationships are known more accurately and over greater distances. In such societies movements gather enormous power as relative after relative becomes Christian.[12]

For this reason

> it is essential that the leaders of the Churches and missions strive
> to see life from the point of view of a people, to whom individual
> action is treachery.[13]

On a basis of suggestive but generally overlooked statements in
Acts and in the Pauline epistles McGavran indicates how large a
role the family and family connections within a People being
discipled probably played in the missionary strategy of the
great apostle. We shall have to omit further discussion of this
subject, however. One question still calls for attention before we
conclude this section. It concerns the spiritual integrity of
People Movements.

McGavran realizes that the long missionary practice of
emphasizing individual conversion, as also the attainment of a
relatively high degree of moral standing before converts may be
baptized, is apt to stand in the way of a serious encouragement of People Movements. He therefore asks whether People
Movements require a lowering of standards for admission into
the Church, or a greater or less degree of indifference to the
sincerity of the conversions that take place group- or family-
wise. The principle that is to be determinative here is the
following:

> the Christianization of a People requires reborn men and women
> A mere change in name accomplishes nothing. While the new
> convert must remain within his people, he must also experience
> the new birth. "If then ye be risen with Christ, set your affections
> on things above, not on things on the earth." The power of any
> People Movement to Christ depends in great measure on the
> number of truly converted persons in it. We wish to make this
> quite clear. The Christianization of peoples is not assisted by
> slighting or forgetting real personal conversions. There is no
> substitute for justification by faith in Jesus Christ or for the gift of
> the Holy Spirit.[13]

This does not take away the need, however, of distinguishing,
as McGavran repeatedly does, between Discipling and Perfecting.

Too often this has been forgotten in missionary practice. Not infrequently spiritual and intellectual standards have been set for the receiving of baptism that can hardly be called reasonable. The order of the Great Commission, particularly as reflected in Acts, is: Discipling, baptism, teaching. McGavran shows here, we believe, the true alternative to Pietistic individualism, on the one hand, and to the German conception of *Volkskirche*, on the other. Not the already sanctified life nor a mass decision to enter the Church, but belief in Christ and the desire to live the sanctified life are the conditions of baptism.

In order to justify and promote People Movements to Christ, it is not necessary to justify or condone the imperfections that attend them. In order to defend his conception of *Volkskirche* Warneck places the benediction of divine sanction on historical mass movements into the Church. It is hardly open to question that much of the conversion of Europe, accompanied as it was by political and even military factors, was not a conversion after the scriptural pattern. In the New Testament faith is an assumption and prerequisite of baptism and in the mass baptisms attending the conversion of Europe this was only too often not the case. It will hardly do to see the New Testament pattern reflected in such conversions on the ground that "the facts of history are also an exegesis of the Bible".

Rather than have recourse to a confusion of history with scripture, it would seem better to acknowledge scriptural precept for what it is—holy, just, and good; and history for what it is—a very imperfect reflection of the divine will. Here the eschatological vision to which we have again and again alluded should help us. The command of Christ to disciple the nations was given by our Lord as He stood *wholly* within the End. It was the risen, glorified and exalted Lord who gave the command to disciple the nations. The perfection of the command corresponds to the perfection of the *eschatos* from which and in which it was given. Its execution does *not* take place in the fully realized End. The outpouring of the Spirit brought into being a situation in which the new aeon is inextricably intertwined with the old. It is in *this* context and in *this* situation that the command is carried out. In fact, it is carried out by men and women who are themselves wholly conditioned by the conjoined aeons. The old man of the flesh and the new man of the Spirit conjointly constitute their present being. The early Church, laboring so consciously in the power of the Spirit, realized to a large degree the ideal set forth in the command. But let us here, too, be scrupulously honest. From the beginning there were evidences of the old aeon in the Church. There were the murmurings of the Grecian widows, the deceit of Ananias and Sapphira, the unhappy tensions between Paul and Barnabas and between Paul and Peter, the agitations of the Judaizers in the Church, the divisions and immorality in the Church at Corinth. Scripture does not condone these tragic things. It judges them, implicitly or explicitly. Yet out of them good things usually came. The risen Lord is the Lord of history whose thoughts and ways do not cease to be higher than our thoughts and ways. We shall therefore gratefully receive from Him whatever of good He gives us through the onward rolling ages of our ambiguous history and, placing ourselves under the judgment of His word, repent for the imperfect conditions which our divided selves create for the channeling of his goodness to us and to the world that yet awaits redemption.

The great merit of McGavran in emphasizing the place of the *oikos* in missionary strategy can hardly be overestimated. The elimination of mass conversion by reason of historical forces, notably the broad spread of education, democratic principles, and religious liberty, make a falling back on the family as the basic social unit of conversion natural and necessary. It is noteworthy, therefore, that McGavran in describing *modern* group movements in Chapter VI repeatedly refers to the "chains of families" in terms of which these People Movements took place.

The converted family is not, of course, the only means of enlarging the Church. The New Testament also speaks of the conversion of individuals, and of groups concerning which we are not explicitly told that they were constituted largely of families. It is necessary to avoid all schematization lest the spontaneity of the witness be lost. Living examples may never become the instrument for the construction of a-prioristic theories. Only let not the great emphasis that Acts places on the family unit in a People Movement to Christ in the context of missionary witness be lost on us as we reflect on the vast importance of social ties in the life of the convert and of the Church in which he must live the new life of the Spirit. For, in a unique sense, approaches to a People through the family in its organic relationship to the People are, as McGavran has called them, veritable "highways of the Spirit".

Chapter 9

PENTECOST AND THE WITNESS OF THE CHURCH IN UNITY

ONE of the most remarkable aspects of the ecumenical movement which is now so intensely engaging the mind of the Church is its origin in missionary co-operation. The ecumenical movement did not take its rise in the established or "sending" Churches, but among missionaries, missionary organizations, and the Churches they brought into being.[1] On the mission field denominationalism tends to lose its urgency, and even the credal *raison d'être* of denominationalism loses some of its cogency. The reason for this is not difficult to see. In the loneliness of a foreign land, in the face of common problems and difficulties, missionaries from different ecclesiastical backgrounds tend to be drawn together. On the mission field the supreme concern is to find an opening for the elemental realities of the Christian faith. The theological and historical backgrounds that were factors in bringing the sending Churches into being are, therefore, not invested with that primary importance that is associated with them at home. But especially is the desire for Christian and ecclesiastical unity on the mission field understandable from the viewpoint of the younger Churches. They nearly invariably constitute a very small minority in an overwhelmingly pagan environment. Confronted by a colossal mass of non-Christian religion and *mores*, by the power of age-old cultures, by indifference and not infrequently by hostility, the younger Churches are more aware and appreciative of the faith that unites them than of the differences that divide them. The things that draw them to each other, moreover, frequently commend themselves to their understanding much more than do the denominational and credal differences that separate them. The being drawn to each other is born of a sort of Christian instinct. The divisions that exist between them, on the other hand, are often regarded as things that have been imposed, the rightness of which may live deeply in the sending Churches, but which may appear as something less than essential to the men and women who are not the product of the theological and historical factors that brought the differences into being.

The younger Churches and the missionary community as a whole do, therefore, so readily fall into what J. H. Bavinck has aptly called the danger of "stable relationships" so characteristic among the older Churches. Where the "stable relationships" obtain everyone is friendly to everyone else, there is a general agreement to disagree, there is no longer unrest about the fact of separation, because separation has come to be accepted as a matter of course, there is not even prayer any more for the restoration of lost unity. At the growing edge of the Church these un-Christian luxuries cannot be afforded because to afford them means to stand in the way of the Church's witness and to jeopardize the Church's very existence. That denominational differences exist on the mission field is, of course, a patent matter. That they cannot be disposed of as simply superficial importations is equally patent. But that they are accepted there in the same sense in which they are accepted at the home base is less than true. For this reason voices expressing pain over existing divisions and urging more striving toward unity and the reconsideration of the things that divide have never ceased to come from those who are deeply concerned about the spread of the gospel in the missionary areas.

One of the great benefits of an active missionary program in which the entire congregation or denomination participates is its reflex effect on the witnessing Church. Church founding is certainly a most central factor in any scriptural missionary endeavor. Therefore serious mission work involves constant re-evaluation of obtaining conceptions concerning the nature of the Church and of the Churches in relation to each other. If the ecumenical movement has anything at all to teach, it is certainly the unquestionable fact that the mission field has brought the older Churches to a serious re-examination of the brokenness of their situation. If the striving after unity is a necessary and legitimate pursuit on the mission field and among the younger Churches, can it be less than necessary and legitimate at the home base of the missionary endeavor? Can a fundamental principle of action for the becoming Church be a matter of indifference for the long established Church? The question that arises at this point, therefore, is the legitimacy of the striving after unity, unity understood not only as spiritual, but also as outward and visible, and expressing itself in the largest possible degree of open fellowship and, where feasible, organizational unity. An inquiry into the missionary significance of Pentecost may not seek to escape a treatment of the ecumenical problem. Notwithstanding divisions that exist on the mission field, it cannot be denied that the need for unity has long been an emphasis *precisely where the Spirit has historically exercised and continues so powerfully to exercise His witnessing and life-transmitting function.* In view of this we ask: Does there come to expression in the missionary emphasis on unity of witness an aspect of the Spirit's being and work that has to a large extent been lost sight of in the ecclesiastical areas where the "stable relationships" can be "afforded"?

It is not intended to attempt here anything approaching a comprehensive treatment of the question. We shall endeavor to understand in its scriptural context the "most ecumenical passage" in the Bible, John 1: 22, 23, and in this passage fix our attention not so much on the idea of unity as on the factor that brings the unity into being, namely, *the glory that Christ has received from the Father.* The passage in question reads:

> And the glory which thou hast given me I have given unto them: that they may be one, even as we are one, I in them, and thou in

me, that they may be perfected into one; that the world may know that thou didst send me, and lovedst them, even as thou lovedst me.

Clearly, the unity of the Church is here presented as a powerful missionary weapon. This unity, which the world must be able to see, must bring it to acknowledge that Christ is the Sent One of the Father. But wherein does this unity consist, and from what does it take its rise? It is necessary to examine the generally disregarded conception of the "glory of Christ" in order to answer this question. In this section, therefore, we shall concern ourselves with the question of the "glory" of Christ. Four matters call for attention in the discussion of this subject.

    A. *The* kabod Yahweh *or the glory of the Lord in the Old Testament*
    B. *The glory of Christ in its New Testament references*
    C. *The relationship between this glory and the Spirit of Christ*
    D. *The meaning of the glory of Christ for the witness of the Church in unity*

A. *The kabod Yahweh*

The Greek word *doxa*, meaning glory, has had an interesting history. It is derived from a word which in classical Greek means "opinion". This opinion can be subjective or objective in character. It can mean that which I think concerning a matter, or that which is thought by another about me. In Greek philosophy the former, i.e. the subjective meaning, predominated and developed itself in two directions. It could mean, on the one hand, the views or teachings of the philosophers and, on the other, an uncertainly held opinion and even a deceitful appearance which is the opposite of the truth. Because the objective sense generally connoted a favorable evaluation, *doxa* in its objective use came to bear "fame" as a prominent meaning and occupied a place in Greek usage next to "honor".[2] The word *doxa* in classical Greek could therefore mean (*a*) "opinion", whether in the subjective or objective sense, and (*b*) "fame", a meaning derived from the objective sense of the root word.

When the translators of the Septuagint cast about for a Greek word for *kabod*, glory, they fixed on the word *doxa*. In so doing they effected a modification in its Greek usage that was of unusual significance. The word *doxa* in its subjective sense was wholly abandoned, and its objective meaning of "fame" was elaborated to include the ideas of glory, splendor, majesty, magnificence, greatness. *Doxa* appears some 280 times in the Septuagint, approximately 180 of which are translations of *kabod*, the remainder rendering 24 other Hebrew words all of which bear a meaning closely akin to *kabod*.

In general Hebrew usage *kabod* meant honor, more specifically, that which gives standing, eminence, importance.[3] In the Old Testament it is used to indicate the greatness or glory of both men and God. Abraham's *kabod* lay in his cattle, his silver, and his gold, Gen. 13: 2; Joseph instructed his brethren to tell his father concerning all his *kabod* in the land of Egypt, Gen. 45: 13, there is a *kabod* of Moab, Isa. 16: 14, of Jacob, 17: 4, of Kedar, 21: 16. The *kabod* conception in the Old Testament reaches its highest expression in the frequently appearing phrase, *kabod Yahweh*, the glory of the Lord. The *kabod Yahweh* appeared to the Israelites in the wilderness journey and is intimately associated with the cloudy pillar and the tabernacle, through both of which it conveyed manifestations of the divine presence.[4] It is also expressly associated with the speaking of God.[5] It receives its most pregnant meaning, however, from its identification with the divine being. When Moses desired to see God's glory, God said to him, "Thou canst not see my face, for man shall not see me and live. And Jehovah said, Behold, there is a place by me, and thou shalt stand upon the rock: and it shall come to pass, while my *kabod* passeth by, that I will put thee in a cleft of the rock, and will cover thee with my hand until I have passed by: and I will take away my hand, and thou shalt see my back; but my face shall not be seen" Exod. 33: 17–23. Isaiah complains, "Jerusalem is ruined and Judah is fallen because their tongue and their doings are against Jehovah to provoke the eyes of his *kabod*", 3: 8. In both of these passages *kabod* is clearly not an impersonal attribute but a representation of the divine being. In Isa. 59: 19, "So they shall fear the name of Jehovah from the west and his *kabod* from the rising of the sun", the identification of the *kabod Yahweh* with the name of Jehovah makes *kabod* even more strongly than in the preceding citations a synonym for Jehovah. Attention must also be called to the vision of overwhelming power with which Ezekiel begins his prophecy, in which one in the likeness of a man sat on a throne of great majesty. This was the appearance of the likeness of the *kabod Yahweh*. The distinction between the divine being and the radiancy that surrounds it is in this theophany so undefined that *Yahweh* and the majesty that flows forth from Him seem to be indistinguishable. There is in this also a clear association of the Spirit with the *kabod Yahweh*. When the voice that issued from the throne spoke to Ezekiel, "the Spirit entered into me . . . and set me upon my feet, and I heard him that spake to me" 2: 2.

The *kabod Yahweh* conception of the Old Testament, there-fore, presents the idea of great power and majesty from the heavenly regions, it is associated with the tabernacle where God manifested Himself in an especial manner, it is a means of revelation, it is at times clearly identified with God's eyes, His name, and even with His very being. In it we meet the revela-tion, attributes and being of *Yahweh* Himself.[6]

This revelation, imposing though it is, awaits its highest manifestation in the eschatological future. The *kabod Yahweh* is the object of religious hope, it is the content of coming universal revelation. Especially Isaiah is the prophet of the coming glory, and the glory concerning which he prophesies stands in the clear framework of the universal dissemination of the grace of God. For Isaiah future salvation for the nations and honor for Israel are indispensable aspects of the *kabod*

Yahweh conception. The way-preparer of Jehovah cries, "Every valley shall be exalted, and every mountain and hill shall be made level, and the rough places a plain, and the *kabod Yahweh* shall be revealed, and all flesh shall see it together" 40: 4, 5. Zion's light is come and the *kabod Yahweh* is risen upon her, "For behold, darkness shall cover the earth, and gross darkness the peoples, but Jehovah will rise upon thee and his *kabod* will be seen upon thee. And nations shall come to thy light and kings to the brightness of thy rising" 60: 1–3. The time will come in which God shall gather all nations and tongues and they shall come, and see His *kabod*, 66: 18.[7] In the Old Testament the *kabod Yahweh* is an integral part of the eschatological expectation. It is the adumbration of the glory of the ministry of the Spirit in comparison with which the *kabod* on the face of Moses was without glory, 2 Cor. 3: 7–11.

B. *The Glory of Christ*

The "glory of Christ" is found in the New Testament as a property of Christ as heavenly being. In Matthew and Mark Christ's glory is related exclusively to His eschatological appearance in judgment.[8] It is also intimately related to the glory of the Father in which He will appear to judge the world.[9] In Luke the heavenly character of Christ's glory is more complex. It appears as antecedent glory in the "glory of the Lord" that shone round about the shepherds at the Angelic announcement of His birth, 2: 9; as an anticipatory glory which Jesus shared with Moses and Elijah at His transfiguration, 9: 28–32; as the eschatological glory in which He will appear at His second coming, 9: 26, 21: 27; and as the glory on which He entered immediately upon His resurrection from the dead, 24: 26. In the synoptics, therefore, the glory of Christ bears a pronouncedly heavenly and eschatological emphasis.[10]

In the epistles of Paul and of Peter the heavenly character of Christ's glory is further indicated. Christ's is the glory and the dominion forever, 1 Peter 4: 11, He was received up in glory, 1

Tim. 3: 16, He is the Lord of glory, 1 Cor. 2: 8, God raised Him from the dead and gave Him glory, 1 Peter 1: 21, His appearing will be in glory, Titus 2: 13; 1 Peter 4: 13.

Our interest is, of course, specifically in the Johannine conception of the glory of Christ. It would seem at first glance that John departs from the New Testament rule of ascribing only distinctly heavenly glory to Christ. He clearly ascribes glory to the earthly Jesus. The apostles had beheld Jesus' glory, 1: 14, the first miracle performed by Jesus was a manifestation of His glory, 2: 11, the sickness of Lazarus subserved the glory of God and the glorification of the Son of God, 11: 4. It must be remembered, however, that John's Gospel is wholly governed by the motif of demonstrating and witnessing that Jesus is the Son of God. For John the deity of the Incarnate One was evident even in His earthly ministry, and it came to expression in the signs and wonders which He did. Even so, Christ's heavenly provenance was not evident to all who saw His wonders, but only to those who believed on Him. "This beginning of his signs did Jesus in Cana of Galilee, and manifested his glory; and his disciples believed on him" 2: 11. The glory manifest in the earthly Jesus is for John, therefore, a heavenly, a supernatural glory.

The glory of Christ is referred to by John in a fourfold way. It is the glory which Christ had with the Father before the foundation of the world, 17: 5, it is a glory that He manifested on the earth (see above), it is a glory that He was yet to receive, 7: 39, 12: 33, 17: 5, it is a glory which He had not yet received and had not yet conferred on the Church, but which He considers as already His and as already hers, 17: 22.[11] These four modes of reference to the glory of Christ in actuality indicate two kinds of glory. These are: the glory of the eternal Son of God which is an *underived* glory, and the glory given to Christ as a reward for His mediatorial work which is a *derived* glory. The glory that Christ had with the Father from eternity is the glory that shone through the form of His humiliation on earth. Therefore John says of the earthly Jesus, "and we beheld his glory, glory as of the only begotten of the Father" 1:14. The reference here is to the eternal Logos who was with God and who was God, 1:1, 14, 15. Especially in the signs and wonders which Christ wrought on earth was the glory of the second Person of the Trinity reflected and made manifest to the eyes of faith.

The second kind of glory of Christ is the derived glory, the glory *given* to Christ. It is the glory for which He prays, "Father, glorify thou me with thine own self with the glory which I had with thee before the world was" 17:5. This verse emphasizes on the one hand the given, the derived character of the glory that Christ received, and, on the other hand, its oneness with the glory that He always had as the eternal Son of God. How to understand the mysterious relationship between these two glories it is not possible to say. It can only be said that the Mediator as the God-Man received at the resurrection a glory He had not had before the resurrection, and that this glory, while one in kind and quality with the glory of the eternal Son of God, is a *given* glory. It is to this glory that Jesus refers in 17:22 as a glory which He has already received and already conferred on his own: "And the glory which thou hast given me I have given unto them." Jesus' work is on the point of attaining its climax in cross and resurrection, but He considers it as already performed and the reward for it as already given. He prays in the certainty of victory and for the moment projects Himself into the time of victory.[12]

The question to which we are particularly concerned to find an answer is: Precisely (or, approximately) what is this "glory" that Christ has received from the Father, which effects the unity of the Church, and through which unity men are brought to acknowledge that Christ is the Sent One of the Father? A fruitful dealing with this question must be preceded by one other brief inquiry. It has repeatedly been noted that the glory of Christ of which the New Testament speaks is a highly eschatological conception. As such its relationship to the

Spirit, who is at the heart and center of all eschatological reality, invites exploration. Does the association which the New Testament establishes between glory and Spirit shed any light on the glory which Christ has, according to John 17: 22, conferred on the Church?

C. *The Glory of Christ and the Holy Spirit*

Paul indicates a close connection between glory, Spirit, and the resurrection of believers and of Christ. There is one glory of the sun, another glory of the moon, and still another of the stars. So it is also with the resurrection of the dead. The body is sown in dishonor, it is raised in glory. It is sown in weakness, it is raised in power. It is sown a physical body, it is raised a spiritual body. The first Adam became a living soul, the last Adam became a life-giving spirit. As we have borne the image of the earthy, so we shall bear the image of the heavenly, 1 Cor. 15: 41ff. In this passage the glory of the resurrected state is put on one level with the spiritual and with power, both of which are concepts that bear the closest conceivable relationship in the New Testament to the Holy Spirit. Moreover, it is equated with the heavenly, and is inseparable from Christ as an alive-making spirit. These connections suggest a pregnant relationship between Spirit and the "glory" concept.

When we read in Rom. 8: 11, "if the Spirit of him that raised up Jesus from the dead dwelleth in you, he that raised up Christ Jesus from the dead shall give life also to your mortal bodies through his Spirit that dwelleth in you", and in Rom. 1: 4 that Christ was "declared to be the Son of God with power according to the Spirit of holiness, by the resurrection from the dead", then it is strongly suggested in Rom. 6: 4 that the "glory of the Father" is to be identified with the Holy Spirit: "that like as Christ was raised from the dead through the glory of the Father, so we also might walk in newness of life." In connection with this verse, and with reference to the glory of Christ, Geerhardus Vos writes:

In a few other passages the resurrection of Christ is ascribed to the Spirit indirectly, being represented by an act of the power, the glory of God, both of which conceptions are regularly associated with the Spirit, cf. Rom. 6: 4; 1 Cor. 6: 14; 2 Cor. 13: 4. . . . But apart from the resurrection the *doxa* is to Paul the specific form in which he conceives of the exalted state of Jesus, and this *doxa* is so closely allied to the Spirit in Christ also, as to become almost a synonym for it.[13]

John relates glory, Spirit, and the resurrection of Christ no less specifically than Paul relates them. In 7: 38, 39 he writes, "He that believeth on me, as the scripture hath said, from within him shall flow rivers of living water. But this spake he of the Spirit, which they that believed on him were to receive: for the Spirit was not yet, because Jesus was not yet glorified." With this passage must be taken 12: 20ff. Certain Greeks who had come to attend the feast of the Passover desired to see Jesus. When He was told of this Jesus responded, "The hour is come that the Son of Man should be glorified. Verily, verily, I say unto you, Except a grain of wheat fall into the ground and die, it abideth by itself alone; but if it die, it beareth much fruit." The glorification of Christ in the second passage is referred by some to the death of Jesus.[14] This is a misunderstanding of John, however, and a departure from the consistent use of *kabod* in the Old Testament and *doxa* in the New Testament in their reference to the divine being. The glorification of Christ in the second as well as in the first passage refers to His exaltation in and after the resurrection. It was at the resurrection that the Spirit was given to Jesus, and this receiving of the Spirit enabled Him to give the Spirit to the Church from which rivers of living water would flow to the world. The glorification of the Son of man, 12: 23, makes possible the transmission of His life through the Spirit to all the nations whom Jesus saw coming to Him in the form of certain Greek proselytes. It means the dawning of the day when the Spirit whom He will send forth will gather the universal Church through the proclamation of her ambassadors.

It must be noted, in the second place, that Paul intimately relates spirit and glory in connection with the *witness* of the Church. In 2 Cor. 3 he directly relates the Old Testament *kabod Yahweh* to the glory of the new covenant by way of contrast between the ministry of the two covenants in terms of their glory. In the brief space of only five verses, 7–11, the word glory appears no less than ten times, and the central object of its reference is Paul's apostolic office and, therefore, in its abiding significance, the ministry of the gospel, namely, the ministration of the Spirit. "But if the ministration of death, written and engraven on stones, came in *glory*, so that the children of Israel could not look steadfastly on the face of Moses on account of the *glory* of his face, which was passing away; how shall not rather the ministration of the Spirit be in *glory*? For if the ministration of condemnation hath *glory*, much rather doth the ministration of righteousness exceed in *glory*. For verily that which was *glorified* was not *glorified* in this respect because of the surpassing *glory*. For if that which passeth away was *glorious*, much more that which remaineth is *glorious*." We see here on the one hand the superior excellence of the glory of the ministry of the Spirit over the Old Testament *kabod Yahweh* that illuminated the face of Moses at the highest point in his ministry and, on the other, the impressively intimate connection between glory, Spirit, and the Church's proclamation. Further, if the *kabod Yahweh* was a revelation of the divine being then this must in a heightened and intensified form be true of the glory of the ministration of the Spirit.

Wherein does this glory consist? That it does not come to expression in visibly radiant and glorious light is apparent. Rather, it is the glory of the immaterial, invisible splendor of the gospel. It is the "great boldness of speech" that streams from the person of Christ's ambassadors in contrast to the glory that Moses veiled from the eyes of the children of Israel, 2 Cor. 3: 12, 13. It is the "manifestation of the truth" so that the light of the gospel of the glory of Christ may shine down upon men,

4: 1–6. It is the power of the Spirit working in the apostles, the gifts of the Spirit evident in the body of believers, the power of love and self-sacrifice that is everywhere released by the preaching of the gospel. Therefore the glory of the ministry of the gospel may be regarded as lying especially in the operations of the Spirit which are mediated through the ministration of the Spirit.[15]

Finally, glory in its relation to the Spirit comes to expression in the *membership* of the Church. In the same great chapter of 2 Corinthians which we considered above Paul relates both Lord and Spirit to the present glory of believers and to the eschatological glory that awaits. "But we all, with unveiled face, beholding as in a mirror the glory of the Lord are transformed into the same image from glory to glory, even as from the Lord the Spirit" v. 18. The transformation of the believer into the image of Christ advances from the glory that now is to the ultimate glory that is yet to be revealed. This transformation is effected by the Lord the Spirit. The glory of the ministry of the Spirit, the glory of the Lord, and the ever advancing glory of believers seem in the end almost indistinguishable. This is not difficult to understand once it is plain that the relationship between glory and Spirit is so intimate as to constitute if not a relationship of identity then certainly a most intimate connection. The Spirit from whom the glory informs the whole being of the risen Lord, bears the witness of the Church, and is organically one with the believers in that He constitutes their life.

The relationship of glory to the Spirit in terms of the life of believers is also indicated in other parts of the New Testament. When Christians are reproached for the name of Christ they are blessed, because "the Spirit of glory and of God" rests upon them, 1 Peter 4: 14. Remembering that "the Lord is the Spirit: and where the Spirit of the Lord is there is liberty" 2 Cor. 3: 17, we are warranted in attaching a particularly pregnant Spirit-associated meaning to "the liberty of the glory of the children of God" Rom. 8: 21. Similarly, the frequent association of the Spirit with power[16] gives a distinct Spirit reference to glory when Paul prays that the Colossians may be strengthened with all power according to the glorious power of God, Col. 1: 11. He also prays that the God of our Lord Jesus Christ, the Father of glory, may give to his readers the spirit of wisdom and revelation in the knowledge of Him in order that they may know, among other benefits, what is the riches of the glory of His inheritance in the saints, Eph. 1: 17–18. The primordial source of all glory in the Church is "the God of our Lord Jesus Christ, the Father of glory", but the glory that He gives is mediated by the Spirit.

With these associations between glory, Spirit, Christ, and believer before us we can now turn to a consideration of the glory of Christ which He has conferred on His Church in order to effect her unity as a means of witness in the world.

D. *Pentecost and the witness of the Church in the unity of the Spirit*

When we now in conclusion ask: What is the glory which Christ gave to the Church and which effects her unity as a means of drawing the world to Christ? the temptation is to say, the glory of Christ = Spirit. This answer we cannot well make because in the Old and New Testaments *kabod* and glory appear as *manifestations*, as *revelations*, as *reflections* of the divine being. While we may not forget that God manifests, reveals, and reflects *Himself*, therefore His *being*, it must be remembered that a manifestation, a revelation, a reflection, implies a manifesting, revealing, reflecting *subject* as well as a mani-fested, revealed, and reflected *object*. We therefore posit: the relationship between the glory of Christ and the Holy Spirit is so close, so intense, so intimate, that we conceive of it as stopping short only at the point of unqualified identification. It is akin to the relationship that Paul discerns between the Lord and the Spirit in his "Now the Lord is the Spirit", and "the Lord the Spirit", 2 Cor. 3: 17, 18.

The life that results from faith in Christ, union with Christ, the power of Christ, and the power of God Himself, are wholly Spirit-effected realities in the life of the believer. The glory of Christ is the manifestation of the life of the Spirit in the body of Christ as it comes to expression in and as a result of the witness of the Church to the crucified and risen Lord. *This is the glory that effects the unity of the Church.*

Attention must now be called to the following specific considerations:

1. It is the Holy Spirit who effects the unity of the Church. The wonderful fellowship of the early Church was a direct outgrowth of Pentecost. Believers were of one heart and soul and had all their things in common. When Ananias and Sapphira sinned against this fellowship they sinned against the Holy Spirit, Acts 4: 32–5: 4. The Holy Spirit is the Spirit of communion, 2 Cor. 13: 14, and the source of gifts that make for unity, Gal. 5: 22, 23. Jew and gentile have access by one Spirit to the Father and are built together for a habitation of God in the Spirit, Eph. 2: 18, 22. Believers must give diligence to keep the unity of the Spirit in the bond of peace, Eph. 4: 3. The fellowship of the Spirit, with exhortation in Christ, consolation of love, tender mercies and compassions, requires that believers be of the same mind, have the same love, be of one accord, Phil. 2: 1, 2. Just as the body is one and has many members, so it is with Christ. For in one Spirit all have been baptized into one body, whether Jews or Greeks, whether freemen or slaves, and all were made to drink of one Spirit, 1 Cor. 12: 12, 13. This passage reminds us of the Spirit-effected indwelling of the believer "in Christ" in terms of which Paul gives pregnant expression to the unity of Christ's body. We are one body in Christ, Rom. 12: 5, all are one in Christ Jesus, Gal. 3: 28, those who were afar off have been brought near in Christ Jesus, Eph. 2: 13. Directly through His own operation and indirectly through the mystical incorporation of believers in the one body of Christ the Spirit is the unity-effecting Agent in the Church.

2. The fact that the Spirit is the unifying element in the Church brings us directly to Pentecost. There is between the Church and Christ only one point of connection. As we can meet God only in Christ, so we can receive Christ only through the Spirit poured out at Pentecost. The whole Old Testament redemptive process moves to its concentration point in Christ, and Christ's merits are dispensed to men only through the Pentecostal gift of the Spirit. Therefore the glory of Christ as the unifying power in the Church, coming to expression in her Spirit-borne witness and life, lies at the heart of the gift bestowed on the Church at Pentecost.

3. It should particularly be noted (a) that the prayer of Christ recorded in John 17 follows immediately on chapters 14, 15 and 16 in which Jesus promises the coming of the "other Paraclete", and (b) that the whole of Christ's prayer is permeated with the thought of the declaration of God's word to men, which is the very activity in which the work of the Paraclete will consist. The unity of the Church is not effected by the bare passive indwelling of the Spirit of glory, but by the exercise of the ministration of the Spirit in the proclamation of the gospel, and in the Christian life that flows forth from the acceptance of the gospel. The unity of the Church that leads the world to acknowledge that Christ is the sent One of the Father is the unity of witness and life which the glory of Christ, that is, the power of the Paraclete, the witnessing and life-giving Spirit, works in the Church.

4. The glory for which Christ prayed in 17: 2 clearly had as its purpose the transmission of eternal life to men: "Father, the hour is come; glorify thy Son, that the Son may glorify thee, even as thou gavest him authority over all flesh, that to all whom thou hast given him, he should give eternal life." Jesus' mention of His desire to transmit eternal life to men in connection with reference to His glory and His authority is strikingly parallel to the giving of the Great Commission on the ground of the authority that has been given Him. In John

17: 2 Jesus glorifies the Father by giving life to all men whom God has given Him by virtue of the authority and the glory which the Father has conferred on Him. In Matt. 28: 18f. Jesus commands the disciples to preach the gospel to all the nations by virtue of the authority that has been given Him. The connection that has earlier been established between the Spirit, on the one hand, and the Great Commission, the lordship of Christ, and the transmission of the life of the Spirit through the preaching of the gospel, on the other hand, would seem to warrant the conclusion that in both John 17: 2 and 17: 22 Jesus intimately relates His glory to the Spirit as the bearer and power of the proclamation whereby life eternal is conferred on men.

The foregoing too brief review of the meaning of the glory of Christ may serve to indicate that the unity of the Church which it brings into being is an intensely *spiritual* unity. It is a unity created and sustained by the Spirit whom Christ has conferred on the Church. It is therefore quite unwarranted and essentially meaningless to emblazon on the banner of ecumenical striving the fragmentary slogan "that they may all be one" if there is no deep regard for the nature of the glory through which alone the oneness can come into being. It is equally illusory to imagine that the oneness for which Christ prayed has been at all measurably advanced by the mere fact that two denominational fellowships become, through an ecclesiastical fiat, one fellowship. It is necessary always to remember that the true unity of the Church rests upon and arises out of the glory of Christ, and that this glory is the power of the Holy Spirit manifesting itself in the witness and life of the Church.

If the kind of unity that liberal and uncritical evangelical Christianity so often espouses is here rejected by Christ, there is another kind of unity that is hardly more acceptable to Him. This is the unity that is so dear to the churchmen of strict orthodoxy. It is the idea that the unity of the Church is *only* a spiritual unity, and that the brokenness of the Church, while regrettable, is not wholly incompatible with this spiritual unity. This is the conception that underlies the "stable relationships" obtaining between denominations that have been rent asunder out of a united life once enjoyed. It is the conception that underlies an easy-going denominational live-and-let-live. It is the conception that makes possible the complacency which no longer has either prayer or concern for the restoration of lost unity.

As the obsession to reduce the many denominations to few denominations appeals uncritically to the words "that they may all be one", so the indifference to the co-existence of many denominations rests on an ignoring of an element in Christ's prayer that stands in the immediate context of His expressed desire for the unity of the Church. This element consists in the words, "that the world may know that thou didst send me". That is to say, the unity for which Jesus prayed is a unity that *the world*, which has no spiritual discernment, *must be able to see*. The glory of Christ is not a latent, passive power of the Spirit. It is an *active* power, and *demands expression*. It demands an expression that will surprise and astound the world. Standing amid the ruins of their own broken homes, hopes, ideals, social structures and even national societies, the men of the world must see one fellowship in which there is no brokenness, no division, no hopelessness, but rather the unity and power of *one* body, *one* fellowship, *one* hope, *one* society. This must draw men to inquire after the source of this unity, this power, this hope, this holy fellowship. And their inquiry must lead them to discover this source in Christ the Head of the Church, the Sent One of the Father. To this interest and to this acknowledgment the world must be brought by the *visibly united* witness and the *visibly* united life of the people of God. For if the spiritually undiscerning world does not see *with its eyes* that which is so manifestly wanting in its own life, how shall a hidden spiritual unity bring it to this insight?

The unity of the Church is, according to Jesus' own words, a great missionary instrument given to the Church. Nowhere is this instrument more needed than on the mission field. Nowhere has its absence been so felt as on the mission field. Nowhere has our betrayal of this unity come to more painful expression than on the mission field. No one can deny that, however great its spiritual and doctrinal aberrations may be, the *visible unity* of the Roman Catholic Church has been one of her most powerful attractions for men. Nor can anyone deny that however great the spiritual integrity and doctrinal purity of much of Protestantism may be, its well-nigh limitless divisions have perplexed and even repelled men. Can we say that the hard-to-measure spiritual unity in the midst of Protestant fragmentation constitutes a closer approximation to the unity Christ desired than does the outward unity of the Roman Catholic Church in the midst of her spiritual deformation? Only the chauvinistic will give an unhesitatingly affirmative answer to this question.

The Church must therefore unceasingly confront herself with the demand of Christ for *complete unity*, that is: a unity in the Spirit expressed in the ministry and life of one visible body of Christ. Where *this* unity does not exist we fall short of the glory of God. For the Son was glorified in order that through the bestowal of His glory on the Church He might make the Church *one*, as He and the Father are one, that thus He might glorify the Father.

Chapter 10

QUENCH NOT THE SPIRIT!
(Pentecost and the Practice of Missions)

If the Holy Spirit given at Pentecost is so centrally the origin and the undergirding, informing and empowering principle of the missionary witness of the Church, it would seem reasonable to expect that He should also have the greatest significance for the *concrete manner* in which the actual missionary work of the Church is performed. It is indeed not possible sincerely to acknowledge the dominant place which the New Testament gives to the Spirit in the missionary proclamation of the early Church without also acknowledging His radical significance for the missionary task of the contemporary Church. The doctrine unfolded in scripture has not been given simply to stimulate intellectual reflection and to provide opportunity for exegetical exercises, but it has been given to penetrate from the mind to the heart and to extend from the heart to attitudes, words and deeds. And surely this can be true in no area of doctrine more than in that area which acquaints us with the Spirit of *life*, the Spirit of *power*, the Spirit of *witness*, the Spirit of *fellowship*, all of which speak of the dynamic of *action*.

In reading missionary literature, especially that of a devotional kind, one will frequently find reference made to the indispensable need of the Spirit in missionary witness. He must give the power, He must create the spirit of missionary devotion, perseverance and self-sacrifice, He must open the hearts of hearers, He must establish the spoken word. True though all these observations are, the impression is generally left that the Spirit will manifest His power wherever men witness sincerely in the name of Christ, regardless of the means employed to effect their witness. Presumably, the only condition that exists for obtaining the blessing and power of the Spirit is the desire for the conversion of men and the glory of God.

It is but seldom suggested that this desire has frequently found, and frequently finds, expression in missionary methods and approaches that contradict the nature of the Spirit and the divine laws that govern His operations. Paradoxically, the good desire which is, in itself, born of the Spirit, may find expression in a manner that is calculated to quench the Spirit. The failure to see this springs from an illegitimate division in Christian missionary thinking and action between the goal to be achieved and the means used to attain it. It is supposed that the goal is more important, more fundamental, than the methods that are employed to reach it. Therefore once the end to be achieved has become clear, the way that is to be followed to reach it is considered to be a rather secondary matter. The Lord sets the aim, but we may determine the methods. John R. Mott has described the situation perhaps as closely as it can be described:

> Missionaries, native Christian workers, and leaders of missionary activities on the home field, while they differ on nearly all questions pertaining to plans, means, and methods, are absolutely united in the conviction that the world's evangelization is a divine enterprise, that the Spirit of God is the great missioner, and that only as He dominates the work and workers can we hope for success in the undertaking to carry the knowledge of Christ to all people.[1]

The fatal fallacy in the assumption that means, in distinction from ends, may be subjectively determined is that it is not legitimate to separate means from ends. Intelligent prosecution of a task in things natural pays the closest attention to methods employed and seeks to determine the laws that govern the most effective realization of a given end. This same care ought to be shown in things spiritual. We may and must distinguish in our minds between means and ends. But we may never create a disjunction between them. Particularly is this true in God's kingdom. In Christ ends are not more important than means, ends are not more basic than means, ends do not in Him occupy a higher level of reality or enjoy a larger measure of divine sanction than the means that ought to be employed to reach them. In Christ ends do not come into being suddenly or in relative indifference to the methods that are employed to effect them. Ends are, in Christ, always *consummations, realizations*, the total outcome of a process. The process that flowers in the end-result, in the realization, in the consummation, is the area in which *means* are employed. Means are therefore ends in process of realization. The consummation cannot possibly be more perfect than the realizing means. It stands to them in a relationship of strict and unalterable correlation. The means *determine* the end because the means are the end in process of becoming. The missionary means we employ are an expression of the now present kingdom of God. Clearly, the manifestation of the present kingdom ought not to stand in contradiction to the kingdom that will one day be revealed in its perfection.

All ends that Christians envision must reflect the perfection of the consummate End of all things, because our ends have meaning only in the light of this End. Likewise, all means employed to achieve the ends envisioned should reflect the adaptability and the suitability of the perfect Means which God used to effect the End. The Means that He used is Christ, and through Christ His world government and the effectuating power of the Spirit. The Means employed to achieve the End were not a secondary matter with God, but reflect the finished wisdom of the eternal counsels of the blessed Trinity. The Means used by God to effect the salvation of men and of the world places us before the fathomless abyss of the question, *Cur Deus Homo?* which even angels cannot comprehend. Christ, who is the End, is also the Means, and Christ, who is the Means, is also the End. In Christ the End is here. The Church as witnessing community lives in this End. It lives also, therefore, in the divine Means which is Christ in the Spirit. Therefore all her means and methods must in some way reflect the divine Means and Method. Let us not cut asunder what God has joined together.

If there has been much disobedience perpetrated in the spirit of obedience, if there have been missions by the sword, by political power, by privileged position, by dollars, pounds, guilders, francs and Reichsmarks, if there have been, and if there are, missions based on the notion of white superiority, of western individualism, of the finality of western Christendom, if our methods have often quenched and grieved the Spirit— all this God forgives and overcomes, and even uses, because there was in it all an element of obedience which He does not despise. It is not we who gather the Church, but He, through His word and Spirit. We may be bound by our limited vision, the Spirit is not bound. The perfect Means, availing Himself of our very imperfect means, will achieve the perfect End that lies very far beyond the horizon of the imperfect ends we envision. This is the comfort and the hope of the missionary community. But it is no less its peril. A doctrine that gives comfort in the awareness of the imperfection of our limited best may easily become a doctrine whereby we rationalize complacency, inertia and fruitlessness. But the price of complacency in God's kingdom is great. It is no small matter if on the one foundation that has been laid we build houses of wood, hay and stubble that shall be burned in the time of testing. It is no small matter if a grieved Spirit must achieve His ends without us, or in spite of us because we stood in His way and did not yield ourselves as supple instruments for His use.

So long as God's kingdom is in process of becoming, that is, so long as God gives His Church a task to discharge in history, we shall have to concern ourselves with the question of missionary method. Essentially this means: how must the Church that now is express her witness in such a manner that she may most effectively contribute to the manifestation of the perfect universal Church that one day shall be? Is there a norm to guide her in answering this question? Rather, is it possible that there should *not* be a norm to guide her in answering it? Is it possible that the Holy Spirit has left to her own judgment how the Church shall most effectively mediate to men the central gift of the Spirit, namely, His own life?

It is one of the supreme ironies of the history of the Christian Church that Paul, who was first and last a missionary, has been regarded by the frequently missionarily indifferent older Churches as first and last a theologian, and that his letters which were "letters to young Churches" have been regarded as primarily theological treatises. Likewise, Acts has been viewed as a dramatic and interesting piece of Church history that could be conveniently appealed to to justify this or that form of Church government while its profoundly missionary character was hardly recognized.

The inevitable results of such an inversion of values have long been evident. Whereas the early Church preserved herself by witness and expansion, the later Church frequently succumbed to the temptation, inherent in her view of the New Testament, to preserve herself by an exclusive emphasis on the strengthening of her internal structure through elaborate instruction in doctrine and by laying down credal boundaries beyond which no one could venture with impunity. In the course of this development the Holy Spirit *as Spirit of witness* was allowed to recede into the background, at least in His missionary aspect. But since the Spirit is a Spirit of witness not only to the Church but also to the world, the limitation of His witness to intra-Church witness prevented Him from fully and powerfully expressing Himself in the Church that wanted Him only in part. As a result the Church was cast upon a period of spiritual lethargy and ineffectiveness manifesting itself in unwholesome

o   209

preoccupation with herself, in sharp and loveless controversies, and in well-nigh total unconcern for the vast unconverted world outside her doors. When the Church tries to bottle up the Spirit within herself she acts contrary both to her own and to His nature. For it is the nature of the Church ever to be enlarging her borders, and it is the nature of the Spirit to transmit His life to ever-widening circles. When the Church does not recognize this law of her being and of the being of the Spirit, the Spirit is quenched and He withdraws Himself, and the deposit of religiosity that is left becomes a putrefaction in the lives of those who have grieved Him.

A return to or a deepening of missionary concern in the Church is inescapably dependent upon a return to or a deepening of the understanding of the Spirit and to greater obedience to His promptings. But then we must not in the first place turn to the doctrine of the Spirit as that doctrine is found in works on Christian doctrine. These will help us but little. We must turn to the doctrine of the Holy Spirit as that is unfolded *in the New Testament*. The doctrine there unfolded is that the Spirit is a *Spirit of life* who transmits His life through *witness*. This witness knows *no boundaries*, because it is the Spirit of the *Son of Man*, of the Logos who became *universal flesh*, and who died for the sins of the *whole world* so that *whoever* believes on Him may have *life*. *That* is the Spirit who was given to the Church at Pentecost. That *alone*, that *exclusively*, is the Spirit given at Pentecost. There is no other Spirit than *this* Spirit. All His manifestations in the Church in love, joy, peace, long-suffering, study, fellowship, self-denial, are fruits of the preaching that is borne by the witnessing Spirit, who has given Himself not only to be enjoyed and possessed, but to be shared and imparted, wherein alone lies the true enjoyment and possession of Him.

There is one man who, more than any other, has had an appreciation for the missionary significance of the Spirit given at Pentecost. This man is Roland Allen. One sometimes hears

Allen referred to as a radical proponent of the so-called indigenous missionary method. Nothing could be farther from
the truth. Such a judgment rests upon a fragmentary or
erroneous reading of him. Allen did indeed stand for "indigenous" missionary methods, but least of all because he was
particularly enamored of the three slogans, self-support, self-
government, self-propagation. He saw little virtue in these
emphases as they are commonly held. How else shall we read
such a passage as the following?

> These efforts [at transfer of control from the top] to undo the evil
> caused by over-direction in the past are themselves tainted with
> the same evil. They are imposed from above. Just as at first we
> concentrated all authority in our own hands and directed every-
> thing for the people from above because we despised the stage of
> infancy as impotent, so now we impose the forms of independence.
> These modern changes are imposed by us just as the earlier forms
> were imposed by us. It is we who say "You must be independent:
> you must be self-supporting and self-governing, you must have
> missionary societies", just as before we said "You must accept our
> guidance in finance, in organization, in missionary effort". Even
> today when we appoint the native archdeacons and bishops and
> establish councils, and encourage the missionary societies, we
> show that we are conscious that the people are not ready for
> them, by a fearful caution providing every conceivable safeguard
> to prevent them from doing anything that we might not approve.
> This is at once a confession of failure and a confession that the
> plan designed to correct the failure is of a piece with the old.[2]

Allen had boundless confidence in the power of the Spirit.
He believed that the Spirit was first and foremost a witnessing
Spirit, of which His revelation at Pentecost was the dramatic
manifestation. He believed that from this Spirit all the goodness
flows that is in the Church. He believed that the Spirit is a
Spirit who places men *at liberty*, who makes men truly *independent* of other men because He places them in a position of
total dependence upon Christ. *Therefore*, he believed that the
Church could not but be witnessing Church, and *therefore*

he believed that Christians and the Churches which they constitute must be free from dependence upon or domination by other Christians and other Churches. An independence which does not grow on this solid root of the Spirit he could only see as the exchange of one form of spiritual domination for another.

In all his writings Allen's overriding concern was to show that missionary method, far from being a secondary or indifferent matter, is a matter of supreme importance. The manner in which the missionary task is discharged, he held, must be determined by the nature of the Spirit who wholly informs and conditions the missionary witness of the Church. A method which is at variance with the nature of the Spirit cannot expect to be successful. When the method whereby the witnessing task of the Church is executed contradicts the nature of the task to be discharged, a working at cross-purposes ensues which can only result in failure. "The end must be implicit in the beginning."

In the remaining pages of this final chapter some indication will be given of what Pentecost should mean for the discharge of the missionary task. An extensive exposition is neither possible nor necessary. The areas that will be touched upon, however, are crucial. It is for the writer a source of particular satisfaction that the practical conclusions to which his exegetical study lead find, as will appear, such unequivocal support in the noble spirit whose missionary experience and observation drove him to the scriptures to determine why the witness that developed so fruitfully in apostolic times now often moves forward so cumbrously and with so little result.

We shall discuss the subject of Pentecost in its relation to the practice of missions under the following heads,

A. *The need of instruction in the nature of the Spirit*
B. *The indigenous Church*
C. *The Spirit, the word, and institutions*
D. *Comprehensive approach or comprehensive message?*
E. *Unity in witness*

A. *The need of instruction in the nature of the Spirit*

Although emphasis on the Church has not been prominent up to this point, it has been the constant assumption that normally and ideally the witness to Christ is borne by *the Church*. When we speak of the Church we do not refer simply to her institutional expression. We understand the Church to be the body of believers manifesting itself, on the one hand, as an organism expressing itself in institutional form and, on the other hand, as an institute serving the needs of the organism. The Church must therefore be seen not as an institute alone, nor as an organism alone, but as the one body of Christ consisting of two correlative aspects.

It is to *this* body that the Holy Spirit poured out at Pentecost has been given. He was poured out on the apostles and on the disciples who stood under the spiritual authority of the apostles. Through the witness of the apostles, through the witness of men appointed by the apostles, and through the witness recognized by the apostles, the Church expanded. Because the Spirit indwells the Church, the Church is a witnessing Church. Because He indwells the Church, He indwells every member of the Church, and therefore every member of the Church is in his nature a witnessing member. The *whole Church*, therefore, is witnessing Church, whether officially and corporately through the offices of the institute, or through her members personally and individually.

This is the kind of Church we meet in the New Testament. It does not know a witness by the apostles that ignores or has little appreciation for the witness of individual members of the Church. It does not know a witness by the members of the Church that does not recognize the authority of the apostles. The New Testament knows nothing of a distinction between the Church, on the one hand, and missionary effort and organization outside of or within the Church, on the other hand. The Church in her entirety, the Church in her official and unofficial, in her organizational and in her organic aspects, is a missionary body. Through this one Church, and through these two mutually complementary aspects of her one indivisible being, the one witness of the Church comes to expression.

The Church was first established and organized with a world-wide mission for a world-wide work. It was a living organism composed of living souls deriving their life from Christ, who was its head. It was an organism which grew by its own spontaneous activity, the expression of that life which it had in union with Christ, the Saviour. Its organization was the organization fitted for such an organism; it was the organization of a missionary body. Consequently there was no special organization for missions in the early Church; the Church organization sufficed. It was simple and complete. There was abundant room in it for the expression of the spontaneous individual activity of its members; for every member was potentially a missionary; and the Church, as an organized body, expected that activity and knew how to act when its members did their duty. With the activity of its members, it grew simply by multiplying its Bishops.[3]

The Protestant Churches have, since their inception, wandered far from the missionary ideal set forth in the New Testament. They have through default permitted to come into being that characteristic phenomenon known as the missionary society. The voice of the Spirit cannot be silenced. His work continues. When the Church organization and organism, as a whole, proved deaf to his promptings, as a whole, the Spirit began to work through some *part* of the Church. So it happened that the refusal of the Church to acknowledge the Great Commission as still binding upon her led "friends of missions", "mission enthusiasts", people who were "mission-minded", to bring into being *missionary societies*. These societies have done the work that the Church in her totality should have performed. The missionary society is, scripturally speaking, an abnormality. But it has been a blessed abnormality. As such, it has been at once evidence of the power of the Spirit and a judgment upon the Church. It has been the salvation of hundreds of thousands, it has prevented the witnessing Spirit from being wholly quenched, and it has spread the faith and the Church to the ends of the earth. But it has meant that the Church allowed her proper task to fall into the hands of groups of her members. It has meant that the Church permitted the obedience that she should have rendered in her entirety to be rendered by the proxy of a few.

> The new modern missionary organization is an addition. With us the Church had largely ceased to be self-expanding: its members had, for the most part, forgotten its missionary character. . . . But the missionary spirit was not dead, and it demanded expression. . . . If we compare our modern missionary work with the missionary work of the early Church, this is what differentiates them: with us missions are the special work of a special organization; in the early Church missions were not a special work and there was no special organization.[4]

At this point Churches that believe in and practice denominational missions may be tempted to feel that they do not fall under the reproach of having departed from the norm of the New Testament. Their mission work stands under the authority of synod or general assembly. It is borne by the offerings of the Church. It is administered by boards and commissions whose members are appointed to represent the entire Church. Does not this reflect the New Testament pattern of missions performed by the Church? It could. But too often it does not. How fully do the decisions of these bodies reflect *the mind of the Church*? How adequately do these bodies inform the Church of the issues at stake, and of the circumstances surrounding them, so that there may be relevant discussion in the Church, and intelligent prayer and giving by the Church? How truly can it be said that *the Church* does what the general assemblies and the boards do?

It is so easily forgotten, and so utterly important to remember, that the Holy Spirit has not been given to synods, assemblies, conferences, boards and presbyteries, just as He has not been given to so many disparate individuals. *The Spirit has been given to the Church in the totality of her manifestation as organization and as organism.* Not to the organization alone, nor to the organism alone, but to the organization as it serves the organism, and to the organism as it comes to expression in the organization. Therefore the official bodies of the Church and her members individually have full and legitimate claim upon the guidance and power of the Spirit only when they stand in communion with the total manifestation of the Church of which they are a part. An ecclesiastical missionary administration that functions apart from or in relative indifference to the Church as an organism has neither right nor reason to suppose that it is standing in the New Testament tradition of missionary witness. Because the Spirit of life and of witness is not divided, the Church as His life-transmitting organ of witness may not be divided.

It is particularly necessary that denominational missions remember this principle. They, doubtless more than the missionary society, are tempted to suppose that they are scriptural in the pattern of missionary administration which they follow. They may, and sometimes do, stand even farther from this pattern than the missionary society does. There was, at least originally, no alternative to the organization of societies if the missionary witness to Christ was to go forth. But there would seem to be no reason why a mission board or commission should not endeavor fully to draw the Church into its confidence, thereby making itself a true instrument and voice of the Church. Because this is so frequently not done, or not done adequately, Allen is entirely right when he speaks of

> a Board of Missions for the Church which is nothing more than a department of Church organization, and is in its spiritual character almost identical with a missionary society within the Church.[5]

If the Church is to return to a true appreciation of her missionary character and thereby to a fuller discharge of her missionary duty, the nature of the Spirit and her own nature as a bearer of the witnessing and life-giving Spirit will have to be emphasized more than has been done in the past. This must be done especially *by the Christian pulpit.* We must cease preaching the Great Commission as a command to be obeyed but must present it *as a law that expresses the nature and that governs the life of the Church.* So long as the Church is seen as a body that meets for edification and praise which *also* has the task of obeying the missionary command, no great deployment of missionary power is to be expected. Nor can the Spirit enter upon a full exercise of His function in the Church so long as He is regarded as the Spirit of regeneration and sanctification who must *also* provide the power required to obey the command. Pentecost was not given to provide the Church with a missionary *donum superadditum.* The outpouring of the Spirit is in and by reason of its very nature the effectuation of the Great Commission in the life of the Church. For this reason there is no record of missionary activity between the giving of the Great Commission and Pentecost, and for this reason missions is in Acts *the central theme* of the Church's activity *after* Pentecost.

There can, of course, be no objection to speaking of the Great Commission as a command. We have repeatedly done so in the discussion of it. But it is not, as it is so often presented as being, an external command. It is not, like the commands of the law, a command which men are impotent to obey. It is a command that has been given because the Church *has the power to obey it,* because the Spirit *has been given* to the Church, because it is of her *essence and nature* to be a witnessing body.

In the gospel the Spirit which expresses Himself in the command is given to the soul to whom the command is addressed. The command is an expression of the mind of the Spirit. It is an instruction in the character of the Spirit given. . . . So the command to preach the gospel . . . is clearly associated with the promise of the presence of Christ with his people, "Lo I am with you always"; with the gift of power from on high, "Ye shall receive power"; with the coming of the Holy Ghost, "He shall bear witness, and ye also shall bear witness"; but the promise of the presence of Christ, the gift of the indwelling Spirit . . . is the assurance that those who are commanded will be able to obey. It is the promise of the motive power to which the command appeals. The voice of Christ without the soul speaks to the Spirit of Christ within the soul. Christ first gives the Spirit and then the command. He first comes to us, and then commands us to go.[6]

Unfortunately, large sections of the Church do not know and have not known that the Church is in her very essence, because she is indwelt by the Spirit, a witnessing body. This has not been known as it should have been known because it was not taught by the Church as it should have been taught. Therefore it is pre-eminently the task of the pulpit to inform the Church of her nature. When the simple intellectual understanding of this much neglected truth strikes deep root in the Church a wonderful change in her attitude to missions may be expected. This change may be expected because the Spirit who indwells the Church will respond to His own voice. The intellectual comprehension will in the mysterious manner of the Spirit become a spiritual apprehension, and spiritual apprehension always finds expression in corresponding action.

A gift of grace does not do away with the need of knowledge. Grace received must be recognized, known, accepted, surrendered to, cultivated, proved by experience. We must "know the things that are freely given us of God" (1 Cor. 2:2).... We have all been taught that the Spirit of Christ is a Spirit of Holiness. We have all been taught to recognize the signs of His Presence in terms of virtuous conduct. We have not been taught to recognize the signs of His Presence in ourselves in terms of missionary activity. . . . What wonder, then, that Christians who have been taught a one-sided truth about the Holy Ghost should be unconscious that they are denying Him, when they deny that side of His nature which they have never been taught.[7]

When the Church is again taught this truth she will become what she ought to be, and once was—a wholly witnessing body. She will learn that the "world" into which she must "go" is not simply a geographical area but also, and very particularly, a spiritual area. Obedience to the Great Commission will not be seen as something that only "missionaries" can execute who go to far-away lands. It is an obedience that must be expressed by the whole Church. Wherever the Church is, she stands in the midst of the world. Jesus expressly prayed that the Father would keep His own *in* the world, not that they be taken out of the world, John 17: 15. Jesus never left the small country of Palestine, yet He was pre-eminently sent "into the world". The understanding of this truth will not leave Christians who seldom travel far from home under the illusion that there is no world for them to go to, because they will know that they are always in it. And Christians whose work calls them to foreign lands will not regard the Christian witness in those lands as a task to be borne only by the missionaries, but they will understand that they always carry their witnessing nature and therefore their witnessing task with them.

As the witness of the Church goes forth unitedly from the institute and from the organism, each witnessing according to its own nature, the problem of the limits of each will solve itself. The conflicts that often find expression here usually arise from the sin of omission on the part of one or the other. When official Church bodies show no interest in missions, those of her members who are not deaf to the promptings of the Spirit begin to undertake a witness in which the institute should have shown initiative. Thereupon the institute reacts, usually on the ground of an infringement of its authority and with appeal to "let everything be done decently and in order". Then the conflict is on that has no end because each stresses a duty that the other is not concerned about, and each ignores a duty that the other emphasizes. On the other hand, it is not unusual to see the institute concerned about the inactivity of the members of the Church in social, economic, educational and other efforts, and in its concern undertaking to stimulate and guide them not simply by the witness and admonition to which it alone is called, but by itself providing the organization, the program, and even officers-after-a-sort for the expression of lay activity. In the end this leads to an ecclesiastical hegemony against which the membership rebels, for it is the true function of the institute to serve and not to dominate the organism.

In the New Testament we find a remarkable mutual complementing of institute and organism. The Church could never have spread as rapidly as it did had the members of the Church left the expansion of the faith to the office-bearers alone. Nor would it have spread so rapidly if the organized Church had not encouraged and accepted the fruits of lay witness. The institute recognized that believers had the Spirit and acknowledged the fruits that their witness brought into being. It accepted converts into the membership of existing congregations or it organized them into new congregations. Believers, on the other hand, recognized the authority of the institute and did not dream of a Christianity that did not come to expression in membership in the organized Church. The way into the Church was through baptism administered by duly authorized persons. Whoever was baptized was regarded as being in Christ and was a member of the Church, whoever was not baptized was not regarded as being in Christ and could not share in the life of the converts and of their churches.

The Church which appropriates this doctrine will not be wanting in a truly witnessing membership, nor in lay workers who shall declare and reveal the love of Christ at home and in the regions beyond, nor in ordained missionaries to organize the fruits of the total witness into congregations of believers worshipping and living under the preaching of the word, the administration of the sacraments, and under the spiritual authority instituted by Christ. For the Spirit of witness is also the Spirit of love. He expresses His love in the witness, and the witness in love. In love He seeks the lost, and these He seeks to the uttermost ends of the earth because His love is as boundless as His life which sustains and renews the entire creation. For He is the Spirit of the Son of Man, the Logos made flesh, the Savior of the whole world.

B. *The indigenous Church*

The pattern describing the growth of the Church of New Testament times is a very simple one. *The Church grew by the addition of converts to existing congregations and by the organization of converts into new and fully independent congregations.*

The importance for us of this simple pattern can hardly be overestimated. It involves the rejection in principle of the method by which we of the West have in many places pursued the missionary task since the days of William Carey, and points to a better way. A characteristic feature of our approach in significant mission areas has been the withholding of a fully independent Church life from the converts which we gained by our witness. Too often we have placed them and the Churches into which they were formed in a state of dependence upon the missionaries and the mission. Our approach has frequently departed from the New Testament pattern in this crucially important respect: it has made missionary control of the Church which its witness brought into being a normal and extended stage between the beginning of the witness and the coming into being of truly independent Churches. It has inserted a protracted stage in the missionary pattern of which the New Testament knows nothing.

Now it is least of all a serious matter that we should do some things of which the apostles never heard. The New Testament is not a book of regulations to govern our behavior, whether missionary or otherwise. The freedom of Christian men is a gift of the gospel, it is the cornerstone of the Reformation, and it ought to be the glory of the missionary both to exercise and to transmit this freedom. The defect of our approach in many places has been that it withheld from converts the freedom Christ has gained for them. We have been eager to give to our converts the Spirit of regeneration and sanctification, we have exerted ourselves to give to them the Spirit of knowledge and of understanding of the scriptures. We have not always shown the same eagerness to surrender them to the

Spirit of liberty and of witness. We endeavored to transplant the patterns of Church life by which we grew up. We often feared spontaneity. It has therefore been a feature of much missionary practice to retain control of the churches that were coming into being. Often the spiritual center of the mission field was not concentrated in so many free and fully functioning congregations, but in mission stations. Thence emanated the directives for the life of the converts and of their Churches.

The price that we have had to pay for this restriction of the liberty of others and for this duplication of self has been a high one. To effect what we effected we have had to suppress something fine in the newly-won believers. We could not allow to come to full expression the Spirit of liberty and of witness that was given to the Church at Pentecost. We saw at length in the preceding study that not a part of the Spirit was given at Pentecost, but that *the whole Spirit* was given. This we have not fully appreciated. For it means that if we transmit to others the life of the Spirit we must not hinder them in fully expressing the freedom and joy of life; if we are eager to see them gather knowledge in the Spirit we should also be eager to see them express the knowledge they have gathered; if we exert ourselves to give them the Spirit of holiness and of life we should be eager to give them the Spirit of liberty through which that life comes to expression. Life means spontaneity and freedom, liberty to be one's self, independence from others. That individuality, that particularity, that distinctiveness of personality and character that God has given to each man, is in the Spirit hallowed and given divine right of existence. The life that the Spirit gives is a renewal of the life that exists. And where men live in societies with age-old customs and usages the renewal of its individuals will mean a renewal of the social patterns in which they live. But it will be a renewal of the existing patterns, just as the renewal of the individual is a renewal and purification of the existing individual. In cultivating the spiritual life of the converts and in giving form to their ecclesiastical life we have too often forgotten this very principal significance of the gift of the Spirit.

When we turn to the book of Acts and to the epistles of Paul we find no trace of this missionary method. Paul did not try to bring into being gentile churches after the Jewish pattern. No small portion of his energy was spent in resisting pressures to do this. He did nothing to make his churches "acceptable" to Jewish Christians. He did not set a Jewish missionary over a gentile congregation to keep it in dependence upon him for years on end. He did not believe in long delays before administering baptism and in appointing elders when there were sufficient believers to form a church. He did not manage the finances of the converts he brought to Christ, nor did he take upon himself the discipline of the delinquent. In short, we find the missionary work of Paul and of the early Church characterized by a complete absence of a characteristic feature of our missionary approach. Paul gave immediately what we often hoped to achieve eventually, he gave without reserve what we frequently gave by dosages and stages.

It must not be supposed that Paul and we achieved the same end, but that he achieved immediately what we hope to achieve after an extended period of time. No greater error could be made than is expressed in such a supposition. If the end is implicit in the beginning then the beginning will be explicit in the end. As we sow, so shall we reap. When we begin with independence we shall end with independence, and this independence will express itself in the framework of the communion of the saints, which is a holy inter-dependence. But when we begin with dependence, we shall end in dependence, as we have indeed so often ended. This dependence, however, is against the nature of the Spirit who lives in the believers and not infrequently leads to open or covert revolution or, if not to this, to less than a full deployment of the power, talent, and devotion that is latent in the suppressed presence of the Spirit.

The Church of Jesus Christ is a new creation, her life is a life in the Spirit, her Lord is Christ alone, and the norm for her life is the scriptures alone. The Church is a revelation of the new aeon, her life is lived in the End which is already here. The younger Churches are not, therefore, a creation of the missionaries, their life is not derived from the Churches that brought them into being, their lord is not the authority of the older Churches, nor is the norm of their life the historically conditioned creeds, customs, usages and ecclesiastical structures of the older Churches. The younger Churches are not revelations of the older Churches, nor is their life lived in the life of the older Churches. Where Christ lives, there the Spirit which He sent lives, and this Spirit is the Spirit of spontaneous life and witness. Where Christians and churches are allowed to be what the unfettered Spirit makes them, where they are set free from men and placed in full dependence upon Christ, there we may expect her witness to flourish and her numbers to grow.

When the spirit and method characteristic of the missionary activity found in the New Testament are allowed to govern our missionary approach there will still be room for, there will, indeed, of necessity be, wide variety in the specific manner in which the approach will be carried out. The Spirit in the missionaries desires to be no less free, spontaneous, and organic in His operations than He desires to be in the lives of those newly found by him. But whatever the specific approach, there will be a common desire to place converts and their churches at liberty, there will be a common desire to let them be masters in their own house, there will be a common desire to see the end envisioned find concrete expression at every stage of the development of the younger Church. And there will be common striving concretely to realize these common desires.

The most rapidly developing group of Churches in the world today is doubtless that grouping known as the Pentecostal movement. In somewhat more than a generation it has swept beyond the boundaries of its American origins into every corner of the world. The movement is so massive that as a matter of religious and ecclesiastical significance it has been called, next to Protestantism and Roman Catholicism, Christianity's "third force". Lesslie Newbigin in his book *The Household of God* gives theological standing to this idea by calling upon the Church everywhere to see the inadequacy of dividing Christianity between the dominant emphases of message (Protestant) and structure (Catholic). There is also the factor of *spirit*. These three, message, structure, and spirit, must characterize the Church of Christ everywhere. It is this often forgotten or neglected factor of spirit in its outreach that makes Pentecostalism the power it is. In a telling passage Newbigin writes:

> The apostle asked the converts of Apollos one question: "Did you receive the Holy Spirit when you believed?" and got a plain answer. His modern successors are more inclined to ask either "Did you believe exactly what we teach?" or "Were the hands that were laid on you our hands?" and—if the answer is satisfactory—to assure the converts that they have then received the Holy Spirit even if they don't know it. There is a world of difference between these two attitudes.[8]

The Pentecostal emphases are on the simple preaching of the gospel, prayer, the gift of the Spirit which is accompanied by "speaking with tongues", faith healing and prophecy. When one views the worship of a typical African congregation that is still close to the missionary situation out of which it developed, one is struck by the staid and almost somber character of the service. Everything is done in unvarying order, the responses are only those that are called for, and every meeting is like the preceding. Such worship is not a contraction of the western spirit, for we are inclined so to express ourselves. But are they African? Is there any way in which the African love of rhythm, chant and joyful response can come to expression? Is there the spontaneity of the free spirit?

There can be little doubt that the success of the Pentecostal witness lies in no small degree in its appeal to this "expressive" aspect of the human spirit. On the other hand, its message is almost entirely soteriological in the narrow sense of the word. The implications of the gospel for state, society, education, and culture come to altogether inadequate expression. The Pentecostal emphasis on the local body of believers hardly does justice to the structuration of the universal body of Christ. Message, structure and spirit must in a full-orbed Christianity find simultaneous expression.

As we observe the growth of the Christian witness in the New Testament, the unusual phenomena of tongues and miracles recede into the background, and the power of the message with the response of faith stands to the fore. We do not find in the New Testament either a despising of orderly worship or the placing of a special premium on the ecstatic. Paul would have both the staid Jerusalemite and the tongue-speaking Corinthian be themselves, and whether it is one or the other, "let everything be done decently and in order". These words come at the end of a chapter on how to conduct worship in tongues and prophecy, 1 Cor. 14. Perhaps it has been a great fault of us western missionaries that we have not been able to conceive that the ecstatic can be decent and orderly.

C. *The Spirit, the word, and institutions*

The task of missions is to be instrumental in transmitting the life of the Spirit. An essential aspect of this task is the establishing of the institutional Church to safeguard, strengthen, and further extend the life that has been brought into being through the witness.

In order to transmit His life the Spirit, according to the norm of the New Testament, uses only one means. This means is the kerugma, the witness, of the Church. The apostles and other office-bearers preached and baptized, and the members of the Church expressed the hope that was in them. This preaching was not merely the announcement of hitherto unknown

226

matters. The lives of those who preached Christ were in their total manifestation an eloquent recommendation of the truth of the spoken word. It was therefore the living word, the heartfelt preaching, the verbally borne kerugma, that revealed Christ to men and brought into being the greatest expansion of the faith in the history of the Church. In the command of Christ, in the work of the apostles, in the witness of the Church, in the believers' participation in the spread of the gospel, this activity of the verbal proclamation stood central. In particular instances this proclamation was supported by the working of miracles, chiefly on the part of the apostles. But as a rule, especially in the gentile areas, it was simply the power of the word that gained for the Church her great victories. Paul's counsel to Timothy is representative of the manner in which the Spirit everywhere transmitted His life: "Preach the word, be urgent in season, out of season; reprove, rebuke, exhort, with all long-suffering and teaching. For the time will come when they will not endure sound doctrine. . . . But be thou sober in all things, suffer hardship, do the work of an evangelist, fulfil thy ministry" 2 Tim. 4: 2-5. Paul's rhetorical questions in Rom. 10 underscore this emphasis: "How shall they call on him whom they have not believed? and how shall they believe in him whom they have not heard? and how shall they hear without a preacher? and how shall they preach except they be sent? even as it is written, How beautiful are the feet of them that bring glad tidings of good things!"

In marked contrast to this method stands the method which we have so largely employed during the past one hundred and fifty years. We, too, have preached the gospel, and no small amount of devotion, self-sacrifice, and perseverance has gone into its world-wide proclamation. But we have done much more than this. We have established schools, colleges, and universities; we have erected dispensaries and hospitals; we have taught people how to farm more efficiently, we have prepared them for positions in business and in the government; we have built

YMCA's and YWCA's. We have had a considerably larger missionary program than the early Church.

Are those added elements a legitimate expansion of the preaching of the gospel which was entrusted to the Church by Christ? Is the introduction of our (more or less) Christian culture in the missionary areas simply an elaboration of the principle of gospel preaching, in the sense that a radio gospel broadcast is an elaboration, or is it the introduction of an alien or ambiguous element in the witness of the Church?

Here we wish to remember that a missionary is never able to divest himself from his own culture. He carries it with him. It is part of his character and personality. Its diffusion in greater or less degree in the area of his witness is an inevitable concomitant of his witness. But the diffusion of his culture and of the techniques of his own civilization does not thereby become a part of his witnessing program. It is simply an inevitable and generally unconscious factor that accompanies his witness. It is quite another matter, however, when characteristically western institutions are deliberately made the vehicle through which it is attempted to secure an entrance for the gospel. Then we are no longer concerned with an inevitable concomitant, but with a consciously chosen method.

We wish also to remember that the successes and vicissitudes that have accompanied the missionary witness of the Church through the centuries have often stood in intimate association with political and social factors, with cultural cross-fertilization, and similar circumstances. The expansion of the early Church stands in close association with a number of these as they came to expression in the then existing Roman Empire. Such important factors as a single governing authority, the prevalence of the Greek language, empire-crossing roads, religious toleration, and the Diaspora, were undoubtedly conducive to the spread of the Christian religion. They were not created by the Church, however, but were providential circumstances of which the Church availed herself. The Church does not live in a vacuum but in a world governed by her Lord. It is her task to recognize this and to adjust her witness to the circumstances which His government brings, or allows to come, into being.

The question therefore remains whether the Church herself may, other than through the proclamation of the gospel, seek to find an entrance for it.

Those who received the message of the early Church were not able to use it for any other end than the end for which it was proclaimed. This end was the salvation of men, and the service of God and of man in which this salvation found expression. When Simon the sorcerer sought to receive the gift of the Holy Spirit for his own ends, Peter censured him with one of the most scorching rebukes found in the Bible, Acts 8: 18–24. The institutions that we have established on the mission field have invited a very different use of them than was intended. In the effort to exemplify the gospel and in the hope of finding an entrance for it we have offered education and know-how of all sorts which drew to our institutions men who desired least of all to receive the gift of the Holy Spirit. They often desired and found only intellectual and material advancement. We hoped through our institutions to spread throughout the region of their service a "Christian spirit", a "sympathetic under-standing of Christianity", we hoped that everywhere a "Christian influence" would be diffused. It was seldom seriously asked how there could be a Christian spirit without the Spirit of Christ, or an understanding of Christianity that did not involve a believing knowledge of the gospel. Especially was it forgotten that a Christian influence that bears no or only little relation-ship to the Church and is therefore not constantly renewed and strengthened through the administration of the word and the sacraments cannot be a living and enduring influence. It has not infrequently happened that men trained in mission schools have later used the knowledge they gained in them against the advancement of the Christian religion. It is quite certain that Paul would have very great difficulty in understanding how the following situation could result from *missionary* activity:

> Our schools were started to produce subordinate professional workers for the Church; they expanded to become the principal training-grounds from which were recruited those who filled positions in the world of the *compradore*—the Customs Service, the Salt *Gabelle*, the Postal Administration, and the foreign firms and the Chinese banks and business houses which were associated with them. Many of the more ardent spirits were stirred by their shame at their country's weakness and their anger at the wrongs it suffered at the hands of foreigners. They considered that the education they were receiving might possibly be designed for the gradual reform of Chinese society, but, if so, for reform in the interest of the West in whose *bona fides* they had lost all trust. They did not believe it could assist the revolution of China in the interest of the Chinese people. They went over in the end to the Communist Party, in which there are surprisingly large numbers of people with this close but extremely partial acquaintance with Christian missions. Others, again, became Christians. But the Church has been mainly among the poor and ignorant, and the rank and file of the ministry not such as are able to attract and hold educated young people; moreover, the schools and colleges have been dominated for the most part by a highly liberal version of Protestantism, while the Churches have been mainly fundamentalist. Few educated young people have found a permanent and satisfying home in the Church. They have tended rather to drift into the "Christian Movement". A man retained the Christian name with a steadily decreasing Christian content, because he was outside the corporate life and discipline of the Christian community. In the end, much more often than not, he ceased to be effectively a Christian at all; the larger cities were full of ex-Christians of this kind, among them a large proportion of those Christians in high positions in the Kuomintang Government of Chiang Kai-shek who were so much praised in the West a few years ago. . . .

Whether they are viewed therefore from the angle of their creative contribution to the needs of Chinese society, or their provision of leadership from the Chinese Church, the educational institutions on which we have lavished so much time, money, and loving hard work, seem for the most part to have made a poor return. The case of the hospitals is not substantially different.[9]

This development was not accidental. Education has a character and urge of its own and cannot with impunity be made a mere instrument of evangelism or a servant of organizational Church requirements. Education is found in one form or another in every society and seeks to serve the total need of the society. Human institutions, even the most conservative Christian kind, have their own natural laws of development and self-expression. They all arise out of the created order of things, and their functions are conditioned by this fact. The proper function of schools is to mold minds and character, of farms to produce food, of hospitals to heal bodies. Redemption so renews the human agents who are engaged in these activities that the educating and the farming and the healing will be done out of motives and for the ends envisioned in the created order. Redemption intends to permeate man's natural activities with spiritual motives and ends. It does not intend that activities so reclaimed, *in casu* Christian institutions, shall, without serious qualification, be subordinated to and made an instrument of the missionary witness of the Church.

The Church in her institutional expression is the only institution in this world that does not arise out of the created order. She arises exclusively out of the *redemptive* order. She is not explainable in terms of the natural order, as are all other human institutions. Her function is to transmit the life of the Spirit through the word and the sacraments, and this life, constantly renewed and strengthened, must find expression in the world that God has made and in the activities to which man is called by virtue of his creation. The Church is not an institution that stands next to other institutions. She stands above them and has significance for all of them. She provides the life and the dynamic for their true functioning. This is the unique task of the Church. It is not her function to educate, or to farm, or to heal, or to pursue scientific investigations. The Spirit that is in her is a Spirit expressing Himself exclusively in *witness* and in *life*. When this witness is received by men the life of the Spirit that indwells them or begins to indwell them will express itself in the activities in which they are called to engage. The witness always precedes the life because the life arises from the witness believed. The tree precedes the fruit, the presence of Christ precedes a variously deploying Christianity, the Spirit of Christ precedes a manifestation of the Christian spirit.

> I believe that we should gain enormously if we could see that missionaries of the gospel ought to have not many activities, but one activity.
>
> I venture to insist that missionaries of the gospel have only one proper activity, the ministration of the Spirit of Christ. The material, social, political, physical advancement of the nation is not their proper, direct work. Their sole work is to bring to Christ those whom He has called and to establish His Church; and the social, political, physical, material progress of the people must spring out of that, and be the direct fruit of the Spirit in them.[10]

It is therefore encouraging to note that in contemporary missionary thinking there is a serious re-evaluation of the place both of institutions and of the Church in missionary witness. Nothing has quite so brought this about as the unhappy experience of the Christian mission in China. No area in the world has seen so varied a deployment of missionary initiative and over so wide an extent as China. Nowhere have missionary institutions had a larger and longer opportunity to prove themselves than in that populous land. Nowhere has the end-result of this activity been so generally disappointing, and with respect to no area of missionary witness is the significance of the Church now more appreciated. It is not possible lightly to read over the following words by a competent observer:

> As Communist control moved southward toward us living in the Yangtze valley there were many informal meetings of Chinese Christian leaders with missionaries in which we discussed what was happening and what we thought was going to happen to the Christian enterprise. In these meetings it was common prophecy that Christian hospitals and missionary doctors stood the best chance of long survival. There was a similar expectation for our schools and missionary teachers. Frequently it was said that our local churches, with their small and comparatively poor congregations and their isolated pastors, had the poorest chance of survival. How wrong we were!
>
> For see what happened. Our schools and hospitals and other social service institutions are being taken over. But our churches continue. In many places, membership has grown and become spiritually more meaningful. For decades our schools and hospitals had dominated our horizons. They were tangible. Their output was commercially and politically in demand. We poured our major investments into them rather than into the development of local churches for enrichment of the content of Christian fellowship. Yet it is Christian fellowship which survives. As in the case of the early Church, it is these local fellowships that are the germinating centers for the life of the Chinese Church of tomorrow.[11]

Another observer writes:

> In the light of the present situation, what is the task of the missionary of our generation? The first job of the new missionary is to shift from the "influence theory of evangelism" to a more direct form of evangelism. "In the future I believe that our emphases should be on direct Christian evangelism and on those projects which make the greatest contribution to the building of the Christian Church", wrote John Bennett after his return from Asia. A missionary institution will be judged by whether or not it is a channel for the proclamation of the gospel and whether or not it adds to the growth of the Church. If it is primarily an agency for cultural penetration and sharing, then its existence is not justified. The urgency of our mission, the brief time at our disposal, and the limited resources at hand do not permit us to

indulge in such extravagances as the spreading of western culture.[12]

It is true that the author of the former of these two quotations justifies the large institutional work that has been done:

> . . . our missionary investments in Church institutions in China have paid in terms of the things they were intended to accomplish. If we now lose control of all of them—and I think that is to be expected—the investment has been worth making.[13]

The question is, what did we intend to accomplish? If it was the founding of a strong Church we have, in the author's own evaluation, been far from successful. But if this end was not attained, then any other ends that were envisioned or achieved cannot but come to stand in a very ambiguous light. Missionary fruits that are not gathered into the Church are scattered fruits, their life is only in themselves, is not renewed and re-invigorated by the regular ministration of the Spirit, and sooner or later it dies. To the extent that the missionary witness of the Church of Christ fails to found the Church, strong and independent, to that extent it fails of achieving its purpose.

In other places the fruit of the Christian missionary witness as it comes to expression in institutional work has not been so put to the test as in China. It is therefore not possible to say what a testing-time would reveal in other areas. But is there good reason to believe that the evaluation that has been rendered would be more favorable than the evaluation that has been rendered over China? Did not China provide a very large and representative cross-section of the Christian mission? ". . . can a China missionary be free of the fear that what was true of China is true still of India and Africa?"[14]

These strictures on institutional work do not mean, of course, that institutions, notably medical and educational, cannot play a role in the missionary work of the Church. The ministry of healing has, perhaps more than any other avenue, provided a directly visible expression of missionary love. It has usually been found that an effective manifestation of missionary concern with physical suffering required an institutional framework. Woven through the service rendered by the institution were a spirit and attitude that strengthened and demonstrated the witness of the mission as a whole. When the institution has come into being, however, a danger has also come into being. This danger is that the institution will gradually grow away from its original purpose as a manifestation of the truth of the witness and will become instead a philanthropic activity that no longer bears a direct relationship to the witness. It may lose, or may measurably lose, sight of the spiritual character of the service which it renders. This will, in the end, cause those who are served to look more to the techniques and skills of the medical personnel and to the independent power of the medicines that are administered than to the life and love that motivate the service that is rendered, and to the Creator and Redeemer whose goodness makes the service possible.

Only spiritual discernment will be able to decide when a hospital or a dispensary is becoming an end in itself and is ceasing to serve the gospel witness. Extension of plant, refinement in treatment, multiplication of staff, increase in "efficiency", all harbor the imminent danger of undermining the purpose for which the hospital exists. The Spirit is easily obscured by our many activities, the great Physician is, in the eyes of those whom we serve, easily overshadowed by the human physician and the medicines which he administers.

In educational work the problem is even more complex. The existence of physical suffering on the mission field leaves a missionary community that has it in its power to alleviate it no choice but to do so. The existence of ignorance does not make the same emergency demand for remedial missionary action. The initiation of educational work is not therefore always such a self-evident matter as the initiation of medical work may be. The question therefore arises: Under what circumstances is the erection of a school by the mission warranted?

When Christian parents in non-Christian areas desire for their children an education that shall be in harmony with the home and church life of the children, but do not possess the necessary know-how to undertake this work, or are unable to secure qualified teachers, there would seem to be every reason for the mission to help them discharge their responsibility. When such a school comes into being it will, in all essentials, be a school of the parents, however much it may for the time being be under missionary sponsorship and control. It will be an expression of the life that the witnessing Spirit has brought into being, to which the missionary community may for a time give form and content. It means the first step in the direction of an indigenous Christian education. The school arises from the Christian community, it will serve it and will make increasing deployment of its powers possible, it will strengthen the growing Church, and will make possible an increase in her evangelistic witness. And, very importantly, the school will be *a school*. It will not be regarded as primarily an evangelistic agency, although the spiritual impact of the school, both on the children and in the community, will be incalculable.

It is quite another question whether missions or churches themselves ought to bring schools into being with a view to serving evangelistic ends with them. A great deal of experience in this direction has been extremely disappointing. The money, time, and energy devoted to such schools have been out of all proportion to the fruits that have been realized in the way of conversion. On the other hand, the fruits that have attended them in many areas forbid an *a priori* exclusion of this means of supporting the missionary witness. It must be remembered, however, that it is not of the nature of a school to evangelize. It lives under the law of its own being. The function of a school is to educate. Education in order to be education in the fullest sense of the word must be Christian education. Christian education, however, assumes Christian educands as

236

well as Christian teachers. The Spirit who speaks through the teacher must be responded to by the Spirit who lives in the pupil. Mission education always stands in danger of moving in one of two directions. It tends either to lose its consciously evangelistic aim or to cease being fully education. That is to say, either education or evangelism tends to assert itself at the expense of the other. A frequent development has been that the evangelistic emphasis ceased to be an organic and permeating element in the totality of the educational process and became confined to specific activities. The school became an educational institution in the usual sense of the word, but there were a chapel period, a course in Bible, and sundry religious activities. Rare is the pedagogical spirit, and still rarer is the school, that is able so to unite the educational and the evangelistic emphases that the school remains fully a school while the evangelistic emphasis permeates the teaching in such a manner that it brings forth fruits of conversion.

The missionary witness of the Church comes to men as the oral proclamation of the gospel, supported by the life, spirit, and attitude of the witnessing agents. The two are one and inseparable. This is the pattern of witness found in the New Testament. Institutional work is not a normal, self-evident part of this witness, but neither does this witness exclude the use of institutions. Institutional work should not be regarded as a normal, self-evident part of the witness because it is not of its nature to be evangelistic but to serve men in the area of things natural. On the other hand, the witness often requires the use of institutions because in the concrete situation of missionary activity they may serve powerfully to illuminate, strengthen, and expand the witness. The Spirit has set norms for the manifestation of His life in nature and in grace, and these norms we cannot ignore with impunity. Therefore the greatest care must be exercised in integrating institutional work in the missionary program. But the Spirit also stands above the norms as we are able to comprehend and define them, and therefore can, without abrogating these norms, use institutional work that recognizes them to advance the witness that goes forth from Him. There is no easy formula, no rule of thumb, to guide us here. Our safety and our fruitfulness lie in recognizing and in acting in accordance with the total need that meets us in the area where the witness must be proclaimed.

D. *Comprehensive approach or comprehensive message?*

During the past twenty-five years an emphasis in missionary method has come prominently to the fore which is known as the Comprehensive Approach. It is to be distinguished from institutional work in this respect that, whereas the latter endeavors to render particular services through particular activities, the Comprehensive Approach seeks to exemplify the meaning of the gospel for the whole of the community served. As Christ is the Savior of the whole man, and of that man in all of his relationships, so the missionary approach must be a total one and must confront man with the meaning of the gospel, concretely displayed, for the whole of his existence.

Because the areas served by missions are for the larger part rural areas, the Comprehensive Approach has come to be a significant factor particularly in agrarian communities. It has therefore received its classic formulation in a Statement entitled "The Christian Mission in Relationship to Rural Problems in Asia and in Africa" by the Jerusalem Meeting of the International Missionary Council, 1928. We quote here the introductory part of the Statement:

> The one inclusive purpose of the missionary enterprise is to present Jesus Christ to men and women the world over as their Redeemer, and to win them for entrance into the joy of His discipleship. In this endeavor we realize that man is a unity, and that his spiritual life is indivisibly rooted in all his conditions—physical, mental and social. We are therefore desirous that the program of missionary work among all peoples may be

sufficiently comprehensive to serve the whole man in every aspect of this life and relationships.

More especially we desire to bring home emphatically both to the mission boards and to the indigenous churches the necessity of a comprehensive program for those larger sections of the population in any country who labor for mankind in field or factory and who, in many parts of the world as at present ordered, are without many of the conditions necessary for that abundant life which our God and Father desires for all His children.[15]

The practical way in which this program is to be realized is "to select suitable rural centers and demonstrate in them an intensive form of work that may eventually spread over wide areas as the Church grows in power and in influence". In these centers "there should be established missionary institutions for rural education". The plan concentrates on the local community as "the natural and most effective social unit of organization for rural progress the world over". In these natural human groupings it "should be the aim of the Church to help correlate all forces in the fundamental and inclusive task of creating a real Kingdom of God. . . ."[16]

What this means for the concrete task of missions has been set forth by J. Merle Davis.

Christianity's concern is with *all of life* and with every condition of the individual and society which either restricts or supports the possibility of man's reaching the fullness of the stature of Christ and realizing His concept of the Kingdom of Heaven. . . . A practical concern for health, diet, sanitation, agricultural improvement, land tenure, home and family life, housing, education, literature, cottage industries, co-operatives, worship, evangelism, Christian stewardship and preaching are all inseparable parts of the Christian evangel. But these things must be conceived as indivisible elements of the gospel and must be *integrated* in the program of the Church.[17]

The premise underlying this conception of the missionary approach is a very basic one. It is that man's spiritual life "is indivisibly rooted in all his conditions—physical, mental and social". This statement will hardly bear close scrutiny. Had it been stated that man's spiritual life is affected by his conditions, we would agree. But it is hardly true that his spiritual life is *rooted* in his conditions. It is rooted alone in his relationship to God. It is the glory of the life of the Spirit that it *transcends* and *overcomes* conditions. In the Bible and in the history of the Church many of the finest testimonies to the power of the Christian faith are found in a setting where conditions were at a minimum—persecution, loneliness, poverty, sickness. The heroes of faith recorded in Heb. 11 did not exercise their faith under favorable conditions. Allen writes:

> . . . as a missionary from India expressed it to me the other day, it is impossible for those people in their ignorance and degradation to receive our message until they are freed from the bondage and degradation in which they are kept by their heathen overlords.
>
> That is a very serious position to adopt. It subordinates Christ to conditions. Historically, it is not true. Men in those conditions have become Christians, and very good Christians too, before the conditions of their life were changed, not only in India, but elsewhere. . . . In the mission field we need to revise our ideas of the meaning of Christian life. A Christian life is a life lived in Christ: it does not depend on conditions. I mean that the life of a slave-girl, the concubine of a savage heathen, amidst the most cruel and barbarous surroundings, herself the instrument of the most vicious and immoral practices, may be a truly Christian life. Christ transcends all conditions.[18]

It may be argued that although the premise underlying the program proposed by the Comprehensive Approach is invalid, we need not therefore discard the program. It could stand on the premise that Christ is a total Savior. One wonders, however, what becomes of the "Christian evangel" when a "practical concern" for cottage industries, co-operatives, agricultural improvements, etc., is given a place alongside of evangelism and preaching, and when the one as well as the other must be an *integral* part of the service of the Church. What relationship does this "evangel" still bear to the New Testament conception of the gospel, and to the kerugma and the witness whereby it is made known? The Church has not been charged with the reformation of social and economic conditions. She has been charged with the task of declaring the power that is in Christ, the new life which, when it lives in men, will issue in social and economic improvement. This task the Church discharges through the proclamation of the gospel. For this reason every true missionary is a walking social revolution. This is the teaching of the New Testament, and one can seek to justify the elaboration of this task into the Comprehensive Approach only by reading into the New Testament what is not there.

The gospel of which we read in the New Testament does not come to men in the form of a Comprehensive Approach, but in the form of a *comprehensive message*. The gospel is good news for the *whole* of life. The Spirit renews humanity and the natural world. He renews the life that He gave at creation. The result of His work is a new creation flowering in a new humanity, a new heaven, and a new earth. The renewal of the Spirit is cosmic. This is the message of the gospel. A more comprehensive message is not conceivable. This message, moreover, is not simply the message of a future salvation. It is the message that describes a present reality. In Christ the End is here. In Him the new creation exists. The lives of believers are taken up in the new aeon which is Christ in the Spirit. Because believers live in Christ they seek to manifest His life and live according to the norms of His kingdom. Out of this fact alone the transformation of conditions arises which can properly be described as a manifestation of the kingdom of God. Social renewal is preceded by the renewal of individuals who understand the comprehensive significance of the gospel.

In confining himself to the proclamation of *this* gospel the missionary does not stand aloof from the needs of the people he serves. On the contrary, the proclamation of the gospel, faithfully performed in relation to their life, as the missionary by careful observation and study has come to know and understand that life, is the true solution of their deepest problems. In discharging this ministry the missionary will show himself a friend and a brother of the people whom he serves. His proclamation will be supported by a confidence-inspiring life and attitude. When he has gained their confidence they will seek his counsel, and he will be able to venture counsel. A wholesome influence for social betterment can go forth from the missionary community when it shows the relevance of the gospel that has been preached to mal-conditions in their midst. The nature of their need and problems may lead missionaries to engage in one or other exemplary activity. Women missionaries especially have great opportunities here because of the more intimate contact they are able to establish with the home life of the people. But such activity is not a separate program which, outfitted with all manner of specially trained personnel, techniques and equipment, stands alongside of the ministry of the gospel. It grows out of the ministry of the gospel and is dependent for its success on the intimate personal relationships that have been established and on the hold which the gospel has on the hearts and minds of the people concerned.

The danger is never remote that many-sided missionary activity will obscure the activity of the Spirit. It endangers the very nature of the witness. It is of the essence of true Christian witness to point to Christ, but inherent in the program proposed by the Comprehensive Approach is the danger of drawing attention to the activities that are undertaken, to their techniques and results, and of making them the central object of interest. What is even more dangerous is that our new and often rather elaborate activities will overshadow and seem to make less significant than they are the evidences of the life of the Spirit in the converts as it strives to find expression in and through them. The Christians we have gained will be constantly tempted to contrast their achievements with ours and to measure their spiritual stature in terms of this contrast. In reality, the awakening life of the Spirit in them is the pearl of great price which we seek, for it is the evidence of Christ having been born in them. Similarly, the surrounding unconverted masses will be distracted from noting the small but perceptible differences in spirit and in attitude that have arisen in their converted neighbors by the attention-drawing activities of the mission in which they suppose that what Christianity "really is" comes to manifestation.

The missionary who pursues his task according to the norm of the New Testament will not consider it his immediate concern to lift the level of life in the area he serves, but to transmit the life of the Spirit through the proclamation of the gospel, and to secure the continued nourishment of this life in the service of fully constituted churches. Where this is faithfully done all else will follow and normally does follow in due course. What does not subserve this task has no place in the missionary witness of the Church. Institutional work and exemplary activities of various kinds are not excluded from the means that may be used to transmit the life of the Spirit and to bring the Church into being. But the entering upon these activities, their scope and their duration, will be determined by the need which the central service has of their help. The task of the missionary is not directly to effect the needed social, political, and economic transformations, but to bring into being a Christianity so aware of its responsibility that it will as a natural and self-evident matter identify itself with the problems that exist and contribute the Christian answer to their solution.

One further caution is prompted by the contemporary movement toward national independence in the former colonial areas, and its inevitable concomitant of the increasing independence of the younger Churches. It is a law of missionary life that as the close of missionary service in a given area approaches, the directly evangelistic personnel is the first to depart, then those who are engaged in educational, medical, and other tasks of a more technical nature. This leaves the remaining personnel without the stimulation that normally arises from the presence of colleagues who devote their lives exclusively to the direct spread of the gospel and to the building of the Church. The only way in which to maintain real relevance of their work to the essential purpose of the missionary enterprise, namely, the building of the Church, is to associate themselves as fully as possible with the growing Church, its life, its work and its witness, lest they become teachers, doctors, nurses, builders, agriculturists whose service becomes an essentially truncated missionary witness.

E. *Unity in witness*

The Church that comes into being at any given place is the child of the witness that produces her. The early Church spoke a witness that was undivided, and the Church she brought into being throughout the Roman Empire was undivided. In our day the witness of the Church is divided, and throughout the world we are bringing into being a divided Church. Here we meet a remarkable difference between the early Church and the Church of our time. Paul knew one body, one Spirit, one hope of his calling, one Lord, one faith, one baptism, one God and Father of all, Eph. 4: 4–6, whom he served as a member of the *one* Church. We know one body, one Spirit, one hope of our calling, one Lord, one faith, one baptism, one God and Father of all, whom we serve as members of *many* Churches. It would seem that we must think more frankly, more courageously, about this disparity than we have done in many sections of the Church.

We confess, "I believe a holy catholic Church". Yet we practice denominationalism. It simply will not do to deny the existence of a conflict here between confession and life on the ground that the unity of the Church which we confess is a spiritual, not a visible unity. In examining the concept of the "glory of Christ" John 17: 22, it became very evident that the unity which the glory of Christ brings into being is not only a spiritual but also, and very emphatically, a *visible* unity. It is a unity which *the world* must be able *to see*. Such a unity the early Church manifested, and the New Testament knows no other Church than a Church which lives in *this* unity. Incipient divisions that threatened the unity of the Church met the severest opposition of the apostles. Nowhere does the New Testament devaluate the *visible* unity of the Church. It assumes it everywhere and protects it where it is threatened. Moreover, the *Apostolicum* was not first confessed in or after the 16th century, but it was in substance confessed by the Church of the first centuries when the Church as yet knew nothing of denominationalism. Doubtless none would be more surprised to hear that the confession of the one Church had reference only to spiritual unity than a Christian of the second or third century. He would say to us: you confess your faith in the same words with which we confessed ours, but you no longer mean as much as we meant when we spoke those words.

We have therefore no right to say: the ecumenical question confronts us with the dilemma: confessional truth or ecclesiastical unity. This dilemma is not legitimate because ecclesiastical unity *is a part* of the confessional truth to which we hold, or should hold.

We must further note that there are clearly discernible in the ecclesiastical world of our time four factors that stand in the way of a united witness. These are: (*a*) non-theological elements such as the cultural and historical background of the Churches, (*b*) credal differences, (*c*) differences in church polity and liturgy, (*d*) differences that affect the very nature of the Christian faith. This last factor first calls for attention.

There are many Christians on whom the ecumenical movement, particularly as it comes to expression in the World Council of Churches, has made a great impression. They see in it a groping toward a recovery of lost glory and a testimony concerning the one body of the one Savior in the midst of a tragically broken world. But they also see that in this movement men are given positions of influence and are allowed to be spokesmen who openly call into question central beliefs in the Christian faith. By "central beliefs" we do not have reference primarily to such questions as the precise manner in which the creation account is to be understood, or to problems of biblical criticism. All Christian circles that are refreshed by scholarly alertness recognize that there are problems here. By the "central beliefs" we refer especially to the doctrine concerning the person and work of Christ. Here, too, difference of opinion is possible with respect to certain aspects from which the person and work of Christ may be viewed. But there is *no* room for a difference of opinion with respect to the reality of Christ's atonement, His physical resurrection from the dead and His return to judge the world at the end of time. When these things are denied or called into question the gospel is denied. It is not possible for the Spirit of Pentecost to transmit His life through a witness that implicitly or explicitly denies that His own life is real. To speak of a life of the Spirit apart from the crucified and physically risen Lord is an unqualified contradiction in terms. That is to say, it is an unqualified contradiction in terms if there is any concern to base our witness on the testimony of the New Testament.

There are many Christian leaders who would support such bodies as National Christian Councils, the International Missionary Council, and the World Council of Churches if they would first "cast out" the liberals from their ranks. In this way, they feel, a united witness at home and especially on the mission field would be measurably advanced. It is open to serious question whether this is the most fruitful attitude to take to the problem of unbelief in the ecumenical movement. It shows too little understanding of the responsibility which conservatives themselves have for the existence of liberal Protestantism. There are conservative denominations that have come into being as a result of a liberal-conservative controversy which, after the separation, have shown very little, if any, concern for the spiritual welfare of the body with which they were formerly united. Where the separation was of a wholly voluntary nature it must indeed be questioned whether it was justified at all. When liberalism in the parent body is thus given still freer rein to develop, the new denomination mistakenly assumes that it is without responsibility for this. Instead of viewing the further development as something that it might have prevented or limited it regards it as an added justification for its separation.

Moreover, the ecumenical bodies mentioned are composed not of so many individuals but of Churches and/or organizations. Whatever may be said of particular leaders in these Churches or organizations, it would be hazardous to say that the bodies which they represent stand outside the Christian circle. The Church does not consist of ministers, professors, and board secretaries, but of the body of believers. Though Christians are not spiritually one with individuals who deny or question truths without which the gospel is not the gospel, are they therefore not one with the entirety of the body or bodies out of which these individuals come? This question must certainly be faced when it is refused to place these bodies outside the Christian pale. And if there is a spiritual solidarity here, why should it not come to some sort of organizational expression? The undeniable attractiveness of the World Council of Churches is that it offers an opportunity for such expression on a world scale.

It would seem, therefore, that the real criticism that is to be made by conservatives of such a body as the World Council of Churches is not in the first place that liberals have seats in its official assemblies. Its failing is that it does not unambiguously affirm the essentials of the Christian faith. We say "unambiguously" advisedly. The message of Evanston to the Churches and to the world is a message that evangelicals can heartily subscribe. But when it is remembered that influential voices in the World Council of Churches have a wholly this-worldly conception of the Christian hope, and have openly and often

247

pleaded for it, the absence of a rejection of this view in explicit statement leaves the impression that it is a tolerated conception. We are not here concerned with two emphases of the same hope. The hope that Christians have in Christ for this life roots in the fact that Christ is already now in the eschatological glory. But it is precisely for *this* Christ that liberalism has little appreciation.

Evanston has shown that American liberal theology finds little acceptance by the Church in the world. It has given many American Churches represented in the World Council seriously to think. What good reason can be adduced why conservative Churches everywhere should not join the World Council of Churches and strengthen the hands of that clear majority in the World Council which has sent a thoroughly biblical message into the world?

The other three factors, namely, the non-theological, credal, and governmental-liturgical, that stand in the way of a witness in unity, or of a measurable approach to it, all exist within the framework of a commonly held Christian faith. For this reason they are resolvable. We who have these differences are in Christ. In Him we are one. Perhaps we shall advance farther on the road of ecumenical co-operation and to various concrete expressions of unity in witness if we will begin with the fact of our unity in Christ while not being blind to the things that divide, rather than begin with the fact of our divisions while not being blind to the unity that we have in Christ. We shall then perhaps more quickly arrive at an understanding of the incongruity that exists between our confessed spiritual communion and the brokenness of our external communion. Roland Allen has in this connection spoken a significant word:

All who receive the Spirit are in reality and truth one. They are united by the strongest and most intimate of ties. They are all united to Christ by His Spirit, and therefore they are all united to one another. Men may separate them, systems may part them from the enjoyment and strength of their unity; but, if they share the one Spirit, they are one.[19]

The difficulty today is that Christians acknowledge that others have the Spirit, and yet do not recognize that they ought to be, and must be, because spiritually they are, in communion with one another. Men who hold a theory of the Church which excludes from communion those whom they admit to have the Spirit of Christ simply proclaim that their theory is in flat contradiction to the spiritual fact. Their theory separates those whom the Spirit unites.[20]

If men believe in the existence of this unity, they may begin to desire it, and desiring it to seek for it, and seeking to find it. If, when they find it, they refuse to deny it, in due time, by ways now unsearchable, they will surely return to external communion.[20]

We are, of course, specifically concerned with the expression of this unity in missionary witness and consequently with its ultimate expression in an ecclesiastical situation of spiritual and external unity among the younger Churches. The question that must therefore frankly be faced here is: Do we contribute to the progress and eventual conquest of the gospel by burdening the new-born Christians with our historically risen divisions? Surely a Christianity that is divided into scores of confessional and governmental groupings which all stand more or less apart from each other is wrong *somewhere*. Must we bring *this* Christianity, which is *unquestionably* wrong *somewhere*, to the mission field?

It is, of course, possible for each Church to say that she is right, or as nearly right as it is possible for a Church to be in this imperfect world, and that all others, whatever their merits, stand on a lower level in the scale of truth, and that therefore unity is dependent upon the acceptance by others of *her* position. When every Church says this about herself and about other Churches an impasse has clearly been reached that can be resolved only at the last trump when the Lord himself will put our folly to nought. For folly it is, and folly that appears nowhere so foolish as on the mission field. Recently a Dutch director of missions visited Indonesia where, in the course of his travels, he came to a village of a few hundred people, the greater part of whom were pagan, in which he found three Reformed churches. Two of these represented denominations found in the homeland, and the third was a splinter group from one of these. He acquainted the Church at home with this discovery through an article in which he quite appropriately stated that he had "met the devil". This is an extreme example, but it must be admitted that what has happened in one village in Indonesia has in a less noticeable but on a vastly larger scale happened on most of the mission fields of the world.

A true attempt to resolve the divisions of Protestantism ought not to begin by doubting the validity of one's own confession, but by calling into serious question the legitimacy of existing divisions, and by recognizing the unity that Christians have in Christ. It is wholly conceivable that some of the things that now divide will be recognized as not having right to credal standing and must therefore be left to private judgment. It is also conceivable that when we meet each other in the unity that we have, and in the doubts that we ought to have, a finding of each other on more fundamental matters will take place, as Roland Allen has suggested, "by ways now unsearchable". This cannot, of course, be achieved by a churchmanship that refuses to acknowledge that external unity is a demand of Christ. Such a leadership, however, quenches the Spirit of the glory of Christ who has been given to the Church. For this Spirit has been given that the Church may be one, that *the world may know* that Christ is the Sent One of the Father.

There is no area in the life of the Church where the possibilities of realizing this unity are greater than on the mission field. Among missionaries of different denominations there is usually a greater degree of co-operation than there is between their respective Churches at home; and where, among the younger Churches, traditions of the western Churches have taken root they are not yet so firmly rooted that a growing together belongs to the realm of possibilities that lie wholly beyond the range of present horizons.

Any effort to bring into being a more united missionary witness will do well to remember that *it is the central task of missions to be instrumental in transmitting the life of the Spirit to those who do not yet enjoy it.* The transmission of this life must be sharply distinguished from all other transmissions that are bound to accompany the proclamation of the gospel by men of one milieu to men of another. This distinction must not fail to recognize, however, and to recognize seriously, that Christ nowhere exists as an abstraction. He comes to expression in concrete men and women, living their lives in concrete, historically and theologically conditioned Churches, all of which have been led to confess Christ in a particular manner. This particularity, moreover, comes to expression not only in creeds and church-polity and liturgy, but also in attitudes and mentalities, both of which are very real, however unmeasurable and intangible they often may be. It is not possible for missionaries not to carry this theological, ecclesiastical and spiritual framework with them, nor to prevent it from influencing their presentation of Christ to men in greater or less degree. Missionaries who do not take theological and ecclesiastical commitments seriously are not, in this respect, in a more favorable situation than those who do, for it means that they do not take seriously two important forms through which they have grown in Christ, or it means that they come out of Christian circles that have not seriously concerned themselves with the fullness of the revelation given in scripture. In either case they are impoverished by their indifference and this cannot fail to be reflected in the ministry they render.

The answer to the problem of how to transmit the life of the Spirit without imposing the forms wherein this life has flowed to us does not lie in being indifferent to these forms. It lies, rather, in distinguishing carefully between the life of the Spirit and the particular frameworks in which it has been ministered to us. It lies, further, in recognizing the cultural, religious and social backgrounds of those to whom we minister the life of the Spirit. Where these distinctions are made and these recognitions exist, the way is open for the creation of a *new* framework, neither wholly ours, nor wholly theirs, wherein the Spirit can most effectively transmit His life and wherein the new Christian community can most effectively express its own genius. This new framework will not be the creation of the missionaries alone, nor will it be the creation of the young Church alone. It will be the result of a *common effort*, for the missionary will recognize that men who have the life of the Spirit working in them ought to express it in terms of their own personality and backgrounds, and those who have newly come to Christ cannot be indifferent to the experience and insight of the Church which has ministered Christ to them. When the missionary so views his part of the task in giving stature to Christ in non-Christian areas he will realize that there are many elements in his background which those whom he serves cannot profitably use, because they are wholly strange to the long history and theological discussion that have made those elements meaningful for him. He will therefore feel constrained to make the limiting of himself an essential part of the giving of himself. He will doubtless discover that the limiting of himself is the most difficult part of giving himself unreservedly.

An unavoidable by-product of this self-limitation of the missionary will be a de-emphasizing of denominational differences. A de-emphasizing of denominational differences, however, does not of itself bring unity in witness into being. True unity does not arise out of whittled-down differences but out of a united, commonly held aim. Since the common effort that engages the witness of the Church focuses on the bringing into being of new Christian communities, it is in terms of *this* aim that the unity in witness can best come to expression. That is to say, the unity in witness is best expressed not so much by the establishing of a common missionary program and message, which would probably be an artificial undertaking, but more indirectly by unitedly facilitating the achieving of true unity among churches served by diverse missionary agencies. Here it is necessary to see what the transmission of the Spirit means in its broadest dimensions.

The missionary is in his very nature a passing figure. He goes to return, he comes to depart. He mediates a birth, and when that has been done his work approaches its end. He has the task of transmitting a life that will develop without him. In effecting this transmission the missionary will be concerned with more than he can give directly. A very necessary part of his work is to help create conditions that will enable the Christians and the Church which they constitute to share the Spirit with others, both in giving and receiving. This means the opening of the doors to as large a measure of Christian fellowship and service as possible. It means the fostering of a truly ecumenical situation where this does not now exist, it means a striving from ecumenicity to ecclesiastical unity in every area where this can fruitfully be done. This effort flows from the confession, "I believe in the Holy Spirit, I believe in a holy, catholic Church".

It is by no means inconceivable that a larger self-limitation on the part of the sending Churches as they come to expression in the missionary community, and a larger effort to create avenues of communion between the younger Churches, will bring into being a more united and creative Christianity than we of the West have so far been able to foster among them. Far from endeavoring to duplicate the divided Christianity of the West in Africa, in the Orient, in South America and in the islands of the sea, we should strive that the Churches in these areas may not fall into the sins of the parents, but that they may present to future generations a greater manifestation of the glory of Christ in their ordered and united Christian witness and life than we have.

This task urgently requires renewed reflection on the meaning of the Holy Spirit for the missionary proclamation of the

Church. He it is who bears the witness of the Church, His is the life that her witness transmits, His the communion that unites the saints, His the unity that makes the Church one. For He is the life of the new creation, He is the power of the new aeon, He is the glory of Christ. This is the Spirit who was given to the Church at Pentecost. This is the Spirit who prosecutes His witness, powerful yet gentle, in ways manifest and hidden, in all places and through all times, until every tongue shall confess that Jesus Christ is Lord to the glory of God the Father.

Notes

CHAPTER I

1. Reprinted in facsimile from the edition of 1792, London, 1891.
2. *Institutes of the Christian Religion*, Book IV, Chapter 3, paragraphs 4 and 5.
3. *D. Martin Luthers Werke*, kritische Gesammtausgabe, Weimar, 1897, Vol. 31, pp. 210 and 211. Luther manifests a vigorous missionary vision in terms of gradual extension and personal witness. When one reads Luther on this subject it is difficult to believe that he would not have acted more sympathetically than did later Lutheran theologians to pleas made on behalf of missions.
4. *Dr. Martin Luthers sämmtliche Werke*, Erlangen Ausgabe, 1846, Vol. 12, p. 193.
5. M. Bucer, *Von der waren Seelsorge*, Straszburg, 1538, p. 46.
6. A. Saravia, *De Diversis Ministrorum Evangelii Gradibus, sicut a Domino fuerunt instituti, et traditi ab Apostolis, ac perpetuo omnium Ecclesiarum usu confirmati*, London, 1590, cf. pp. 37–39.
7. Joh. Gerhard, *Loci Theologici*, Lipsiae, 1885, Locus XXIII, Cap. V, par. 220, p. 145.
8. Quoted from W. Gröszel, *Justinianus von Welz, der Vorkämpfer der lutherischen Mission*, Leipzig, 1891, pp. 78–79.
9. A. Fuller, *The Gospel Worthy of all Acceptation*, 2nd ed., Clipstone, 1801, p. 35.
10. A. Fuller, *ibid.*, pp. xv–xvi.
11. George Smith, *Life of William Carey*, London, 1885, p. 48.
12. William Ellis, *History of the London Missionary Society*, London, 1844, Vol. I, p. 13.
13. William Ellis, *ibid.*, p. 25.
14. Eugene Stock, *History of the Church Missionary Society*, London, 1899, Vol. I, pp. 3–5.
15. William Knight, *Memoir of Henry Venn*, 2nd ed., London, 1882, p. 398.
16. Richard Lovett, *James Gilmour of Mongolia*, 4th ed., London, n.d., pp. 42, 43.
17. John R. Mott, *The Evangelization of the World in this Generation*, London, 1900, p. 5.
18. Gustav Warneck, *Evangelische Missionslehre*, 2nd ed., Gotha, 1897, Vol. I, p. 91. (E.T. *Outline of History of Protestant Missions*, London, 1901.)
19. Johann Warneck, *Paulus im Lichte der heutigen Heidenmission*, Berlin, 1914, p. 16.
20. J. Van Den Berge in his dissertation (Free University, Amsterdam), *Constrained by Jesus' Love*, Kampen, 1956, makes a fair comment when he observes about this part of my thesis that the missionary command "was never the one and only motive", and that it was "closely integrated with motives of love and expectance", p. 165. However, Dr. Van Den Berge himself notes here and in other places that it was the Great Commission which often occasioned and provided integration for the urging of other motivations.

CHAPTER 2

1. Nikolaus Adler, *Das erste christliche Pfingstfest*, Münster i. W., 1938, p. 133.
2. M. Meinertz, *Jesus und die Heidenmission*, Münster i. W., 1925, p. 196.
3. G. Warneck, *op. cit.*, pp. 184, 185.

4. O. Pfleiderer, *Das Urchristentum*, 2nd and enlarged ed., Berlin, 1902, Vol. I, p. 493. (E.T. *Primitive Christianity*, London, 1909.)
5. K. F. Nösgen, *Kommentar über die Apostelgeschichte des Lukas*, Leipzig, 1882, p. 108.
6. Th. Zahn, *Die Apostelgeschichte des Lukas*, Leipzig-Erlangen, 1922, p. 363.
7. A. Wikenhauser, *Die Apostelgeschichte und ihr Geschichtswert*, Münster i. W., 1921, p. 277.

CHAPTER 3

1. Roland Allen, "The Revelation of the Holy Spirit in the Acts of the Apostles", *International Review of Missions*, Vol. VII, April, 1918, p. 162.
2. Roland Allen, *ibid.*, p. 162.
3. Eucherius of Lyons, *Instructionum ad Salonium*, Liber I, J. P. Migne, *Patrol. Lat.*, Vol. 50, p. 809.
4. *The Commentaries of Isho'dad of Merv*, edited and translated by Margaret Dunlop Gibson, Vol. IV, No. X, in *Horae Semiticae*, Cambridge University Press, 1913, p. 9.
5. Theophylactus, *Expositio in Acta Apostolorum*, J. P. Migne, *Patrol. Gr.*, Vol. 125, p. 533.
6. John Calvin, *Commentary on the Acts of the Apostles*, on chapter 2: 2, 3, 4.
7. Martin Luther, *Episteln Auslegung*, Stuttgart, 1866, pp. 9, 10.
8. Benedicto Aretio, *Commentarii in Sacram Actuum Apostolicorum Historiam*, Berne, 1607, p. 22.
9. Joannis Lorinie, *In Actus Apostolorum Commentaria*, Coloniae Agrippinae, 1609, p. 85.
10. Liberto Fromondo, *Actus Apostolorum Commentaria*, Louvain, 1654, p. 47.
11. Ed. Zeller, *Die Apostelgeschichte*, Stuttgart, 1854, p. 84.
12. Alexander Duff, *India and India Missions*, Edinburgh, 1840, p. 378.
13. K. F. Nösgen, *Der Heilige Geist, sein Wesen und die Art seines Wirkens*, Berlin, 1905, note 27, p. 133.
14. Adolf Harnack, *Beiträge zur Einleitung in das Neue Testament*, Vol. III, *Die Apostelgeschichte*, Leipzig, 1908, pp. 4ff. (E.T. *New Testament Studies*, III, *The Acts of the Apostles*, London, 1908.)
15. Ed. Zeller, *op. cit.*, pp. 97ff.
16. O. Pfleiderer, *Das Urchristentum*, 2nd ed., Berlin, 1902, Vol. I, p. 478. (E.T. *Primitive Christianity*, London, 1909.)
17. Joh. Weiss, *Ueber die Absicht und den literarischen Charakter der Apostelgeschichte*, Marburg, 1897, p. 56.
18. K. L. Schmidt, *Die Pfingsterzählung und das Pfingstereignis*, Leipzig, 1919.
19. Adolf Harnack, *op. cit.*, *Einleitung*.
20. F. J. Foakes Jackson and Kirsopp Lake, *The Acts of the Apostles*, Vol. I of Part I of *The Beginnings of Christianity*, London, 1920, pp. 322, 323, 328.
21. Richard B. Rackham, *The Acts of the Apostles*, 14th ed., London, 1951, p. 19.
22. F. F. Bruce, *Commentary on the Book of the Acts*, Grand Rapids, 1956, and London, p. 58.
23. H. L. Strack and Paul Billerbeck, *Kommentar zum Neuen Testament aus Talmud und Midrasch*, Munich, 1924, pp. 604, 605.
24. Cf. Preface.
25. Albert von Ostertag, *Uebersichtliche Geschichte der protestantische Missionen von der Reformation bis zur Gegenwart*, Stuttgart, 1858, p. 4.
26. John R. Mott, *The Decisive Hour of Christian Missions*, London and New York, 1910, p. 193.
27. F. W. Dillistone, "The Dispensation of the Spirit", in *Missions Under the Cross*, IMC, London, 1953, pp. 81–92.
28. H. Kraemer, *Kerk en Zending*, The Hague, 1936, pp. 24–27.

256

NOTES

CHAPTER 4

1. *Weimar Ausgabe*, Vol. 5, p. 367.
2. *Commentary on Genesis*, chapter 1: 2.
3. Genesis 41: 38; Exodus 28: 3; 31: 3; 35: 31; Numbers 11: 17; 27: 18.
4. Numbers 27: 18; Judges 3: 10; 11: 29; 13: 25; Deut. 34: 9; 1 Sam. 16: 13, 14.
5. Numbers 11: 25, 26, 29; 1 Sam. 10: 6–10; 2 Sam. 23: 2; 1 Kings 22: 24; Nehemiah 9: 20, 30; Isa. 48: 16; Micah 3: 8.
6. W. Eichrodt, *Theologie des Alten Testaments*, Leipzig, 1935, Part 2, p. 26. (E.T. *Theology of the Old Testament*, London, 1960.)
7. Otto Procksch, *Theologie des Alten Testaments*, Gütersloh, 1950, p. 468.
8. K. Bornhäuser, *Studien zur Apostelgeschichte*, Gütersloh, 1934, p. 11.
9. Matthew 1: 18, 20; Luke 1: 35, 41; 2: 25–27.
10. Matthew 3: 11; Mark 1: 8; Luke 3: 16; John 1: 33.
11. Matthew 3: 16; Mark 1: 10; Luke 3: 22; John 1: 32.
12. Matthew 4: 1; Mark 1: 12; Luke 4: 1, 14.
13. Matthew 16: 21; Mark 10: 23ff.; Luke 9: 44, 45; John 13: 7; 16: 16.
14. Luke 24: 49; John 7: 39; 14: 17, 26; 15: 26; 16: 13; Acts 1: 8.

CHAPTER 5

1. F. Büchsel, *Der Geist Gottes im Neuen Testament*, Gütersloh, 1926, p. 469.
2. H. Bavinck, *Gereformeerde Dogmatiek*, Kampen, 1910, Vol. III, p. 566; Vol. IV, p. 300.
3. H. B. Swete, *The Holy Spirit in the New Testament*, London, 1916, p. 7.
4. *Ibid.*, p. 21.
5. Karl Barth, *Kirchliche Dogmatik*, Munich, 1932, I/1, pp. 474, 475. (E.T. *Church Dogmatics*, Edinburgh.)
6. G. Vos, "The Eschatological Aspect of the Pauline Conception of the Spirit", in *Biblical and Theological Studies*, by members of the Faculty of Princeton Theological Seminary, New York, 1912, p. 239.
7. *Ibid.*, p. 237.
8. *Ibid.*, p. 227.
9. *The Works of John Owen*, ed. by Wm. H. Goold, Edinburgh, 1852, Vol. IV, p. 407.
10. G. Vos, *op. cit.*, pp. 159, 160.
11. Acts 2: 17; 2 Timothy 3: 1; Hebrews 1: 2; 1 Peter 1: 20; 2 Peter 3: 3; 1 John 2: 18; Jude 18.

CHAPTER 6

1. Roland Allen and Sydney James Wells Clark, *A Vision of Foreign Missions*, London, 1937, p. 132.
2. Karl Barth, *K.D.*, I/1, p. 478.
3. H. L. Strack and Paul Billerbeck, *Kommentar zum Neuen Testament aus Talmud und Midrasch*, Munich, 1924, Vol. II, pp. 560, 561.
4. C. K. Barrett, "The Holy Spirit in the Fourth Gospel", in *The Journal of Theological Studies*, April, 1950.
5. O. Schmitz, in *Theologisches Wörterbuch zum Neuen Testament*, Stuttgart, 1954, Vol. V, p. 792.
6. C. K. Barrett, *op. cit.*, p. 14.
7. *Ibid.*, p. 12.
8. A. Wikenhauser, *Die Apostelgeschichte und ihr Geschictswert*, Münster i. W., 1921, p. 15.
9. *Ibid.*, p. 26.

R

10. G. Wingren, *Evangelische Missions Magazin*, 1947, p. 145.
11. I Corinthians 10: 4; 12: 13; Galatians 5: 6; 6: 15; Colossians 3: 11.
12. A. Harnack, *Lehrbuch der Dogmengeschichte*, 3rd ed., Leipzig, 1894, Vol. I, p. 205. (E.T. *History of Dogma*, London, 1895.)
13. H. Strathmann, in *Theologisches Wörterbuch zum Neuen Testament*, Stuttgart, 1942, Vol. IV, p. 505.
14. K. Barth, *Auslegung von Matthäus 28: 16–20*, Basel, 1945, p. 8.
15. Robert E. Speer, *Missionary Principles and Practice*, New York, 1902, pp. 9, 10.
16. See especially the excellent treatment of this subject in the booklet by Oscar Cullmann, "Die ersten christlichen Glaubensbekenntnisse", Heft 15 in *Theologische Studien*, Zürich, 1943. (E.T. *The Earliest Christian Confessions*, London, 1949.)
17. Jerome on Psalm 17, J. P. Migne, *Patrol. Lat.*, Vol. 26, p. 863.

CHAPTER 7

1. Roland Allen, *Pentecost and the World*, Oxford, 1917, pp. 42, 43.
2. W. Michaelis, "Geist Gottes und Mission nach dem Neuen Testament", *Evangelisches Missions Magazin*, 1932, pp. 7, 8.
3. G. Warneck, *Evangelische Missionslehre*, 2nd ed., Gotha, 1897, Vol. I, pp. 135–57. (E.T. *Outline of History of Protestant Missions*, London, 1901.)
4. Johannes Dürr, *Sendende und Werdende Kirche in der Missionstheologie Gustav Warnecks*, Basel, 1947, p. 52.
5. *Op. cit.*, p. 53.
6. "Mission and Eschatology", *Ecumenical Review*, January 1954, pp. 149–50.
7. Oscar Cullmann in *Christ and Time* (E.T., 1951), p. 82; and G. Vos, *The Pauline Eschatology*, Princeton, 1930, p. 38.
8. *K.D.* IV/1, pp. 810, 811.

CHAPTER 8

1. *Op. cit.*, p. 55.
2. Roland Allen, *Pentecost and the World*, London, 1917, pp. 39–41.
3. Dissertation, University of Utrecht, 1948.
4. Cf. Otto Raum, "Dr. Gutman's Theories on the Kilimanjaro", *International Review of Missions*, 1934, p. 504.
5. Gustav Warneck, *op. cit.*, Vol. III, pp. 249–60.
6. H. Kraemer, *The Christian Message in a Non-Christian World*, London, 1938; J. Merle Davis, *New Buildings on Old Foundations*, New York, 1945.
7. Cf. especially O. Michel in *Theologisches Wörterbuch zum Neuen Testament*, Vol. V, 1954, p. 133.
8. Reported especially in his *Christian Mass Movements in India*, Cincinnati, 1938.
9. D. A. McGavran, *The Bridges of God. A Study in the Strategy of Missions*, London, 1955, p. 1.
10. *Ibid.*, p. 9.
11. *Ibid.*, p. 18.
12. *Ibid.*, pp. 21, 22.
13. *Ibid.*, p. 11.

CHAPTER 9

1. W. R. Hogg, *Ecumenical Foundations*, New York, 1952.
2. In G. Kittel, *Theologisches Wörterbuch zum Neuen Testament*, Vol. II, pp. 236–38.
3. G. von Rad, *ibid.*, Vol. II, p. 240. Cf. also R. H. Strachan, *The Fourth Gospel*, 3rd ed. (n.d.), pp. 103, 104 (1st ed. published 1941).

4. Exodus 16: 9–12; 24: 15–18; 29: 43; 40: 34, 35; Leviticus 9: 6, 24; Numbers 14: 10; 16: 19–20.
5. Cf. texts in Note 4 above.
6. Cf. Helmuth Kittel, *Die Herrlichkeit Gottes*, Gieszen, 1934, p. 162, and G. Kittel, *op. cit.*, p. 248.
7. The eschatological perspective of the *kabod Yahweh* is also suggested by a number of Psalms: 72: 19; 96: 3; 102: 15, 16; 138: 4, 5.
8. Matthew 19: 28; 24: 30; 25: 31; Mark 13: 26.
9. Matthew 16: 27; Mark 8: 38.
10. Cf. G. Kittel, *op. cit.*, pp. 251, 252.
11. In the Apocalypse *doxa* is chiefly referred to God. In so far as it refers to Christ it is related to His eschatological glory.
12. The entire prayer is permeated with the idea of future reality as present fact: vv. 4, 11, 12, 13, 18, 22, 24.
13. G. Vos, *Biblical and Theological Studies* by members of the Faculty of Princeton Theological Seminary, New York, 1912, p. 234.
14. Cf. R. B. Lloyd, "The Word 'Glory' in the Fourth Gospel", *The Expository Times*, 1932, p. 547; R. H. Strachan, *op. cit.*, p. 106.
15. Cf. R. Kabisch, *Die Eschatologie des Paulus*, Göttingen, 1893, pp. 206, 208; C. F. Heinrici, *Das Zweite Sendschreiben des Apostel Paulus an die Korinther*, Berlin, 1887, pp. 170–73.
16. Cf. Luke 1: 35; 4: 14; 24: 49; Acts 1: 8; 10: 38; Romans 15: 13; 1 Corinthians 2: 4; Galatians 3: 5; 1 Thessalonians 1: 5.

CHAPTER 10

1. John R. Mott, *The Decisive Hour of Christian Missions*, London and New York, 1910, p. 193.
2. Roland Allen, *Educational Principles and Missionary Methods*, London, 1919, pp. 41, 42.
3. Roland Allen, *The Spontaneous Expansion of the Church*, London, 2nd ed., 1949, pp. 131, 132.
4. *Ibid.*, p. 132.
5. *Ibid.*, p. 161.
6. Roland Allen, *Missionary Principles*, London, 1913, pp. 24, 25.
7. *Ibid.*, pp. 41, 43, 44.
8. Lesslie Newbigin, *The Household of God*, New York, 1954 (London 1953), p. 104.
9. David M. Paton, *Christian Missions and the Judgment of God*, London, 1953, pp. 38, 39. It must be observed that Paton considers this picture "doubtless somewhat overdrawn for emphasis". So far as his own experience in association with two hospitals and a college is concerned, however, he cannot feel that the overall picture he gives is more than a "modest exaggeration of the real truth" (p. 40).
10. Roland Allen, *Mission Activities Considered in Relation to the Manifestation of the Spirit*, London, n.d., p. 32.
11. Ralph A. Ward, "Do Institutions Ruin Missions?" *Christian Century*, November 14, 1951, pp. 1306, 1307.
12. Theodore F. Romig, "The Missionary at an Era's End", *Christian Century*, December 5, 1951, p. 1402.
13. Ralph A. Ward, *op. cit.*, p. 1307.
14. David M. Paton, *op. cit.*, p. 40.

15. Jerusalem Meeting of the International Missionary Council, 1928, Vol. VI, p. 287.
16. *Ibid.*, pp. 288, 289.
17. J. Merle Davis, "The Comprehensive Ministry to Community Needs" in *The Challenge of Communism to Christianity*, New York, 1948. Quoted from J. C. Hoekendijk, *op. cit.*, p. 278.
18. Roland Allen, *The Spontaneous Expansion of the Church*, p. 112.
19. Roland Allen, *Pentecost and the World*, Oxford University Press, 1917, p. 85.
20. *Ibid.*, p. 87.

Indexes

Index of Authors

ADLER, N., 28, 53, 54, 57, 58
Allen, R., 48, 61, 63, 64, 99, 136, 163, 210 ff.
Andriessen, A., 52
Aretio, B., 51
Ashmore, W., 26

BALJON, J., 57
Barrett, C. K., 105-107
Barth, K., 86, 103 (note), 122, 138, 153
Baur, F. C., 55
Bavinck, H., 78
Bavinck, J. H., 13, 60, 61, 187
Bennett, J., 233
Bornhäuser, K., 70
Bruce, F. F. 57, 58
Bucer, M., 20
Büchsel, F., 78
Bugenhagen, J., 20

CALVIN, J., 18, 19, 23, 51, 66
Carey, W., 16, 17, 18, 22, 23, 27, 221
Chrysostom, 50
Clark, S. J., 99
Cullmann, O., 67, 94, 126 (note), 144, 151 (note)

DAUBANTON, F. E., 63
Davis, M., 174, 239
Dibelius, M. 33
Dillistone, F. W., 61
Duff, A., 52, 53
Dürr, J., 142, 163

EICHRODT, W., 69
Ellis, W., 26
Eucherius of Lyons, 50

FOAKES-JACKSON, F. J., 56
Fromondo, L. 52
Fuller, A., 23

GERHARDUS, J., 21, 52
Grosheide, F. W., 57
Gröszel, W., 22
Grotius, H., 52
Gutmann, B., 170

HARNACK, A., 28, 54, 56, 114, 139, 141, 142
Haweis, T., 25
Heinrici, C. F., 198 (note)
Hoekendijk, J. C., 168, 169, 174-176
Hogg, W. R., 186 (note)
Horne, M. 25

ISHO'DAD OF MERV, 50

JEROME, 131
Jochanan, Rabbi, 58
Judson, A., 26

KABISCH, R., 198 (note)
Kraemer, H., 62, 174
Kuyper, A., 57

LAKE, K., 56
Lawes, W. G., 26
Lechler, G. V., 57
van Limborch, Ph., 52
Lorinie, J., 52
Luther, M., 19, 20, 21, 51, 66

McGAVRAN, D. A., 168, 179-185
Meinertz, M., 28, 29
Melanchthon, Ph., 20
Michaelis, W., 139
Morrison, R., 26
Mott, J., 26, 60, 206

NELSON, R. A., 149
Newbigin, L., 225
Nösgen, K. F., 39, 53, 57

VON OSTERTAG, A., 59
Owen, J., 92

PATON, D. M., 231 (note), 234
Pfleiderer, O., 33, 55
Plevier, J., 52
Procksch, O., 70

RACKHAM, R. B., 57
Richter, J., 63
Romig, T. F., 234 (note)

Saravia, A., 20, 21
Schmidlin, J., 63
Schmidt, K. L., 56
Schmitz, O., 106 (note)
Smith, G., 24 (note)
Speer, R. E., 123
Steinmann, A., 57
Stock, E., 25
Strachan, R. H., 190 (note), 196 (note)
Strack, H. L. and Billerbeck, P., 58 (note), 105 (note)
Strathmann, H., 116 (note).
Swete, H. B., 78, 85

Theophylact, 50

Van Den Berge, J., 27 (note)

Venn, J., 25
Vos, G., 87 (note), 90, 92 (note), 94, 151 (note), 195

Ward, R. A., 233 (note), 234
Warneck, G., 26, 29-32, 36, 40, 44, 46, 63, 123, 139-142, 169-173, 183
Warneck, J., 26
Weiss, J., 55
von Welz, J., 21, 22, 24
Wikenhauser, A., 42, 57, 109
Wingren, G., 113 (note)

Zahn, Th., 41, 54, 57
Zeller, E., 32, 52, 55
Zinzendorff, N. L., 170
Zwingli, U., 20

Index of Bible Passages

GENESIS

Chapter	Verse	Page
1	1	124
	2	66
	28	120
9	1ff.	121
11	1ff.	137
12	3	66, 68
13	2	190
41	38	69 (note 3)
45	13	190

EXODUS

Chapter	Verse	Page
16	9ff.	190 (note 4)
24	15ff.	190 (note 4)
28	3	69 (note 3)
29	43	190 (note 4)
31	3	69 (note 3)
33	17ff.	190
35	31	69 (note 3)
40	34ff.	190 (note 4)

LEVITICUS

Chapter	Verse	Page
9	6, 24	190 (note 4)

NUMBERS

Chapter	Verse	Page
2	28	117
11	17	69 (note 3)
	25ff.	69 (note 5)
	39	117
14	10	190 (note 4)
16	19ff.	190 (note 4)
27	18	69 (note 4)
44	5	117
59	21	117

DEUTERONOMY

Chapter	Verse	Page
34	9	69 (note 4)

JUDGES

Chapter	Verse	Page
3	10	69 (note 4)
11	29	,,
13	25	,,

1 SAMUEL

Chapter	Verse	Page
10	6ff.	69 (note 5)
16	13ff.	69 (note 4)

2 SAMUEL

Chapter	Verse	Page
23	2	69 (note 5)

1 KINGS

Chapter	Verse	Page
22	24	69 (note 5)

NEHEMIAH

Chapter	Verse	Page
9	20	69 (note 5)
	30	69 (note 5)

JOB

Chapter	Verse	Page
33	4	66

PSALMS

Chapter	Verse	Page
33	6	66
51	11	70
	11ff.	70
72	19	192 (note 7)
96	3	192 (note 7)
102	15ff.	192 (note 7)
118	23	158
138	4ff.	192 (note 7)

ISAIAH

Chapter	Verse	Page
2	2	157
16	14	190
17	4	190
21	16	190
40	1	106
	4ff.	192
48	16	69 (note 5)
57	19	37
59	19	191
60	1ff.	192
63	11	70
66	18	192

EZEKIEL

Chapter	Verse	Page
2	2	191
11	19	77
36	27	77

JOEL

Chapter	Verse	Page
2	28	77
	28ff.	77
	32	37

MICAH

Chapter	Verse	Page
3	8	69 (note 5)

HAGGAI

Chapter	Verse	Page
1	14	70
2	5	70

ST. MATTHEW

Chapter	Verse	Page
1	18ff.	71 (note 9)
3	11	71 (note 10)
	16	71 (note 11)
4	1	71 (note 12)
10	17ff.	108
12	18	72
	28	72
16	21	73 (note 13)
	27	192 (note 9)
19	28	192 (note 8)
24	14	99, 148
	30	192 (note 8)
25	31	192 (note 8)
26	53	143
28	18ff.	145, 202
	19	72, 170
	19ff.	28, 148
	20	100, 108

ST. MARK

Chapter	Verse	Page
1	1	124
	8	71 (note 10)
	10	71 (note 11)
	12	71 (note 12)
	34	144
2	5	143
5	43	144
7	36	144
8	38	192 (note 9)
10	23ff.	73 (note 13)
13	10	99
	26	192 (note 8
16	15	28
	15ff.	25
	20	21, 108

ST. LUKE

Chapter	Verse	Page
1	15	71
	35	71 (note 9), 199 (note 16)
	41	71 (note 9)
	67	71
2	9	192
	25	106
	25	71 (note 9)
3	16	71 (note 10)

Chapter	Verse	Page
3	22	71 (note 11)
4	1	71 (note 12)
	14	71 (note 12), 199 (note 16)
	18	72
7	28	87
	48	143
8	22ff.	143
9	28ff.	192
	44ff.	73 (note 13)
11	13	72, 73
24	25ff.	157
	26	148, 192
	27	147
	45ff.	77, 127
	47ff.	107
	49	73 (note 14), 199 (note 16)

ST. JOHN

Chapter	Verse	Page
1	1	124, 194
	14	193, 194
	14ff.	194
	17	87, 104
	22ff.	188
	32	71 (note 10)
	33	71 (note 10)
2	11	193
3	5	72, 73
	5ff.	73, 90, 132
	13	96
	34	71
4	10	90
	24	131
5	33	104
6	16	144
	29	23
	33	90
	35	90
	48	90
	51	90
	63	90, 98, 99
	68	90
7	38ff.	72, 90, 196
	39	65, 73, 77, 78, 79, 193
8	12	90
	40	104
	44	104
	45	104
	45ff.	104
10	10	90
11	4	193
	25	90, 99
12	20ff.	196

266

ST. JOHN—*cont.*

Chapter	Verse	Page
12	33	193
13	7	73 (note 13)
14	6	90, 104
	16ff.	104, 132
	17	73 (note 14), 104
	18ff.	132
	23ff.	132
	26	73 (note 14), 104, 133
15	9ff.	132
	26	73 (note 14), 104, 133
	26ff.	104
16	8	77
	8ff.	104
	13	73 (note 14), 77, 104
	13ff.	104, 133
	16	73 (note 13)
17	2	201, 202
	5	193, 194
	14ff.	201
	15	219
	22	193, 194, 195, 202, 244
	26	132
18	37	104
20	22	50, 74, 86, 146

ACTS

Chapter	Verse	Page
1	2	72
	6ff.	100
	8	28, 46, 59, 62, 77, 107, 109, 122, 133, 149, 166, 199 (note 16)
	15ff.	45
	22ff.	127
2	1ff.	28, 55, 57, 109, 166
	3	52
	3ff.	101
	4	50, 101
	4ff.	135
	14	109
	16ff.	37, 103
	17	51, 65, 149, 167
	21	37
	23	148
	24	127
	33	65, 145
	33ff.	143
	38	51, 166, 167, 172
	39	37, 39, 177
	41	163
	46	181

Chapter	Verse	Page
3	25	37
	26	37
4	4	163
	8ff.	166, 167
	12	37, 38
	20	200
	31	166, 167
	32ff.	200
	33	127
	36	43
5	14	164
	32	166
	42	165
6	7	164
	8ff.	80
7	51	167
	51ff.	80
	55	167
8	4ff.	30
	6	164
	14	164
	17	167
	18ff.	229
	25	164
	26ff.	30
	29	167
	39ff.	167
	40	164
9	15	44
	17ff.	167
	20ff.	44
	23ff.	44
	30	44
	31	30, 42, 167
	32	164
	32ff.	32
	35	164
	42	164
10	1ff.	32, 43, 167
	9ff.	38
	24	165
	28	31
	30ff.	38
	34ff.	39
	36	39
	38	199 (note 16)
	42	39
	44	165
	44ff.	34
	45	40, 41
	47ff.	34
11	1	33, 41
	1ff.	41
	2ff.	33, 41

ACTS—cont.

Chapter	Verse	Page
11	10	42
	12	34, 38
	14	34, 39
	15	124
	15ff.	34
	17	34, 40
	18	33, 35, 42
	20ff.	43
	21	164
	24	164
	25ff.	44
13	1ff.	44
	2	167
	9	167
	15	118
	44	164
	46ff.	44
	49	164
	52	167
14	21	164
15	1	35
	1ff.	29-34
	8ff.	167
	9ff.	29
	16ff.	29
	28	167
16	6ff.	167
	9	167
	15	165
	29ff.	165
	31ff.	172
17	4	164
	6	163
	18	127
	33ff.	164
18	8	165
19	6	167
20	20	166
22	15	38, 45
	21	29, 45
	21ff.	38
24	21	127
26	17ff.	29, 4

ROMANS

Chapter	Verse	Page
1	4	88, 145, 195
	16	99
4	18ff.	81
	25	147
5	5	132
6	4	195, 196
	4ff.	88
7	14	87

Chapter	Verse	Page
7	24	96
8	9	89
	9ff.	92
	10ff.	145
	11	74, 89, 195
	13	88
	15	92
	18ff.	93
	19ff.	96
	21	199
	22ff.	156
	23	91, 92
	26	74
	34	127
9	1	112
	25	159
10	8	21
	9	144
	13ff.	99
11	25	153
12	5	200
13	11ff.	156
15	13	199 (note 16)
	16	89
	30	133
16	3	112
	25ff.	154
	26	159

1 CORINTHIANS

Chapter	Verse	Page
1	2	89
	16	165
	18	127
	30	89
2	1	126
	2	127, 218
	4	111, 199 (note 16)
	8	193
	9	158
	10	160
	12	126
	13	80, 111, 160
	18	126
3	22	126
4	15	112, 126
6	3	126
	11	89
	14	196
	15ff.	89
	17	88
9	16	128
10	1ff.	80
	4	81
	9	80, 81, 114 (note 11)

1 CORINTHIANS—cont.

Chapter	Verse	Page
12	1ff.	81
	3	75, 89, 111
	4ff.	133
	12ff.	200
	13	61, 114 (note 11)
	31ff.	133
	28	19
13	12	156
15	13	127
	14	127
	41ff.	195
	44	145
	46	95
20	31	126

2 CORINTHIANS

Chapter	Verse	Page
1	3ff.	106
	22	91, 92
2	17	89, 112
3	3	111
	3ff.	88
	6	75, 111
	6ff.	99
	7ff.	192
	12ff.	197
	17	81, 88, 198
	17ff.	199
	18	74, 198
4	1ff.	198
5	1ff.	93
	5	91
	16ff.	156
	17	88
6	2	100
12	19	112
13	4	196
	14	200

GALATIANS

Chapter	Verse	Page
1	16	29, 128
2	3ff.	29, 32
	3ff.	29, 32
	7	40
3	5	199 (note 16)
	14	82, 92
	28	200
4	4	95
	19	126
	26	126
	28ff.	81
	6	114 (note 11)
5	17	74

Chapter	Verse	Page
5	22	74
	22ff.	88, 110, 133, 200
	23	133
	25	88
6	15	88, 114 (note 11)

EPHESIANS

Chapter	Verse	Page
1	4	84
	9ff.	154
	13ff.	91, 93
	14	91, 92, 110
	17ff.	199
	20ff.	144
2	13	200
	14	158
	18	74, 110, 200
	22	200
3	1	158
	3ff.	154
	5	160
	5ff.	82, 111
	6	158
	8	159
	8ff.	29, 154, 160
4	3	110, 200.
	4ff.	244
	11ff.	115
	20ff.	112
	30	93
5	8	156
	32	155, 158
6	18	74
	19	158, 160

PHILIPPIANS

Chapter	Verse	Page
2	1	74
	1ff.	200
	10ff.	126
	11	147
	16	99, 125
3	3	74
4	15	124

COLOSSIANS

Chapter	Verse	Page
1	8	110, 133
	11	199
	26ff.	155
	27	158
	28	160
3	5ff.	156
	11	114 (note 11), 168
4	3	160
	17	112

1 THESSALONIANS

Chapter	Verse	Page
1	5	111, 199 (note 16)
	6	74, 111
4	11	129

2 THESSALONIANS

3	10ff.	129

1 TIMOTHY

3	4	166
	12	166
	16	155, 159, 193
4	2ff.	227
	3ff.	129
5	4	166
	8	129, 166
	14	166
	14ff.	129
	17	115

2 TIMOTHY

1	10	99
	16	166
3	1	94 (note 11)
4	19	166

TITUS

1	11	166
2	4ff.	166
	13	193
3	5	74

HEBREWS

1	2	94 (note 11)
2	3	124
	4	110
10	14ff.	84
11	10	138
	40	83, 87

1 PETER

Chapter	Verse	Page
1	2	110
	10ff.	82
	11	40
	12	74, 83, 111
	20	94 (note 11)
	21	146, 193
	23ff.	125
2	2	126
	9	126
4	11	192
	13	193
	14	198

2 PETER

3	3	94 (note 11)
	8	84

1 JOHN

2	1	105
	7	124
	18	94
	24	124
	29	90
3	11	124
4	6	105
	7ff.	132
	8	131
	16	131
5	4	90

2 JOHN

	5f.	124

JUDE

	18	94 (note 11)

REVELATION

6	1ff.	100, 151
	2	146
13	8	84
19	13	100
	13ff.	146
20	4	126
22	5	126

DATE DUE

ЛІІГ 17			
JUL 17			
SEP 9			
MR 15 199			
APR 1 0 199			